making learning visible
children as individual and group learners

making learning visible
children as individual and group learners

Project Zero
Harvard Graduate School of Education

124 Mt. Auburn Street, Fifth Floor
Cambridge, MA 02138 - U.S.A.
tel. +1 617 495 4342
fax +1 617 495 9709
e-mail: info@pz.harvard.edu
http://pzweb.harvard.edu

Reggio Children
International Center for the Defense
and Promotion of the Rights and
Potential of All Children

Via Bligny, 1/A - C.P. 91 Succursale 2
42100 Reggio Emilia - Italy
Tel. +39 0522 513752
Fax +39 0522 920414
e-mail: info@reggiochildren.it
website: www.reggiochildren.it

**Making Learning Visible: Children
as Individual and Group Learners**

© 2001 Reggio Children, The President and
Fellows of Harvard College, and The Municipality of Reggio Emilia

Texts and images (photographs and drawings) of the children of the Municipal Infant-
toddler Centers and Preschools of Reggio
Emilia, since 2003 Preschools and Infant-
toddler Centers-Istituzione of the Municipality of Reggio Emilia.
© 2001 Municipality of Reggio Emilia

Photograph on page 352
© Ted Russell - Image Bank

ISBN 978-88-87960-25-9

Published by:

REGGIO CHILDREN srl
Via Bligny, 1/A - C.P. 91 Succursale 2
42100 Reggio Emilia - Italy
Tel. +39 0522 513752
Fax +39 0522 920414
Cod. Fisc. e P . IVA 01586410357
Cap. Soc. Euro 1.000.000,00
Iscritta al Registro Imprese di RE
n° 01586410357 - R.E.A. n° 197516

On the cover: fingerprint

making learning visible
children as individual and group learners

editorial coordinators	RE: Claudia Giudici, Carla Rinaldi PZ: Mara Krechevsky
texts by	RE: Paola Barchi, Angela Barozzi, Paola Cagliari, Tiziana Filippini, Amelia Gambetti, Claudia Giudici, Giovanni Piazza, Carla Rinaldi, Laura Rubizzi, Paola Strozzi, Vea Vecchi PZ: Howard Gardner, Mara Krechevsky, Ben Mardell, Steve Seidel
art direction and graphic design	Isabella Meninno with the collaboration of Vea Vecchi and Giovanni Piazza
design consultant	Rolando Baldini
page composition	Annamaria Mucchi
photographs by	RE: Vea Vecchi, Giovanni Piazza, Mirella Ruozzi Raffaella Bonetti, Giuliana Campani, Marina Castagnetti, Marina Ferrari, Eluccia Forghieri, Isabella Meninno, Stefano Sturloni PZ: Melissa Rivard and Constance Wolf
drawings by	Children of the Municipal Infant-toddler Centers and Preschools of Reggio Emilia
English translation	Jacqueline Costa, Gabriella Grasselli, Leslie Morrow
printed by	Tipolitografia La Reggiana, Reggio Emilia
original research project	Making Learning Visible: Children as Individual and Group Learners
coordinated by	RE: Carla Rinaldi, Amelia Gambetti, Giovanni Piazza, Vea Vecchi PZ: Mara Krechevsky, Howard Gardner, Steve Seidel
research team	RE: Paola Barchi, Marina Castagnetti, Tiziana Filippini, Amelia Gambetti, Claudia Giudici, Giovanni Piazza, Evelina Reverberi, Carla Rinaldi, Laura Rubizzi, Paola Strozzi, Vea Vecchi PZ: Howard Gardner, Mara Krechevsky, Ben Mardell, Steve Seidel, Janet Stork
organizational team	RE: Francesca Marastoni, Claudia Giudici, Francesca Davoli, Paola Riccò, Luisa Zecca, Emanuela Vercalli PZ: Sara Hendren and Terri Turner

The Making Learning Visible Project is a collaboration between research teams based at Project Zero and the Municipal Infant-toddler Centers and Preschools of Reggio Emilia. The views expressed in this book are those of these teams and should not be construed as representing the views of all members of Project Zero.

Acknowledgments

Project Zero   A number of people have helped us in the course of this project.

The following individuals offered insightful thoughts on early reports produced by the research teams: Ron Berger, Bela Bhasin, Tina Blythe, Mary Eisenberg, Sylvia Feinburg, Tom Hatch, Sara Hendren, Connie Henry, Mindy Kornhaber, Ken Lindsay, Ulla Malkus, Nili Pearlmutter, David Perkins, Miriam Raider-Roth, Polly Smith, Sue Steinsieck, Shari Tishman, and the teachers and administrators at the Eliot-Pearson Children's School in Medford, Massachusetts. We owe special gratitude to Tina Grotzer, who gave us many detailed comments on the propositions.

Elizabeth Dowling helped launch the project and graciously volunteered two summers of her time during its first two years.

Our sincere thanks go to Eve Crevoshay, Anne Kornblatt, Steven Lipsitt, Liz Merrill, Adria Steinberg, and Jesse Winch for helpful observations during the preparation of this book.

David Allen offered invaluable insights and suggestions regarding both the shape and content of the book. We are most appreciative of his wise counsel and support throughout the writing process.

Melissa Rivard generously and adeptly helped us produce many of the images of American educational practice for the book.

We are also grateful to our many colleagues at Project Zero and to the participants in the monthly study group, Rounds at Project Zero, for listening to our thoughts as this work evolved and providing so much encouragement and helpful critical response.

We are indebted to Sara Hendren and Terri Turner for their administrative assistance during the years of this project. We owe special gratitude to Terri, who brought good spirit and a careful eye to countless versions of this manuscript.

Finally, we of the Project Zero research team acknowledge the extraordinary privilege of collaborating with our colleagues on the Reggio Emilia research team. The opportunity to explore together questions and ideas, and to learn with them and through their ways of working, has been challenging and deeply rewarding. We thank them all.

Reggio Emilia   The Reggio Emilia research team would like to thank all the children, parents, teachers, staff, and pedagogistas of the Municipal Infant-toddler Centers and Preschools.

Additional thanks go to the administrative staff of the Municipal Infant-toddler Centers and Preschools of Reggio Emilia, and to the staff of Reggio Children for their invaluable collaboration.

Project Zero &   The Project Zero and Reggio Emilia research teams are especially appreciative of the
Reggio Emilia   many contributions of Leslie Morrow and Gabriella Grasselli. We benefited immeasurably from their expertise as translators in our meetings and in the many documents they translated for both teams.

We are grateful for the editorial expertise of Vivian Wheeler, whose careful and critical eye was invaluable to this volume. We also thank our proofreader, Kathleen Pearsall, for catching many infelicities in the text.

Contents

The titles in yellow refer to a series of "ministories" that weave through the book, which highlight children's learning processes and their sense of wonder and amazement, made visible by the sensitive and attentive eye of the teachers.

Protagonists
Erika, 13 mos.
Elisabetta, 11 mos.
Matteo, 10 mos.
Teacher
Barbara Fabbi
Infant-toddler Center
Bellelli
Photographs by
Marina Ferrari
Mirella Ruozzi
Text by
Tiziana Filippini
Claudia Giudici

Contagious Experiments

Learning to listen, see, observe, and interpret the children's actions, thoughts, and logic of investigation and construction helps us to learn the art of being and talking with them, to understand better the processes and procedures they choose for developing personal relationships and acquiring knowledge. The educators' responsibility is thus to design and construct contexts that sustain these processes and foster relationships, loans of competencies, expectations, imitation, and "contagion."

A classroom at the infant-toddler center has been completely transformed: What wonders and opportunities can this bring?

Here a "papered" room, where the floor has been covered with large strips of roll paper, is the "disorienting" backdrop the teachers prepare for the children one morning.

Matteo, Erika, and Elisabetta are seated on the paper that has been laid out on the floor of their classroom. Matteo is holding a marker that he picked up off the floor earlier. (Markers of various colors have been left there by the teachers so that the children can use them, if they wish, to make colored marks on the large surface.)

But now the unexpected happens. Matteo, with the help of Elisabetta, pulls on the edge of the paper...

until a piece tears off.
The torn piece tends to roll up,...

forming a tube.
The game is becoming very interesting. Matteo, gripping the marker in his hand, observes the new "tube" attentively and then grasps it with his other hand...
He seems to glimpse a possible relationship between the marker and the tube.

Matteo's concentration and muscle tension increase; he raises the tube, tilts it slightly, stares at the opening, and tries to slip the marker into it.
His effort makes the tube tilt too much, and his attempt is unsuccessful.

Before abandoning the endeavor, however, Matteo seems to want to give shape to the possibility he had glimpsed and "embraces" the tube and the marker together.

Erika, who has been watching him from a distance but with apparent disinterest, now moves toward Matteo.
Has she perhaps understood the objective of Matteo's "maneuver"?

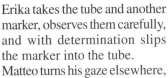

Erika takes the tube and another marker, observes them carefully, and with determination slips the marker into the tube.
Matteo turns his gaze elsewhere, as if he were disappointed or distracted.

Erika, on the other hand, looks steadily at the bottom of the tube and seems to be waiting for something to happen, probably for the marker to come out, but there's nothing there! Since the tube is only slightly tilted, the marker has stopped inside.
What to do? Abandon the endeavor? Shortly afterward...

Erika, under the attentive and curious gaze of Elisabetta, stubbornly grabs another marker and slips it into the tube. This time, the movement of introducing the marker makes the tube tilt higher...

The satisfaction is great, and Erika's efforts and tenacity have been rewarded.

The game is repeated with other markers...

and one after the other the two markers come out at the bottom, confirming the two children's initial hypothesis.

It's a game that Erika and Matteo have probably enjoyed on a number of previous occasions: putting a small object into a larger open-ended one and watching it come out. Could it be that the presence of her friends and the encouraging looks of the teachers make Erika more attentive and confident in her actions?

Time will be their greatest ally. Giving oneself time to pause, to stop for a moment and reflect, often means giving quality to the learning that takes place and the relationships that are formed.

The desire is contagious... Elisabetta, who has followed Erika's experiments with attention and curiosity, now comes and picks up a marker and the tube.

She observes and explores the tube attentively. Is she perhaps checking to see whether the inside of the tube is a "factory" of markers? Or does she want to conduct the same experiment? This would mean being conscious of the coordination of movements needed and the right inclination of the tube. For the moment Elisabetta does not go beyond her visual inspection, and we can only guess at why she does not continue. But we can suppose that all these children, though in different ways, will store this situation in their memory and experiment with it on other occasions.

A Guide for the Reader

As the story of Matteo and his friends reminds us, groups can provide a powerful context for *group*

learning, even for the youngest among us. Certainly this is the case for most adult domains of *learning*

knowledge, in which much of the learning occurs in group settings (think of the science lab,

the art ensemble, the business enterprise). Yet in American schools, most aspects of instruction
assessment

and virtually all assessment practices are focused on individual performance and achievement.

In this book we argue that systematic and purposeful documentation of the ways in which

groups develop ideas, theories, and understandings is fundamental to the meta-cognitive

activity that is critical to the learning of individuals as well as of groups. It is, therefore, worthy
group learning

of serious investigation. The focus of the research reported here is neither group learning nor
documentation

documentation alone, but what happens at the intersection of the two.
learning group

What is a learning group? We define it as "a collection of persons emotionally, intellectually,

and aesthetically engaged in solving problems, creating products, and making meaning—an

assemblage in which each person learns autonomously and through the ways of learning of

others." A good deal of research has been directed at how groups form and function (Claparade,

Dewey, Fabbri, Ferriere, Freinet, Munari, Rogers, and Watson, among others). These and

other studies highlight both the positive aspects of group learning and the risk that "group

ideology" may conceal the internal dynamics at work. If not carried out in a conscious and

responsible way, group work can produce results that are contrary to its intended aims. For

example, if all of the children in a group are considered to be the same or capable of working
collaboration

on a common task in the same way, they may be less inclined to collaborate and more likely to

work in isolation. On the other hand, if a project leads toward overspecialization based on the

preexisting skills of the members of a group, these skills may become fixed and the members'

growth restricted.
questions

We began our own research collaboration with a range of questions related to the nature of

learning in groups and to the ways in which documentation and assessment can support such

16

learning: When does a group become a learning group? Who is part of a learning group in school? What is the relationship between individual and group learning? In what contexts is individual learning enhanced or stifled in a group? Are there cultural blind spots that limit our ability to consider new possibilities and opportunities for individual and group learning?

Questions related to how the process of documenting children's learning informs that learning were paramount. Our hypothesis was that documentation not only allows us to make visible— visible and hence come to know and monitor—the dynamics of individual and group learning, but also is itself a tool that can promote individual learning within the group as well as learning by the group as a whole. In this view, documentation helps to ensure that individual and group learning are interdependent and tightly correlated, while simultaneously retaining the unique interdependent correlated qualities of both. When their learning is documented, children can revisit and thereby interpret revisit interpret their learning experiences and also reflect on how to develop these experiences further. reflect Interpretation and reflection become fundamental aspects of documentation that are not only retrospective, but also are projected toward the creation of future contexts for learning. Documentation is not limited to making visible what already exists; it also makes things exist precisely because it makes them visible and therefore possible. Readers will find many visible and possible examples in this book of how documentation informs teachers' choices for designing learning progettazione contexts (that which is called *progettazione* in Reggio Emilia).*

We identify four features as central to our conceptualization of group learning:

1. The members of learning groups include adults as well as children.

---

* Translator's note: In Italian, the verb *progettare* has a number of meanings: to design, to plan, to devise, to project (in a technical-engineering sense). The use of the noun *progettazione* in the educational context, at least in Reggio Emilia, is in opposition to *programmazione*, which implies predefined curricula, programs, stages, and so on. The concept of progettazione thus implies a more global and flexible approach in which initial hypotheses are made about classroom work (as well as about staff development and relationships with parents), but are subject to modifications and changes of direction as the actual work progresses.

2. Documenting children's learning processes helps to make learning visible and shapes the learning that takes place.

3. Members of learning groups are engaged in the emotional and aesthetic as well as the intellectual dimensions of learning.

4. The focus of learning in learning groups extends beyond the learning of individuals to create a collective body of knowledge.

Another way to distinguish learning groups from other kinds of groups is the degree of intentionality in terms of who is in the group and why it has come together. As the definition proposed earlier in the chapter makes clear, the focus of learning groups is often on solving problems, creating products, and making meaning. But learning groups also share a focus on learning how to learn in a group and epistemological concerns such as understanding the understanding of others and how understandings are developed and modified. When individuals participate in learning groups, they come to see the group as a way to foster individual competencies and discoveries; they learn that the uniqueness of each person benefits from and acquires value in dialogue with others.

The ideas, experiences, and reflections presented here are offered as a challenge to educators; we hope that they will provoke thinking and practice about documenting, understanding, and supporting individuals who learn in groups. We see the audience for this book as educators, researchers, parents—and anyone who is interested in knowing more about how children (and therefore all of us) learn in groups. Although our analysis and reflections are grounded in the theory and practice of the Reggio Emilia schools and the American educational context, the issues addressed here will likely be of interest to readers of any nationality.

ostriches

This book reports on a collaboration between Project Zero, an independent research group at the Harvard Graduate School of Education, and the Municipal Infant-toddler Centers and

Preschools of Reggio Emilia, Italy. In 1997 we joined together out of a mutual desire to explore questions about the nature of learning in groups and how documentation can make that learning visible. These two organizations combine more than sixty years of educational practice, research, and advocacy for children. The ultimate goal of the collaboration is to help teachers and others understand, support, document, and assess individual and group learning. Our book proposes to do the following:

1. Put forth a conceptual framework that we hope will inform future research and practice relative to group learning.

2. Identify seven sets of propositions about how learning groups in early childhood form, function, and demonstrate understanding.

3. Provide examples of documentation of individuals learning in groups.

4. Take a closer look at adults (teachers and parents) in learning groups as documenters of children's learning processes and as learners themselves.

5. Draw on research from Reggio Emilia and Project Zero to reflect further on such issues as the relationship between context and group learning, the role of research and documentation in teaching and learning, and connections among learning groups in diverse settings and age groups.

6. Examine the cultural context that supported the development of these ideas in Reggio Emilia and the United States and identify what we call cultural knots—assumptions, values, and beliefs that frame our understandings and images of individuals learning in groups—which can become barriers to the creation of learning groups.

The structure of our book is not linear; we try to engage and provoke the reader's thinking through the use of multiple voices, perspectives, and "languages."* The sections contributed by the Reggio team make use of the visual as much as the verbal language, thereby trying to

---

* Reggio educators use the term *language* to describe different ways of representing, communicating, and expressing thinking in various media and symbol systems.

create a new language that is more unusual but also particularly effective in communicating the procedures of thinking and acting. Project Zero's contributions, on the other hand, are mostly verbal. Although we identify individual or group authors for the various chapters, all of the ideas described here were generated in the context of our collaborative research. Readers will also encounter, weaving throughout the chapters, a series of ministories made up of images and prose. These provide documentation of individual and group learning, with the children as protagonists, representing a sort of common "thread" that joins the two research teams as we worked to share perspectives and experiences and to understand each other.

The book opens with introductions by leaders of each organization, Howard Gardner and Carla Rinaldi, that provide some of the history and motivation for this research collaboration. Three main parts follow. In the first, we discuss issues of group learning and documentation from the multiple points of view of Reggio educators: *pedagogisti* (pedagogical coordinators), teachers, and *atelieristi* (studio teachers). In the chapter entitled "Infant-toddler Centers and Preschools as Places of Culture," Carla Rinaldi discusses the reasons why early-childhood services should not be considered simply as places for the transmission of culture but can become places where culture is created and shared values are constructed. Tiziana Filippini then offers her reflections on the meaning and value of organization in the Reggio experience as an introduction to the text by Reggio teacher Paola Strozzi, "Daily Life at School: Seeing the Extraordinary in the Ordinary." Strozzi provides the context of daily life that seems to foster individual and group learning by describing the early hours of a day in her classroom. In "Documentation and Assessment: What Is the Relationship?" Carla Rinaldi articulates the critical role played by these two elements in children's learning processes, and delineates how documentation allows for reflection on the processes of individual and group learning. In "Documenting the Documenter," Reggio teacher Laura Rubizzi offers the reader a glimpse into the more subtle aspects of documentation through a brief but detailed "diary" of a documentation process involving three educators: an experienced teacher, an experienced atelierista, and a young atelierista. In "Conversation with a Group of Teachers," Amelia Gambetti highlights some of the struggles that Reggio teachers encounter when they first join learning groups and engage in pedagogical research. Paola Cagliari and Claudia Giudici, in "School as a Place of Group Learning for Parents," attempt to describe briefly the theories and meanings underlying school-family relationships, an essential quality of the educational project of the Reggio Emilia early-childhood services. They discuss how the school, by offering parents a wide variety of contexts, opportunities, and experiences, becomes a privileged place for their learning and growth. Carla Rinaldi, in "The Courage of Utopia," closes this section with some reflections on school as a true place of research, where teachers and students alike reflect daily on the ways they learn and construct knowledge.

In the second part of the book, we present the initial findings of our joint research in a set of propositions about learning groups in early childhood based on the Reggio experience. After an introductory note about the methodology of pedagogical research, we begin with visual and prose documentation of classroom experiences in the Diana and Villetta preschools. "The Curiosity to Understand," contributed by atelierista Vea Vecchi, and "The Fax" and "The City of Reggio Emilia," contributed by atelierista Giovanni Piazza and teachers Paola Barchi and Angela Barozzi, offer stories of individual and group learning, highlighting different aspects of how learning groups form, function, and demonstrate understanding. We hope readers will be able to see for themselves the context from which our ideas emerge and share in the teachers' reflection process, bringing to bear their own critical perspectives as well. In "Form, Function, and Understanding in Learning Groups," Project Zero researcher Mara Krechevsky describes in detail a set of propositions grounded in the Reggio classrooms. The propositions are illustrated with a variety of examples.

In the third part, we cross the ocean and underscore the views of Project Zero researchers on group learning and documentation, building on the team's visits to the Reggio Emilia preschools and its study of the educational theory and practice in these schools, with particular reference to the American context. "Moving across the Atlantic" by Ben Mardell raises several cultural factors to consider as we try to make sense of the ideas transplanted to American soil. In "Four Features of Learning in Groups," Krechevsky and Mardell put forth a definition of learning groups and detail four characteristics of group learning. In the next two chapters, "Understanding Documentation Starts at Home" and "To Be Part of Something Bigger than Oneself," Steve Seidel shares reflections on documentation and assessment and the role of the group in the American educational context. He identifies traditions and beliefs that complicate American approaches to documentation and group learning, but also draws significant connections between American and Reggio practices and theories. Reconsidering American beliefs and traditions in light of the Reggio experience suggests the possibility of new understandings and images of individual and group learning. In "The Question Cannot Be Satisfied with Waiting," Seidel reflects on the role of research in the conception of teaching and learning put forth in this volume. We close with reflections from Howard Gardner and Carla Rinaldi on the meaning of the research we have undertaken together.

The Appendixes provide the reader with additional information regarding the two research groups, Project Zero and Reggio Children, and offer a further look at certain aspects of the experience of the Municipal Infant-toddler Centers and Preschools of Reggio Emilia, which should aid the reader in more fully understanding the related texts in the book. Finally, there are the bibliography and notes. The bibliography related to the Reggio Emilia texts is conceived as a sort of "cultural landscape" in the sense that it does not provide precise references to quotes or mentions in the individual texts. The Project Zero notes, on the other hand, provide all the bibliographical references cited in the relevant texts.

Our book challenges traditional notions of research by viewing schools as places for documenting human learning and development. The multiple perspectives provided here offer different ways to understand ideas that are not adequately represented by one viewpoint or in one language. Thus, the design of the book reflects the nature of our investigation. Our research is based on the notions that theory can result from as well as contribute to classroom practice, and that documentation of learning processes is critical to the research enterprise, as is the presence of multiple perspectives and languages. Rather than prescriptions, we have tried to provide a set of educational points of reference or orientation. By making individual and group learning visible, we hope to contribute to the collective inquiry into teaching and learning and to the creation of what Carla Rinaldi terms "a culture of research."

ostriches

Introductions

Throughout history, a few schools have acquired legendary quality. Their ranks have included Plato's Academy, the Yasnanya Polanyi School set up on his estate by Count Leo Tolstoy, the Laboratory School at the University of Chicago presided over by John and Alice Dewey, and the collection of contemporary schools inspired by the writings and example of Maria Montessori, Rudolf Steiner, and Jean Piaget. To these ranks I have no hesitation in adding the Municipal Infant-toddler Centers and Preschools of Reggio Emilia, as inspired by the work of Loris Malaguzzi and as fashioned over the years by his circle of collaborators and colleagues, several of whom are represented in the essays of this volume.

Howard Gardner

From all over the world, educators have flocked to Reggio Emilia over the last quarter-century to observe firsthand the marvelous institutions for young children that have developed there. No doubt part of the attraction consists in the lovely part of the world in which these schools are situated—the region of Emilia Romagna qualifies as a genuine example of civil society today as well as an area known for its high culture, delicious food, and strikingly effective community organizations.[1] But the chief attraction is the schools of Reggio Emilia themselves: schools in which the minds, bodies, and spirits of young children are treated with utmost seriousness and respect. At the same time these young persons experience pleasure, fun, beauty, and extensive learning.

I first learned about these schools in the early 1980s. My wife, Ellen Winner, and I had the privilege of visiting the schools shortly thereafter and spending a memorable couple of days with Loris Malaguzzi, Carla Rinaldi, Vea Vecchi, Amelia Gambetti, Tiziana Filippini, and Lella Gandini. Since then, I have stayed in touch with the schools, participating from time to time in museum exhibitions and writings that attempt to convey to others "the genius" of the schools. I was well aware, however, that while my admiration of the schools was unbounded, my actual knowledge of how they operated, and why, remained at a novice level.

Thanks to the generosity of a funder who wishes to remain anonymous, my colleagues and I from Project Zero have been given the opportunity to rectify the situation. Over the last three years, I have made three brief trips to Reggio and read and reflected a great deal about the experience; my colleague Mara Krechevsky and her team have made several more extensive trips to Reggio, and members of the Reggio team have made exchange visits to the United States on a number of occasions. We are certainly not at the expert level—research tells us that attainment takes ten years of daily practice—but I trust that individually and collectively, we have advanced beyond the novice level!

To provide a context for the reader of this volume, let me give some background about Project Zero. Our organization was founded in 1967 by the noted philosopher Nelson Goodman. At the time, a decade after the Soviets had launched their satellite Sputnik, a great deal of money was being spent to improve scientific, mathematical, and technical

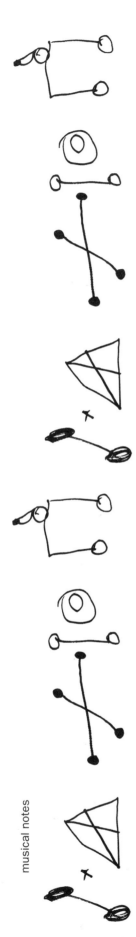

education in the United States. A funder approached the Harvard Graduate School of Education to determine whether there was interest in an analogous, though obviously much smaller, inquiry into arts education. In an inspired move, Dean Theodore Sizer invited Goodman to head the program; and with characteristic acerbity, Goodman christened the fledgling organization Project Zero "because nothing systematic is known about arts education."

In the intervening thirty-four years, Project Zero has become one of the larger, and certainly one of the most long-lived, American institutions that conducts basic research in cognition, learning, and pedagogy, with a continuing special focus on the arts. Over this period, more than one hundred investigators have carried out literally hundreds of studies and projects under this general rubric. Among our better-known undertakings are leadership in "Project Intelligence" in Venezuela, the "Arts PROPEL" collaboration with the Educational Testing Service, a three-year collaborative study of arts education in China and the United States, the ten-year "Project Spectrum," an effort to develop curriculum and assessment of young children, and the longstanding effort "Teaching for Understanding," launched in the early 1990s in the United States and now a well-known intervention in several parts of the world.

My own empirical work in developmental psychology and neuropsychology came together in the early 1980s when I developed "the theory of multiple intelligences" and described it in my book *Frames of Mind*.[2] (By a coincidence, Mara Krechevsky's first job as a young researcher at Project Zero was to help with the proofreading of that volume.) In its thimble-sized version, that theory claims that all human beings have at least eight or nine separate intelligences, ranging from the well-studied linguistic and logical-mathematical intelligences to less well understood forms like musical intelligence, interpersonal intelligence, and the intelligence of the naturalist. While we all share these intelligences as part of our human birthright, we differ from one another—for both genetic and environmental reasons—in our particular profile of intelligences at any historical moment. The fact that we have different spectra of intelligences can either be ignored or exploited in education. The many educational efforts inspired by "MI theory" have generally investigated how the *fact* of our multiple intelligences can stimulate more individualized approaches to curriculum, pedagogy, and assessment.[3]

Following the development of "the theory of multiple intelligences," the educational work of my research group at Project Zero has followed two principal directions. One part of the work has focused on how best to assess student learning, with particular attention to how the multiple intelligences can be observed at work. Project Spectrum and Arts PROPEL represent two efforts proceeding from this perspective. The other part of the work has focused on how to bring about better understanding in various disciplines. Our view of understanding goes well beyond simple memorization of facts and concepts to the appropriate deployment of knowledge in new situations. In our view understanding is a performance in which, using the array of intelligences, one shows oneself—and others—just how one can make use of what one has learned. Our work on teaching for understanding has been the principal arena in which these ideas have been developed.

I mention these three lines of work—multiple intelligences, new forms of assessment, education for understanding—not primarily to offer a personal "vita" but rather to suggest areas in which our Project Zero work overlaps with longstanding concerns of Reggio Emilia. As should be evident in the pages that follow, our colleagues in Reggio are keenly aware of the many ways in which youngsters organize and make sense of experience—not restricted to eight or nine modes of representation, it is they who have celebrated "the hundred languages of children." Educators at Reggio Emilia have never been satisfied with rote forms of learning. Building confidently on the enormous perceptual and cognitive powers and motivations of children, they have helped young children probe deeply into areas that interest them. In the process, they have evoked remarkable performances of understanding—ones that have actually expanded the world's appreciation of what young children can accomplish. Finally, the extensive documentation of student learning that is integral to the "Reggio project" constitutes an exciting form of assessment, whose potential needs to be demonstrated to the rest of the world.

The title "making learning visible" is a triple pun. First of all, it highlights the strong Reggio interest in the world of vision—what one can see, what one can understand, what one can convey to others in graphic form. Second, it reflects the investment in documentation as a powerful means of communicating to all interested parties what has been learned in a significant experience. Finally, and here I speak personally, it represents our best effort to indicate what we have learned from this collaboration. Speaking for myself and my colleagues at Project Zero, I am happy to say that we have learned a great deal and we hope to learn much more. We hope that some of our learning is visible—and audible and palpable—in the pages that follow.

We come from a culture and we are immersed in history, in doctrines, and in economic, scientific, and human facts with which we are openly engaged, at all times, in a difficult and arduous process of negotiation and a struggle for survival.

– Loris Malaguzzi

Carla Rinaldi

I believe that these words of Loris Malaguzzi, the philosopher, founder, and guide of the experience of the infant-toddler centers and preschools of Reggio Emilia, provide one of the most important interpretive keys for understanding this experience but also offer fundamental indications for those who are called on to carry forward the experience.

I also believe that his concept of negotiation with the historical, political, social, and cultural reality represents the primary action that should characterize the very identity of schools, in Reggio as elsewhere. For us, this was and continues to be a daily commitment; it is a difficult one, which requires us to pay close and constant attention to the phenomena that affect school and society, in Italy and beyond.

We feel and we know that the primary aim of schools, including schools for young children, is no longer to educate citizens of a city and of a nation with a well-defined identity, but to educate "citizens of the world" who are conscious of their roots but open to cultural and geographical horizons with no boundaries.

A radical change in a school, in the directions indicated above, can only take place if the school places primary emphasis on paradigms by which each individual can interpret and make use of the contents, the competencies, and the specific understandings that will accompany that person over the course of his or her civil and professional life. Each individual can thus not only learn how to learn, but also become aware of the value of learning as a quality of life itself, in order to organize and multiply the learning opportunities as well as to enjoy them and find pleasure in learning together with others. Each individual must be able to perceive this value and defend it, demand it for himself or herself and for others, in all the contexts of civil and professional life.

Though we in Reggio know that our efforts over all these years have been geared in this direction, at a certain point in our history we felt the need to go deeper.

We felt, and still feel, the need to understand more about the nature of learning in the scholastic environment (and elsewhere), to try to find a closer correlation with the construction of personal identity and of interpersonal relationships. We were strongly convinced that individuality and intersubjectivity are not in opposition but are complementary. However, we were not able to document that conviction with sufficient sensitivity, visibility, and clarity of exposition. We felt that we had a strategy in hand, the one known as documentation, that could help to confirm our declarations and deepen our understandings. The documentation itself could become part of new ways of learning. We knew that this question of learning with others is an important issue not only in terms of pedagogical, psychological, and epistemological research, but also, and most importantly, for its cultural and political significance.

Knowing how to work in a group—appreciating its inherent qualities and value, and understanding the dynamics, the complexity, and the benefits involved—constitutes a level of awareness that is indispensable for those who want to participate, at both the personal and professional levels, in effecting change and building the future.

We had reached this stage in our thinking and examination of the problems involved when we received the proposal from Howard Gardner to carry out joint research with Project Zero. We accepted with great pleasure, fully aware of what this meant, as we were linked to them by a long acquaintance. We had known Howard Gardner and Project Zero for about twenty years. From the start, we held them in great esteem for many reasons, which we were able to understand more fully over the course of time.

I still remember our joy when Dr. Gardner accepted our invitation to come to Reggio in the early 1980s to speak about his book *Frames of Mind*, which had not yet been published in Italian. We had heard about the book for some time from our dear friend and colleague Lella Gandini, one of the "pioneers" who were of great help to us in our dialogue with the United States.

We were quite familiar with most of the psychological and pedagogical literature coming from the United States. The work of many of the giants in the field, such as John Dewey, Jerome Bruner, and David Hawkins, whose influence was critical to pedagogical and psychological research throughout the world, was fundamentally important to the thinking of Loris Malaguzzi and to the Reggio educators. We were also familiar with some of the writings of Nelson Goodman and the provocative idea behind the name Project Zero, which at first glance was somewhat enigmatic.

Howard Gardner's visit to Reggio gave us the first opportunity to deepen our understanding of the project by discussing it with one of its authors and actors. Above all, it was an opportunity to understand better the basic tenets of his theory of "multiple intelligences." The encounter seemed less like a first meeting than a reunion of traveling companions along a road which, despite our differences, turned out to have many surprising aspects in common.

During that period, in the early 1980s, Loris Malaguzzi was developing and refining the theory that characterized and still characterizes the experience of the Reggio preschools: the theory of "the hundred languages." Along with Malaguzzi, we were in the process of designing and preparing the exhibit that still bears this name. We were surprised, but also pleased and excited, by the idea that in another country, in another culture, another author had developed a theory "in the plural."

No longer just one language (the verbal one), said Malaguzzi, but a hundred languages.

No longer just one intelligence, said Gardner, but seven. Apart from the specific number, the important elements were the concepts of plurality, possibility, richness, expansion, and dialogue.

And our views of the child? Once again our thinking was along the same lines: a child who is competent, a child to whom we must offer many opportunities, so that each and every child can find possibilities for his or her individuality and subjectivity to be expressed, enriched, and developed.

School, therefore, is viewed as a very important place, a decisive place for giving all those involved the possibility to be themselves, in the rich originality and wholeness of each individual.

There were many differences between Reggio and Project Zero, as well, but these were equally rich and stimulating; indeed even more so, as they encouraged us to continue the dialogue, to compare the differences, to make them even more fascinating. Then came our encounter with the Project Zero research team: Mara Krechevsky, Steve Seidel, Janet Stork, Ben Mardell, and the others.

I had the good fortune to participate in one of Project Zero's summer institutes and to expand my understanding of the group's theory, but especially to witness the professionalism and political commitment of the members.

I was struck by their discussions about art (Arts PROPEL) and assessment, and I fully agree with their analyses and positions, which were very bold and continue to be very topical. The idea of changing the approach to art and particularly to assessment in a country (like many others) where tests prevail and art is considered to be merely complementary (as also happens in Italy, unfortunately) seemed to be one of the most explicit and effective political statements that I had heard within the American context.

My colleagues and I had often discussed these issues, so when the proposal for the joint research was made to the pedagogical coordinating team, approval was unanimous. The same was true for the schools chosen to be involved in the project, Diana and Villetta. For those who work with children on a daily basis and want to reflect on and dialogue with other points of view, not only to understand what happened but also to make something new happen, for those who know that their professionalism strongly hinges on exchange and dialogue, occasions such as this are eagerly sought and welcomed more than ever with open arms.

When Mara Krechevsky came to Reggio for the first time to define the specifics of the research, it turned out to be quite easy for us to agree on "what to do." We began to see the possibility that a sort of "group epistemology" could be outlined: the group could be (and would seem to be) a sort of "learning system" whose elements were connected interactively—thanks also to the reflections inspired by the documentation materials.

This was the beginning of a challenging experience that has often required us to shift our positions, physical as well as mental and cultural, but that has certainly enriched all of us in a way that now, looking back, seems quite extraordinary.

We hope that this emotion and this passion can be sensed by the reader, who will share with us the results of our experience in being a *learning group*.

RE
PZ

Protagonists
Lorenzo, 19 mos.
Matilde, 20 mos.
Infant-toddler Center
Bellelli
Teacher
Daniela Chiesi
Photographs by
Raffaella Bonetti
Text by
Tiziana Filippini

The Right Hand

Matilde and Lorenzo are outside in the school yard with other friends. They have been together at the infant-toddler center for ten months.

We are lucky to have captured and documented an episode that otherwise would have blended in with other ordinary situations in the daily life at the center.

We see this as an important episode, one that undermines any prejudices or stereotypes that refuse to recognize young children's competencies, including the unsuspected ability to evaluate situations, objects, and skills at a very young age.

The sequence described here shows how young children are able to read and grasp the problems posed by the context, to make hypotheses and predictions, and particularly to organize themselves when attempting to find consistent solutions.

The ability to make a pertinent decision on how to resolve a problem, even a small one, and being able to do so with the complicity and joy of a friend, is a demonstration that suggests to us that children at a very young age not only measure the relationships between things but already show a clear ability to construct meaningful relationships with their peers.

34

A stone, a precious little stone, Matilde's accomplice in play and discovery, involuntarily ends up in a tight spot and it's impossible for her to get her hand in to recover it.

Impossible, that is, for a chubby hand like Matilde's.
She makes a quick evaluation and formulates a hypothesis.

Another child, a smaller friend, could be of help.
Lorenzo seems to be just the one. It shouldn't be difficult to persuade him. Is a hug sufficient?

Yes, it seems to be. Lorenzo, in fact, follows his friend, with whom he has shared many games and adventures, and together they reevaluate the problem.

Lorenzo could be the one to do it. We can try.

Under Matilde's attentive and grateful gaze, Lorenzo slides his hand into the gap.

Matilde's evaluation was correct: Lorenzo's hand is definitely smaller than hers.

His hand is one that Matilde knows well, a friendly and familiar one. She has grasped the difference and knows who and when to ask for help to resolve the problem.

He did it! Here's the stone. The satisfaction is great, and Lorenzo proudly shows Matilde the retrieved stone, pleased that he has fulfilled her expectations. And Matilde,...

though counting on Lorenzo's ability, doesn't neglect a careful recheck, as if this further increases the value of the endeavor.

Yes, that's really the right stone. But how did that happen? It's such a narrow space...

The destiny of the treasure does not seem to be particularly important. Holding hands, Matilde and Lorenzo walk away toward new challenges that will reinforce their feelings of mutual esteem, collaboration, and probable friendships.

Infant-toddler Centers and Preschools as Places of Culture

Carla Rinaldi

I begin with a declaration that I consider to be fundamentally important for more than just the comprehension of this document. The declaration is this: school, including the school for young children, is an educational place, a place of education; a place where we educate and are educated; a place where values and knowledge are transmitted; and above all a place where values and knowledge are constructed. School is a place of culture—that is, a place where a personal and collective culture is developed that influences the social, political, and values context and, in turn, is influenced by this context in a relationship of deep and authentic reciprocity.

Considering school as an educational place is a choice that has always characterized the Reggio Emilia experience, and this choice has assumed topical importance within the contemporary debate regarding the role of the school: Is school a place of education or a place of "formation"?*

Nowadays in Italy, there is often a tendency to favor the use of the term (and concept) of formation. The reasons are not easy to understand. We can suppose that the term formation has been singled out because it is effective in expressing the subjective and self-constructive aspects of education. Or perhaps because it is close—as others maintain—to the concept of professional and vocational training, which is certainly an extremely important element of a scholastic experience, but not the only one. Or perhaps the word formation seems more neutral, more detached from the issue of education in relation to the question of values, which is certainly a pressing issue of our times.

In short, the individual is "formed" and then takes his or her own direction, choosing the values that will sustain the relationships and rapport with the community in which he or she lives.

My personal hope is that the debate will continue, but above all that the concept expressed by the term education can remain strongly tied to the concept and identity of school.

We see school not as the place of instruction or the place of formation (in the vocational/professional sense), but as the place of education. But what do we mean by this? That school, for us, is a place where, first and foremost, values are transmitted, discussed, and constructed. **The term education is therefore closely correlated with the concept of values**, where "to educate" also means—and in certain respects primarily means—to educate the intrinsic values of each individual and each culture, in order to make these values extrinsic, visible, conscious, and shareable.

* In Italian, the word *formazione* in the educational context is used in the more general sense of personal "formation" as well as in the sense of vocational or professional training.

And what is a value? Value is certainly a polysemous word, one of the most polysemous of all, just as education, formation, and subjectivity are contextual terms; that is, they can only be defined in relation to the cultural, political, and historical context.

One consideration is that the term value seems to come not from the philosophical sphere but from the economic and cultural sphere. A possible definition could be: "Values are the ideals that a person aspires to in his or her life." These values act as a point of reference in our judgments and our conduct, and on this basis we conform (or not) our relationships within the social group of reference (community, society, culture). Values define cultures and are one of the foundations on which society is based.

Others may define values as "what makes the human being more human."

These are appealing definitions—intuitively appealing. But what is, and who is, a "more human" human being? And this presupposes another prior question: "Who is a human being?"

In Reggio Emilia, it is a question with which we are very familiar, because we place it at the core of our pedagogical action (though in a substantially modified form) when we ask ourselves, "What is our image of humanity and of the child?"

Values, therefore, are relative and are correlated with the culture to which they belong; they determine the culture and are determined by it.

This apparent digression is actually a fundamental issue for an institution that wishes to define itself as educational. Certainly, when we talk about assessment, the question of values will return as the subject of our reflections and discussions.

What I would like to put forth are some of the values that have structured our experience, but that have also been expressed and renewed by this experience.

The first is the value of subjectivity, which we view in terms of wholeness and integrity (a holistic value). I have chosen the term subjectivity from a number of possible others (such as person or individual) because I think it more clearly highlights the correlational and reflexive aspects involved in the construction of the individual subject. Each subject, then, is a construction (self-constructed and socially constructed) that is defined within a specific context and culture.

A number of studies on the brain have quite spectacularly demonstrated the uniqueness and unrepeatability of each individual and of his or her construction as a subject. Much is known about how the individual develops in relation to the environmental context, and about the strong influence of interactional qualities on the destiny of each of us, particularly in the early years of life.

The methodological implications of this value of subjectivity can be seen in our daily strategies in the Reggio schools: observation and documentation, small-group work, the organization of the space, the presence of mini-ateliers,* and so on.

But I would like once again to underscore the importance of this value of subjectivity in the way that we have described it. In my view, the relationship between subjectivity and intersubjectivity is fundamental not only on the cognitive (and psychopedagogical) level, but above all on the political and cultural level.

I believe that this question is vitally important for the future of humanity itself. The relationship between the individual and others, between Self and Other, is a key issue for our futures. To choose whether our individual construction is independent from others or exists *with* others and *through* others, means resolving not only the traditional pedagogical-psychological debate, but also the one regarding different images of the human being and humanity. It is a question of political and economic choices that can influence the entire educational system, and also the social system.

Here we can clearly see how the sciences, and above all pedagogy, are not neutral but are "partisan," and our pedagogy in Reggio Emilia is a pedagogy of partisanship; that is, it holds certain values.

This value of subjectivity, with the related affirmations regarding the uniqueness and unrepeatability of each individual, is strongly connected to **the value of difference**: difference in regard to gender, race, culture, and religion. Difference because we are individuals, because we are all, in fact, different.

But difference per se is not a value. It can become one if we are able to create a context, a culture, a strategy, and a school of differences.

Dealing with differences is difficult and requires commitment and hard work. In confronting differences, we are faced with otherness, but also with "outside-ness" (extraneousness). Differences are sometimes painful, and always challenging. We tend to be more attracted by the idea of sameness, by that which makes us the same. But this is a great risk, and the questions consequently raised are of vital importance:

- What do we do with the differences?
- How do we avoid the risks of homogenization or standardization?
- Are all differences acceptable? If not, which ones are not?

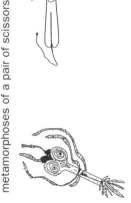

metamorphoses of a pair of scissors

* The mini-atelier is a small studio space connected to each classroom.

- What is the aim of an educational project that seeks to be open to differences? Is it to standardize them?
- What concept of equality are we developing?
- Is the aim to make everyone equal, or to give everyone opportunities to develop his or her own subjectivity (and thus difference) by interacting with others, where this includes elements in common as well as elements that are different?

These questions are of substantial importance at both the pedagogical and the political levels. The inherent risks involve not only education but Western culture in general, which is experiencing massive migration of people, races, cultures, religions.

Globalization, which is fostered by our extraordinary communication systems (television and the Internet, for example), has the potential to create a widespread phenomenon of standardization and encourage the formation of cultural stereotypes. Schools, however, can do an equal amount of damage by encouraging a "culture of normality"; that is, fueling the desire for "normality," for "norms" or "standards," which is so pervasive nowadays.

In my opinion, the only perspective that can translate differences into values is that of integration, but by integration I do not mean fundamentalism. We cannot move toward creating a harmonious unity if this means an overpowering will to impose a single vision, a single way of thinking, a sort of homogeneity without doubts or defeats. Integration is based on multiplicity, and we cannot expect to encounter one single reality without the contrasts and contradictions that are always present in a reality composed of different visions.

The risk that we run, in Italy as elsewhere, is that of fundamentalism and extremism.

In all our lives, somewhat instinctively and without educational input, at some point we begin to recognize otherness. Soon after, in relation to certain others who are "more other," more extraneous, we tend to develop a concept of "others" who are "less other." We are all potentially subject to this attitude, even those who consider themselves to be "above reproach."

The term integration has many possible meanings, and often in daily use it has a meaning and a policy that is very close to the term conformism (for example, having all the children do the same thing based on a principle, or a value, of equality).

In order to educate ourselves, we must try to understand the differences rather than having any pretensions to eliminate them. This means approaching each individual with great sensitivity in terms of his or her particular background and personal history. It means "listening" to the differences (we talk about the "pedagogy of listening"), but also listening to and accepting the changes that take place within us which are generated by our relationships and particularly by our interactions with others. It means letting go of any truths we consider to be absolute and being open to doubt, giving value to negotiation as a "strategy of the possible."

All this means—or *can* mean—greater possibilities for us to change, without feeling divided.

In this definition of the value of differences, we find a richer and more contemporary definition of **the value of participation, or, participation as a value**. In the Reggio educational experience, we have always maintained that participation (feeling a sense of belonging and partaking) is not limited just to the families, though family participation is absolutely crucial. It is a value and a quality of the school as a whole. This means providing for spaces, languages, and, more generally, organizational methods and strategies that make this kind of participation possible, which we have always worked toward in our experience. It means that the educational and pedagogical aims must be clearly stated, but at the same time, participation requires a certain sense of indefiniteness and ample spaces of possibility.

These reflections lead to the affirmation of another value that is part of our experience: **the value of democracy**, which is embedded in the concept of participation.

Once again, the relationship between the individual and the community in which he or she lives can be regulated and oriented in such a way as to exalt either active participation or participation by delegation. The debate is affecting our country as well as each of us individually.

This extremely important issue deserves at least a brief mention, because we must not forget how closely the school is connected to the society in which it is situated. The recurring question is whether the school is limited to transmitting culture or can be, as we in Reggio Emilia strive toward, a place where culture is constructed and democracy is put into practice.

I would also like to mention another value, **the value of learning**. Though some may question the concept of learning as a value, I feel it is essential for our experience, and in a certain sense is its founding principle.

Learning *is* and *can be* a value if we are aware that learning—which is decided by each individual in times and ways that cannot be programmed—is a "relational place" that makes us reflect on the meaning of education itself and leads us to search for new paths in educating and in personal and professional formation.

In educational practice, this means being open to the complex, conflictual, and unpredictable nature of human learning wherever it takes place, both inside and outside the institutional contexts directly involved in education and formation. The entire Italian school system today—with great effort, many contradictions, and many risks—is enmeshed in this process of evolution from a school of teaching to a school of learning.

Learning is the emergence of that which was not there before. It is a search for the self as well as for the other and others that surround each individual.

Educating is thus modified in relation to learning. It means placing the world in front of us, creating an event, and living the various situations. It means educating ourselves.

When we participate in an educational process, in fact, we bring our own growth and development into play, and we do this on the basis of our own expectations and our own designs. There is a constant relational reciprocity between those who educate and those who are educated, between those who teach and those who are taught. There is participation, passion, compassion, emotion. There is aesthetics. There is an aesthetic relationship, as described by Gregory Bateson: aesthetics as a quality of knowledge-building (aesthetics as a value) and, we might add, the value of change, of becoming, and so on.

Then there is **the value of play, of fun, of emotions, of feelings**, which we see as essential elements of any authentic cognitive and educational process.

Learning thus becomes a value because of its power to bring about a synthesis between the individual and his or her context, in a warm relationship between those who learn and that which is being learned, a relationship filled with emotion, curiosity, and humor.

For each of us, the cognitive act becomes a creative act, involving the assumption of responsibility as well as autonomy and freedom.

Knowledge, or better, subjective understanding, becomes an individual responsibility and, in order to be realized to the fullest, a sense of optimism and of the future is needed.

What, then, constitutes formation for us as teachers? It is simply learning: the job of teachers is to learn, because they are teachers. It means keeping our distance from any overriding sense of balance, from that which has already been decided, preconstituted, or considered to be certain. It means staying close to the interweaving of objects and thoughts, of doing and reflecting, theory and practice, emotion and knowledge.

Our task, perhaps, is to seek constantly (though not necessarily ever to find) a balance between the inherent rules and restrictions (some of which are indispensable) and the real emotion and passion of learning.

We are talking about formation for teachers and children alike, rejecting the idea of formation as "modeling," as a passage from one state to another, from various "ways of being" to another "way of being." The aim of this kind of formation is to think and act with reference to the process of becoming, of change. It is an ongoing activity, a permanent process, a quality that must pervade the scholastic institution and that the school, in turn, must grant to all the subjects involved.

Formation toward change, and formation as change.

All of this takes place by means of a choral effort, with the participation of everyone, in full awareness of the restrictions and limits of the institution itself (restrictions of timetables, spaces, and resources), with a commitment that does not delegate to others that which is inherent in formation, which is above all self-formation and group formation.

The scholastic institution thus emerges as the privileged place of education—not the only one, but a special one. Schools must overcome the conflict between the expectation and desire to belong (the sense of belonging) and the need for autonomy and self-affirmation that each of us experiences.

These two aspects, which may seem contradictory and ambiguous, can be extremely generative. Formation for teachers (weekly staff development meetings, for instance) can be a context in which other views can represent both an opportunity and a potential threat, but where negotiation and cooperation can be the ultimate outcome.

It is for this reason that in Reggio Emilia the primary contexts of professional development are inside the schools themselves or in the system-wide professional development program. Not as "contexts" in which one simply describes to the others what he or she has learned, but as places where we can reflect on what has happened inside (as well as outside) the school, in order to self-assess and assess the quality and quantity of learning opportunities that we offer the children, the families, and the teachers themselves—opportunities for learning and sharing values.

What kind of culture should we be working toward and build?
This is a crucial question for all, and particularly for those who work in the educational field.

somersault

44

- Where is the future?
- Where does the "new" reside?
- What kind of future can we construct together?

Because we are now in a phase of increasing globalization, we are inundated with information and kept abreast of events across the entire planet in real time. We are spectators, more than authors, of an extraordinary technical-scientific revolution that is changing the quality of human relationships, the definition of personal identity, and the construction of cognitive processes. New issues will certainly emerge regarding the concepts of privacy, ethics, space, and time.

So is the "new" to be found in the media explosion? I think not, or at least not *only* there. The media revolution will be just one of the possible futures, provided we are able to produce another "revolution"; that is, the new is and will be found where individuals are able to overturn every rigid barrier of culture, class, ethnic group, and wealth.

We will find the new and the future in those places where new forms of human coexistence, participation, and co-participation are tried out, along with the hybridization of codes and emotions. New languages will be generated: planetary languages.

Today's youth are already doing this. Young people are the great precursors and authors of these hybridizations: in music, in fashion, in design, creating new forms and new freedoms. Young people are extremely capable and sensitive in finding these common roots in different universes of thought.

It is necessary for us to learn this unity in diversity, and this diversity in unity. We need the involvement of each diversity in the "pluriverse" of our planet: a cultural and linguistic pluriverse.

Now more than ever, the concept of "the hundred languages of children" seems to be an extraordinary intuition, as well as an obligation for all of us.

How can we make the languages truly one hundred in a "project of alliance" with this cultural pluriverse that surrounds us? What can help us is the now-mature awareness of the unfinished nature of every tradition and of each of us (the value of incompleteness).

The construction of self, of the individual, becomes increasingly defined as a point of intersection and of multiple identities. More and more, the individual will express an intercultural, intersubjective identity. So the quantity and quality of his or her encounters and experiences will become increasingly important.

cartwheel

45

Intercultural education thus represents one of the essential guidelines for defining the quality of our future, to the extent that the interaction between cultures is not only a political issue, but above all a cultural and cognitive issue.

Cultural education is not a separate discipline, nor is it simply the illustration of the customs and religions of a country, though these are certainly important. It is more than this: it is primarily a style of educational-relational thinking. It is what we call "project-based thinking" (*pensiero progettuale*), a way of thinking that is open to others, that is open to doubt and to the awareness and acceptance of error and uncertainty. It is the interweaving of multiple cultural codes, multiple languages, "contagion," hybridization. It plays on boundaries, not as marginal zones (center versus boundary), but as places that generate the new that is born of contagion and interchange.

The new thus seems to lie in promoting an educational process based on the values of human dignity, participation, and freedom.

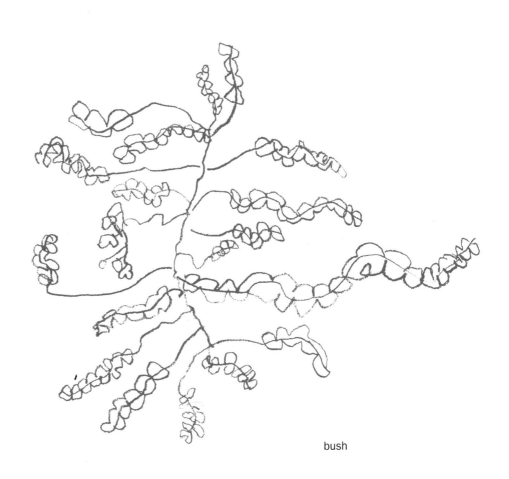

bush

Protagonists
Alessandro, 5 yrs. 8 mos.
Riccardo, 5 yrs. 6 mos.
Silvia, 5 yrs. 4 mos.
School
Diana
Teacher
Paola Strozzi
Photographs and text by
Vea Vecchi

The Right Price

In the exchange of money and goods between buyer and seller, young children perceive *number* as an important element, though perhaps it is only by intuition that they are able to understand the conventional significance of numbers in terms of quantity, code, and value.

Playing the shop game allows the children to give shape to these conventional meanings, putting them in relation to one another. The children exchange money and goods, but also competencies, where each player (shopkeeper and customer) generously offers to the others his or her personal wealth of coins, ideas, and abilities.

The episode documented here demonstrates one of the children's many possible intelligent learning strategies.

48

The children have previously set the values and prices of the goods and printed them on labels that are glued to the products.

The three children involved in the game have different levels of competence in working with numbers. Riccardo is quite skillful and uninhibited. Alessandro has some difficulties, particularly in making change. For Silvia, the way numbers get divided and put back together is still somewhat nebulous.

In order to determine the amount of money Silvia and Alessandro owe him after each purchase, Riccardo, the shopkeeper, adds up the numbers using a method that fascinates Alessandro and Silvia, who both observe him attentively.

He taps each item with his index finger as many times as its sale price, counting aloud at the same time.

As shown in this photograph, Riccardo taps three times on the product whose price is 3, counting aloud: *1, 2, 3;* four times on the product that costs 4: *4, 5, 6, 7;* and so on for all the products sold. Then he says: *You owe me 12.*

Paying 12 is not easy for Silvia. She needs to make the sum using the coins she has in her purse. Riccardo, Alessandro, and the teacher try to help her, but Silvia does not seem to understand how it works.

Then she finds a strategy that helps her to overcome the muddle of calculations. She starts tapping the money with her left hand the way she saw Riccardo doing, and uses her right hand to help by counting on her fingers. Using this method, she is able to pay the correct amount of 12.

Everyone is happy that Silvia has come out a winner in this difficult encounter with numbers.

Alessandro and Riccardo have now tired of the game and want to go on to something else. But Silvia has no intention of giving up her turn as the shopkeeper and experimenting with her newly acquired skills, so she persuades another friend to come and be the customer.

In the various payment stages, Silvia uses her newly developed technique a number of times. She feels so confident about it that she tries to explain it to her friend, using the customer's own fingers to help.

Later, in her comments to the teacher, Silvia says: *Today I learned... you know what? I learned that numbers have to be counted. If you count them you can understand them better, but you have to count with the fingers of your other hand, too; otherwise you can make a mistake. It's hard for me to count without using my fingers. Do you know how I learned it? It was my mind that helped me learn it... and Riccardo gave me the idea, too, a little bit.*

The counting strategy used by Riccardo initially, and then by Alessandro and Silvia, was subsequently adopted by the other children in the class within a fairly short period.
We are almost certain that the success of this strategy was due to its being in harmony with the children's processes, as well as to its musicality with the hand movements and the sound produced, giving the strategy rhythm and visibility.
The aesthetic element often enters into children's choices. Beauty and pleasure are strongly integrated in the knowledge-building processes.

On the Nature of Organization

Tiziana Filippini

Organization, in the Reggio experience, has always been thought of as a constituent part of the identity of the school, an aspect that is bound to the values and choices of the educational project. For this reason, we offer a brief discussion of organization as an introduction to the following chapter, "Daily Life at School." We will examine some of the organizational choices that characterize our educational project and that we feel are particularly important for understanding the broad context that fosters individual and group learning. (For general information on the organization of the Municipal Infant-toddler Centers and Preschools of Reggio Emilia, see Appendix D.)

The quality of learning, especially that of learning to learn in a group, seems to be closely correlated to the quality of opportunities to share and participate in the daily life of the school. Building and maintaining relationships is the guiding thread that accompanies children through the various times, spaces, and activities of daily life; it is the main occupation to which they dedicate energies and passion from the moment of birth. Schools, on the other hand, too often dedicate their energies primarily to curriculum and didactics, neglecting the broad network of relationships and communication that are an integral part of the educational process, and consequently placing little emphasis on the organization of these relationships.

The "places" of education have never reached a clear consensus on the nature and role of organization. Traditionally, schools have constructed their identities and objectives by decontextualizing themselves, by separating the disciplines and fields of knowledge, and by being intolerant of any ambiguity or uncertainty. Organization, which is such an important aspect of the lives of individuals and societies, has generally been relegated to a secondary role of mere functionality, with little recognition of its ethical and educational value.

We believe that organization is in large part responsible for the quality of relationships within the school and therefore for the quality of the educational project itself. Organization involves more than just the structures of the school. What makes the organization is the meaning given and the values ascribed to these structures by the subjects of a school. Organization involves working conditions, schedules, spaces, and decision-making processes, all of which are informed by and inform the values and relationships within an institution. In this way, the organization defines the

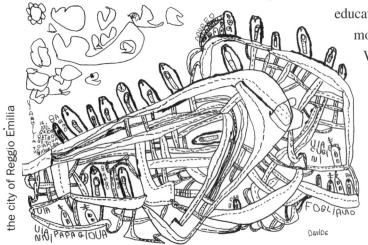

the city of Reggio Emilia

52

possibilities and realities of a school.

It is precisely for this reason that we have never delegated choices regarding organization—and these choices involve administrators, pedagogistas, teachers, school staff, and parents, though in their different competencies and roles.

Our experience has always been particularly sensitive to the constant interplay of theory and practice. We are convinced that the close alliance between the theoretical system and the practical-organizational system does not consist simply of implementing the theory correctly. Rather, it lies in the capacity to experience this alliance as a dynamic relationship in which theory and practice are reciprocally influenced, giving priority not to an "executive" intelligence but to a creative intelligence that attempts to construct, maintain, and renew this relationship of circularity and reciprocity.

We have tried to counter the culture of separation and dualism, starting with our image of the child, which has always underscored connection rather than parceling, and including our systemic view of the school. Seeing school as a system of communication and relationships was an initial choice that continues to characterize and distinguish our commitment to valuing, as well as putting into practice, the dialogic nature of the individual and of knowledge.

Within this systemic approach, which means that each part is involved in reciprocal relations with the others, organization is seen as the progettazione of these relationships (see page 17 for the definition of progettazione). It is as if a school were a large living organism whose parts (children, adults, schedules, spaces, and so on) relate to the whole not only because they are included, but also, we hope, because of a bond that embodies a common sense of belonging, the construction of shared stories, and intertwined destinies. In our experience, the aim of organization is to create a bond of interdependence that can give each subject the meaning of his or her presence and of the presence of the others.

We have tried to find a type of organization that is accepting and supportive but that also fosters these connections. Reciprocal enrichment can be achieved only within the connected and integrated points of view of the individual parts. Thus we have tried to create a network of participation that is the result of many different points of view.

We have paid particular attention to *how* the values and aims are connected to the design and organization of work, schedules, spaces, school environments, activities, staff development, family participation, and relations with the city. This is in order to welcome and give value to the ongoing relationships of interdependence, exchange, and collaboration that develop among the protagonists of the school, who are engaged in integrating their knowledge and contextualizing it.

Another major choice was to create a dialogue of the political, administrative, and pedagogical domains, with the view that this reciprocity would provide the necessary consistency for realizing such a complex undertaking. As it happened, this choice turned out to be crucial at the cultural level, as school personnel developed a broader view that encompassed not only the children but also world events in general. It generated an awareness that the issues of children and childhood cannot be treated separately from the issues of women, men, families, and society.

Our engagement in and commitment to relationships progressively raised our attention to and awareness of the search for the "dimension of the possible" that characterizes the adventure of growing and of education. We feel that this attention to the process of "becoming" is highly fruitful in providing the positive conditions for realizing the educational project and also for continuing to learn; that is, for gradually acquiring the structures necessary for interpreting experience.

A no less important gain can be found with regard to the responsibilities vested in us as educators. In the conscious construction of a dialogue between ideas and practices that embodies the unpredictability and uncertainty of the real pulsing of life, we are constantly faced with the need to make choices, to rearrange elements of our own experience and that of others in sequences that generate innovations.

When all those involved are called upon to contribute to the construction of an educational project, and local discretion and adaptations are both permitted and supported, we can clearly see how the plurality and diversity of the points of view, expectations, and interpretations in a group can become resources for influencing "reality." This brings to light new and unexpected elements that help us constantly to reconsider the limitations and possibilities of the context in which we work. It is our actions that make the difference, and this implies our responsibility to be not so much the interpreters as the builders of the experience.

Declaring that meanings and knowledge are constructed, that they do not exist outside of ourselves, that children like adults are not spectators but actors of their own lives, leads to a conceptual, cultural, and epistemological overturning of the way we view education and the role of schools and teachers. Time and specific working conditions are required to make it possible for schools and teachers to become real and effective sources of learning. In our ongoing and permanent staff development, we place a great deal of emphasis on promoting constant learning and an attitude of research, an openness to change and to discussing diverse points of view. Therefore, the organization of work must enable and support communicative dynamics which, by interweaving individual and collective thought, leads us to experiment with the existence of "possible worlds" and the possibility of constructing new meanings or, better, shared meanings.

We chose to have a working team in the school, where collaboration and collegiality are seen as quality features of the school's identity. The distribution of jobs, as well, is not only a functional choice but is devised so that every person, despite their different roles, can feel that they are included as an active part in the realization of the experience. These choices are both premises and conditions that foster the assumption of responsibility and continuous negotiation toward redefining one's own role and that of the school. Staff collegiality is not taken for granted; it must be supported by professional development initiatives and also requires that times and opportunities be established within the work schedule.

In Reggio, being able to reflect on our actions has been crucial to the development of our approach. Revisiting and reflecting on our actions, to which we give priority in our professional development and which are aided by the documentation process, enable us to take constant stock of and closely examine our experience and understandings. Reflective thinking allows us to step back from ourselves, creating a distance that prevents us from getting caught up in "events," thereby increasing our awareness of what we are learning and also of the dimension of the possible—of that which it is possible to know and to be. This phenomenon permeates the processes of adults and children alike.
The more this reflective process becomes a collegial endeavor (thanks to the organization of the work schedule so that we share our thoughts with our colleagues as well as with the children's families), the greater the possibility of more dialogic approaches that help us to appreciate the intentionality, the values, and the meanings present in the organization.
All this gives substance and meaning in our daily work to the idea that each act of perception is an act of creation that requires both the awareness of one's responsibility as a builder of possible worlds and the awareness that it is one of many points of view; that is, a sense of relativity emerges that strengthens one's desire to seek completeness in others. Right from the start, said Loris

Malaguzzi, children search for completeness, and they realize that this can be achieved not only through internal dialogue but also through dialogue with others. And the same is true for all of us.

The introduction of the atelier and the figure of the atelierista was another choice decisive for the identity of our experience. The benefits lie not only in the specific aspect of arts education, but in the creative process common to all the expressive languages, fostering the sort of "contamination" that gives rise to an original way of conceiving and developing an educational project. Moving from one language to another helps free us from the shackles of repetition, and we discover that we can always encounter new points of exploration and thus of departure.

In the awareness that we are dealing with an organism characterized by interactions that are rapid, complex, and simultaneous, we cannot think in terms of wanting to exercise overall control; we do, however, hold ourselves responsible for choosing and thus designing, to the best of our ability, the qualities of the bonds that we want to bring into existence.

The decision to have two coteachers in each classroom was not based on a goal of greater efficiency as much as on ethical, cultural, and pedagogical factors. The passage from one to two persons creates a basic nucleus of social behavior. A "pairing" of this sort brings into play interdependence and reciprocity of thought and action; and the choices made, which result from agreements, disagreements, and negotiations, become public acts. Moreover, this arrangement eliminates the isolation of the teacher in the classroom and fosters a first nucleus of socialization that, when multiplied by the number of classes and the number of staff, forms a team, or what we might call a breeding ground for human relationships.

To complete our discussion of organization as the progettazione of relationships, we should also mention aspects such as the environment, architecturally and functionally designed and equipped to provide a system of interactions and interconnection; the choice of small-group work as the most effective type of organization for fostering and giving quality to interactions and learning; the continuity of the class group; the time frames of the school day and year; and additional aspects that the reader will encounter in other chapters of the book.

In conclusion, we believe that the educational processes require thinking that can find interactions over broad and multiple dimensions. Therefore, it is necessary to adopt an organizational method and style that are systemic, that enable us to grasp the unity of that which is normally kept separate. For this reason, our professional development projects have always aimed at supporting teachers' curiosity and fostering the pleasure of broadening the cultural context of our pedagogical approach. Within this ecological-systemic vision of the educational project, we attempt to make a close connection between educational issues and general inquiry on human relationships, on the relationship between man and knowledge, man and the world. Our aim is to build philosophical and value-related horizons that are closely interwoven with the emerging culture. Here the interdisciplinary approach is viewed not merely as a meeting of people who come from different disciplines, but as an exchange and collaboration between certain kinds of knowledge and understanding. It embodies and develops an organic, multidisciplinary approach whose nature is both cognitive and ethical. It is a way of living and thinking together that directly and deeply involves the cultural and didactic content.

high jump

Daily Life at School: Seeing the Extraordinary in the Ordinary

Paola Strozzi

From a project by
Marina Mori
Paola Strozzi
Vea Vecchi
School
Diana
Photographs by
Vea Vecchi

What do we mean by context in the field of education? Is it possible to define the word so that its meaning is clear and complete?

Today many of the studies on cognitive development that focus in particular on individual and group learning place at their center the relationship between the individual and the context. Knowledge, according to these theories, should emerge as the product of an activity that is shared and distributed in a context that involves and joins individuals, physical materials, cultural tools, and symbol systems.

The context, redefined in broader terms to include the physical, cultural, and social environment, is no longer considered merely a group of external variables that foster or impede an individual's behavior and thoughts. Instead, according to these studies, the context should be seen as an integral part of the learning and knowledge of each one of us.

Learning and knowledge are therefore made possible, but also conditioned, by the interaction between individuals who are building knowledge along with others, and their physical and cultural environment. The individual and the context thus take on substance. They define each other and give each other identity.

At school, the scholastic context and the individuals who inhabit that context work together to give meaning to the entire experience. Thus, events such as waiting for a special friend in the morning (and knowing you are expected), finding moments to be alone, working on a project "in secret" with a group of friends, interpreting the memories of those who attended the school in the past, the verbal exchanges between adults, and the sounds, tastes, and smells all become expressions of that collaboration between the individual and the context that makes the individual's relationship with the world meaningful.

Many years ago Loris Malaguzzi encouraged us to consider school as one of the places where the search for the meaning of life and of the future takes place. In this sense, I believe, he was speaking about an "amiable school": "Making an amiable school (hard-working, inventive, livable, documentable and communicable, a place of investigation, learning, recognition, and reflection) where the children, teachers, and families are happy is our goal." Visitors who enter the Municipal Infant-toddler Centers and Preschools of Reggio Emilia for the first time are often struck by the care and attention given to the environment, which creates a sense of harmony and "communicativeness."

Perhaps we could say that being attentive to the context means "living the atmosphere," making palpable what is usually invisible: joy, curiosity, interest, affection, autonomy, possibility, responsibility, desire, expectation, tranquillity, satisfaction, intimacy, individuality, belonging. These aspects become visible not because we list them but because we appreciate them and practice them in our daily life.

Scholastic organization in Italy (the environment, human resources management, and didactic programs) is too often the result of noncritical repetition, limited awareness, and a lot of fortuitousness passed off as "creativity" or didactic freedom. We know that children want to spend time with other children, but this fact can overshadow our questioning ourselves as to how children "live" together, what their interests are, and how these interests are communicated and negotiated.

Important processes are involved in a child's production of an artifact. Over the years we have learned to seek out these processes; we have done our best to make them visible, and we have certainly grown to appreciate them. There is also, however, a similar "process" quality in the many events that make up our day. We try to "spy" on these processes because we feel that it is here that much of that search for meaning, which is so important to us, is played out. Whether or not we realize it, our ideas concerning education are transformed every day into gestures, actions, words, and mimicry, much as our thoughts and theories concerning education are nurtured and modified by their encounters with day-to-day practice. It is both our desire and our responsibility to ensure that this happens.

Malaguzzi was very aware of this unity and synergy between theoretical declarations and quotidian practice, and he often urged us to be mindful of these two moments and to be consistent.

There are new philosophies and scientific theories which maintain that every single part of a whole, even the smallest part, represents the whole. These theories can be expressed, for example, by mathematical structures or represented by hologram images. We believe that an effective educational system must have the same characteristics as these structures: each small part should reflect the ideas and the choices that inspire the whole system and, above all, should make the well-being of the entire organizational system possible.

A school, however, is a very complex and fluid organism. It is made up of individuals, spaces, rhythms, desires, expectations, and emotions. It is by no means easy to maintain a high level of awareness regarding something as complex as the life of a school. At the same time, we cannot leave everything to observations that are random or too far apart in time. If we did, we would run the risk of generating schools that are empty systems, or self-serving bureaucratic exercises, or places where children spend a more or less long period of time but where they do not "live."

In Italy, where professional development often separates theory from the organization of work, there is a particularly high risk of creating a school, as Bateson says, "...that disinforms rather than forms, because it takes away from things the pulse of life." This is why we must make frequent assessments of our quotidian life, through critical and attentive listening.

There is little documentation concerning the daily life of a school beyond the didactic activities, yet we are convinced that the quotidian is a "special teacher." We usually focus our attention on what the children have produced. Sometimes the projects themselves are examined; very rarely are the processes analyzed, and then only verbally. This is why at the Diana School we chose to "reread" ourselves and our work by going into the five-year-olds' class one morning and using the camera to document a typical day.

Here we present only a fragment of the "live report" of the five-year-olds, documented with photographs: from 7:30, when the school opens, until 9:00, when all the children have arrived and we decide together how we will spend the rest of the day. The "morning assembly," when the children and teachers plan out their day, is viewed by many of our interlocutors as an essential moment. Probably so, but at times this moment risks overshadowing everything that has taken place before it, which is truly a microcosm of experiences and possibilities. Indeed, in this hour and a half preceding the traditionally more visible start of the school day, we can find many of our declarations concerning the meanings of education.

I believe that by recognizing meaning in the small gestures of the quotidian we can see how visibility and depth are given to important concepts such as the role of the environment, the image of the child, the copresence and coresponsibility of the teachers, the relationship with the families, and so on. We would like these images of our daily life to be seen as a situation of "overall softness," as defined by the research group of Reggio Children and Domus Academy in Milan in their book *Children, Spaces, Relations – Metaproject for an Environment for Young Children*: "A context of overall softness means an ecosystem that is diversified, stimulating, and welcoming, where each inhabitant is part of a group but also has spaces for privacy and a pause from the general rhythms. There is respect for others, listening: a 'strategy of attention.' It is a serene, amiable, livable place."

A school that awaits
7:30 a.m.

The school awaits the children, parents, and staff. It greets them with the early-morning light, which filters through the large windows and from the two inner courtyards. In this environment the natural light dialogues with the colors and surfaces, and transparency underlines the relationships and the exchange of information between the inside and the outside: the season, the weather, and the light at different times of day. The physical environment is inviting. Its furnishings suggest to the children and their parents stories to be created or continued.

Narrations

The documentation panels cover the walls throughout the school as if they were a second skin. The panels make you feel that you are, or invite you to become, a part of experiences and stories. They suggest that future experiences will be valued. The documentation substantiates the value of memory and narration as a right and a vital quality of the educational environment.

Arrival
7:30 a.m.

The children begin to arrive and all are welcomed in the three-year-olds' classroom by one of the teachers. This spot was chosen because it is the classroom closest to the entrance. Its windows look out onto the front gate, so the children who are already present can see who is arriving. There are only a few children until 8:00.
(To better understand the organization of the school, see notes in Appendix D.)

Saying goodbye

The moment when children and their parents say goodbye is extremely delicate. Even when it is quick, it is still full of meanings and emotions that have an impact on the children's sense of well-being as well as that of their parents.

A teacher for each class arrives at 8:00. They rapidly exchange greetings and materials.

Communication alliances between teachers

Welcome

We go into the five-year-olds' classroom with Marina, as children and parents continue to arrive.
In our educational community we consider the moment of welcoming the children to be a value.
"Welcoming" implies listening, openness, recognizability.
A child, parent, anyone who works at the school must feel the sense of well-being that comes from being awaited and welcomed with pleasure.
The school is not a place for anonymous users, but for people who live a portion of their lives together.
Marco has been absent for a few days. His return is celebrated by a group of friends...

Secrets

who want to tell him about a top-secret plan. In order to do this they move into a room off their classroom and close the door. We respect their secret and do not enter.

Waiting

Meanwhile, in the piazza (the large central space in the school), Eleonora waits for the friends she is closest to at the moment…

Communication alliances between the children

and as soon as they arrive, the girls get together to tell each other what seem to be very important things. Children move about the school with confidence and freedom, occupying almost all of the spaces.

Urgencies

There is a palpable sense of urgency to talk, to share things, and to make plans right from the start.

The children spontaneously form groups. The girls seem to prefer groups of three; the boys tend to gather in larger groups. This is an important piece of information to take into consideration when planning activities.

The groups are not stable; they move around, expand, or grow smaller, their interests and participants changing all the while.

Pauses

Sometimes the children like to be by themselves, as does Chiara in the mini-atelier. This space is set apart from the classroom and, like the other smaller spaces we have created in the school, allows the children to be by themselves or in small groups. This dimension of "being" is sought out in certain moments and is appreciated by both children and adults.

Marina begins to look at some notes concerning proposed projects for the day, along with two children who express their own opinions, as the children regularly do in informal moments like this. The adults' behavior conveys to the children that they and their work are taken seriously. The children are always keenly aware of the adults' actions and of the relationships among the adults.

Project hypotheses

The teachers in Reggio Emilia use different tools to plan their work at school. As a general rule, they make monthly and weekly forecasts regarding new or ongoing projects. These hypotheses concern not just the children but also the families, as well as staff development.

There are no ready-made, standardized planning tools in the infant-toddler centers and preschools.
The teachers of each school prefer to discuss, year by year, the efficacy of the tools we have employed. If necessary, we design new tools that are more functional for a certain task, more in line with the thinking strategies of the coteachers.

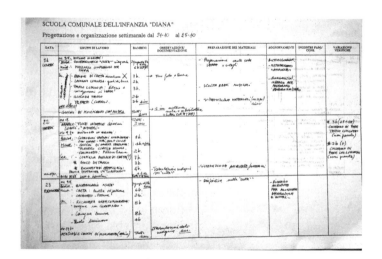

Preparation

The teacher, with the help of some children, begins to organize the material that will most likely be needed during the morning, based on the weekly forecast.

The fact that the teacher and children together prepare the material is not simply a question of practicality; it is part of the educational project itself.

This preparing together stimulates expectations, curiosity, and desire, and it broadens the scope of the forecast and the search for tools.

The children sense this, which explains their interest in helping.

Intelligent materials

Our environments are like landscapes of possibilities and suggestions. The entire school fosters relationships among the children themselves and between the children and the materials. If we value the children's desire and pleasure in carrying out investigations, either by themselves or in groups, then we must make sure that the sort of materials we provide allow this to happen. If, for example, we propose to the children an experience with the overhead projector, they have to be able to find and use materials that are transparent, opaque, colored, and not colored; that is, materials that do not impose a direction but that pose questions and elicit hypotheses and the desire to experiment.

The class's other teacher arrives with a bouquet of flowers and is greeted by a group of children. The entire staff is attentive to the aesthetics of the school. Caring about the environment where you live contributes to creating a sense of belonging and to showing respect for those who live there; it is an integral part of the educational process.

Belonging
8:30 a.m.

There are tasks the children take turns doing, like taking care of the plants…

Attention and care

and helping out in the kitchen. Sometimes these sorts of activities become possible offers for the morning's work.

Coresponsibility

To ensure the well-being of both the children and the adults in the school, as well as the professional growth of the teachers, a strategic choice was made in the mid-1970s to have two teachers present in a class who are equally responsible for that group of children. In those days it was not easy to eradicate the archetypal figure of the individual teacher whose so-called didactic freedom often resulted in human and cultural solitude. The teachers' discussions, coresponsibility, and working together provide an important example of social learning that is not lost on the children and their families. The coteachers are together every day from 8:30 until 2:00. At this time of the morning, the presence of two teachers means…

Exchanges

that one can meet with the other classroom teachers or with the atelierista in order to ask for advice, exchange information, or decide who will deal with urgent matters. For the five-year-olds' teachers the process is facilitated by the fact that the children are both used to and capable of organizing themselves in different groups.

The children can take items back and forth between home and school. Permitting this kind of transit of objects—which, after all, are pieces of the children's interests and of their lives—demonstrates simply and clearly that school and home are in continuity with each other. It also demonstrates that the school does not practice unilateral a priori censorship. School is a place for discussion, sharing, and negotiation with the families.

Each child has a backpack with the school logo that encourages and supports these transits between home and school. The children are allowed to bring in anything that interests them; the timing, the method, and the opportunity to play with toys from home are all negotiated individually and as a group.

Personal places

The children each have a place where they can put their belongings.
Other personal places include message boxes, portfolios for their drawings and two-dimensional artifacts, and a storage bin for mail received and other objects. Each child has a drawer with his or her photo and name on it. It is by no means easy to direct this traffic of personal belongings! But we accept negotiation as an important relational element, in spite of how complicated it is, because we can only gain by it; teachers and children feel involved in communication, which is just as authentic as the children's very real and complex interests.

70

Autonomous group organization

8:45 a.m.

By now almost all of the children have arrived. They continue to move around the foci of their various interests, like this group playing checkers. Those watching participate actively by giving advice and, when necessary, by helping to count up points or suggest moves. Many group activities are taking place at once. The children move from being protagonists in one activity to being the audience in another, an audience that helps and learns, thereby becoming a "competent audience."

Group self-organization

Sometimes the children carry out projects they have organized by themselves and that we teachers find out about only by chance. Chiara and two of her friends explain to us that the elaborate drawing on the far left is a page from a book they have written and illustrated called *Life, Death, and Birth.* They tell us that they work on their book every day, drawing a page and then taping it to the preceding pages. Opening to the chapter called "About Life," we find a picture of two women exercising, with the caption, "You have to exercise so that you don't get cellulite!"

Transformations

There is always a lot of activity in the dress-up area right from the beginning of the day. The children play in this area, building real and imaginary places. It only takes a few elements to create situations and "landscapes" and to feel like someone else.

71

Things do not always go smoothly. Our children fight as well, often arguing until someone finally bursts into tears. The teacher is sometimes called in to referee, as in this case. We do not shirk this role, though we do try above all to help the children discuss the situation among themselves in order to solve the problems that gave rise to their argument. The five-year-old boys still sometimes get into fistfights, though less frequently and less violently than they did as three-year-olds. Our educational organization encourages exchanging opinions, feeling part of a community, not being or feeling excluded, and being seen and recognized by the other children and by the staff. The feeling of belonging created lowers aggression levels.

Conflicts

Mingling

The children love to "migrate" to other classrooms.
In this case, two of the "big" children have gone into the three-year-olds' classroom and after having helped the teachers set out the materials for the activities to come, they volunteer to be tutors for the younger children.

Coteacher communication alliances

While the children are involved in different activities, their two teachers find the time, limited but precious, to go over the day's activities together. If necessary, the teachers adjust and reorient these activities based on the events of the preceding day, the children who are present, the interests expressed by the children that morning, and so on.

Flexible schedule
9:00 a.m.

Now that all the children have arrived, it is necessary to tidy up the spaces and put away the materials used, while still showing respect for the activities in which the children have been involved. The various periods of the school day are not signaled by bells or tones. Children who are finishing up an activity or game are free to do so; they will join the group as soon as they have finished.

Group landscape
9:15 a.m.

Everyone has arrived and we get together for the assembly to see who is present, to have a fruit snack, to talk about something of interest, and to decide what to do.
This, however, is not a fixed rule. We sometimes break up into smaller groups immediately if the projects we are working on are clear to everyone, or we can spend the entire morning together or even split into two groups. We need rules, but we also need to be able to break away from them.

Not everything we will work on today is new. Some projects begun days or weeks earlier will be worked on, either by the original participants or by others.

Our kind of organization does not tolerate strict programs or predetermined directions. Once an overall time frame has been set (9:00 for arrival, 12:00 for lunch, 3:30 for snack, and 4:00 or 6:30 for departure), what determines the beginning or end of an activity is primarily the children's interests and desires.

Interests and desires

In the assembly we must choose among the activities proposed and decide who will be in which group. The children have the opportunity to propose other activities as well.

It is not easy to speak one at a time, to be clear, to engage the others. The teacher supports communication when she feels that it has become too fragile.

Assembly

Negotiation of ideas

This important opportunity gives the children an even stronger sense of participation and of building an experience together.

"So ideas fly, bounce around, accumulate, rise up, fall apart slowly, or spread, until finally one of them takes a decisive hold; it flies higher and conquers the entire group of children." (Loris Malaguzzi)

Group identity

The formation of groups is important: the characteristics of the individuals who make up a group determine whether or not an activity will proceed smoothly.

Other chapters in this book will explore this particular aspect in detail.

Workshop　It is now about 9:30. As we agreed during the assembly, the children have divided themselves into groups to work on different topics and with different materials. Today there is a group who will send a message to a single recipient, and groups who will continue exploring the qualities of light, shadows, and smells.

One group is finishing up some sculptures that will decorate the wall of an inner courtyard; the children say they are going to "make the wall pretty."

Time and the children's experiences at school flow together in a sort of osmotic relationship, in which every part of the day is important. There are no "fractures of value," no primary and secondary experiences. All of these activities derive from earlier experiences and will generate future experiences.

We will continue to "spy" on how individual and group learning emerges in other contexts and during other moments of the school day. But all with a lightness of spirit!

"The important thing is not to get bored. Let's just let things get done, as we do in our own cultures, but in such a way that no one gets bored... Because school is not a preparation for life, it is a part of life. School can be an honest way of living one's life." (Jerome Bruner, from notes taken during a conversation with a group of teachers in Reggio Emilia, July 1999)

Documentation and Assessment: What Is the Relationship?

Carla Rinaldi

The concept of documentation as a collection of documents used for demonstrating the truth of a fact or confirming a thesis is historically correlated to the birth and evolution of scientific thought and to a conceptualization of knowledge as an objective and demonstrable entity. It is thus tied to a certain historical period and to profound reasons of a cultural, social, and political nature that I will not examine here.

Rather, I find it interesting to underscore how the concept of documentation, which has only recently moved into the scholastic environment, and more specifically into the pedagogical-didactic sphere, has undergone substantial modifications that partially alter its definition. In this context, documentation is interpreted and used for its value as a tool for recalling; that is, as a possibility for reflection.

The didactic itinerary and the learning path that take place in a school assume full meaning for the subjects involved (teachers and students) to the extent that these processes can be suitably recalled, reexamined, analyzed, and reconstructed. The educational path becomes concretely visible through in-depth documentation of the data related to the activities, making use of verbal, graphic, and documentary instruments as well as the audiovisual technologies most commonly found in schools.

I want to underscore one aspect in particular regarding the way documentation is used; that is, the materials are collected *during* the experience, but they are read and interpreted at the *end*. The reading and recalling of memory therefore takes place after the fact. The documents (video and audio recordings, written notes) are collected, sometimes catalogued, and brought back for rereading, revisiting, and reconstruction of the experience. That which took place is reconstructed, interpreted, and reinterpreted by means of the documents which testify to the salient moments of a path that was predefined by the teacher: the path that made it possible for the objectives of the experience to be achieved.

In short, according to this conceptual approach and didactic practice, the documents (the documented traces) are used after and not during the process. These documents (and the reflections and interpretations they elicit from teachers and children) do not intervene during the learning path and within the learning process in a way that would give meaning and direction to the process.

Herein lies the substantial difference. In Reggio Emilia, where we have explored this methodology for many years, we place the emphasis on documentation as an integral part of the procedures aimed at fostering learning and for modifying the learning-teaching relationship.

To clarify further what I mean, a number of assumptions should be

tree

stated that may initially seem far from the issue at hand but that—or so I hope—will aid in understanding that our choice and practice are neither random nor indifferent. In fact, I believe that documentation is a substantial part of the goal that has always characterized our experience: the search for meaning—to find the meaning of school, or rather, to construct the meaning of school, as a place that plays an active role in the children's search for meaning and our own search for meaning (and shared meanings).

In this sense, among the first questions we should ask ourselves as teachers and educators are these: How can we help children find the meaning of what they do, what they encounter, what they experience? And how can we do this for ourselves? These are questions of meaning and the search for meaning (why? how? what?). I think these are the key questions that children constantly ask themselves, both at school and outside of school.

It is a very difficult search and a difficult task, especially for children who nowadays have so many spheres of reference in their daily lives: their family experience, television, the social places they frequent in addition to the family and school. It is a task that involves making connections, giving meaning to these events, to these fragments that are gathered over the course of many and varied experiences.

Children carry out this search with tenacity and effort, sometimes making mistakes, but they do the searching on their own. We cannot live without meaning; that would preclude any sense of identity, any hope, any future.

Children know this and initiate the search right from the beginning of their lives. They know it as young members of the human species, as individuals, as people. The search for the meaning of life and of the self in life is born with the child and is desired by the child. This is why we talk about a child who is competent and strong—a child who has the right to hope and the right to be valued, not a predefined child seen as fragile, needy, incapable. Ours is a different way of thinking and approaching the child, whom we view as an active subject with us to explore, to try day by day to understand something, to find a meaning, a piece of life.

For us, these meanings, these explanatory theories are extremely important and powerful in revealing the ways in which children think, question, and interpret reality and their own relationships with reality and with us.

Herein lies the genesis of the "pedagogy of relationships and listening," one of the metaphors that distinguishes the pedagogy of Reggio Emilia.

For adults and children alike, understanding means being able to develop an interpretive "theory," a narration that gives meaning to events and objects of

sound script

the world. Our theories are provisional, offering a satisfactory explanation that can be continuously reworked; but they represent something more than simply an idea or a group of ideas. They must please us and convince us, be useful, and satisfy our intellectual, affective, and aesthetic needs (the aesthetics of knowledge). In representing the world, our theories represent us.

Moreover, if possible, our theories must please and be attractive to others. Our theories need to be listened to by others. Expressing our theories to others makes it possible to transform a world not intrinsically ours into something shared. Sharing theories is a response to uncertainty.

Here, then, is the reason why any theorization, from the simplest to the most refined, needs to be expressed, to be communicated, and thus to be listened to, in order to exist. It is here we recognize the values and foundations of the "pedagogy of listening."

The Pedagogy of Listening

How can we define the term listening?

Listening as sensitivity to the patterns that connect, to that which connects us to others; abandoning ourselves to the conviction that our understanding and our own being are but small parts of a broader, integrated knowledge that holds the universe together.

Listening, then, as a metaphor for having the openness and sensitivity to listen and be listened to—listening not just with our ears, but with all our senses (sight, touch, smell, taste, orientation).

Listening to the hundred, the thousand languages, symbols, and codes we use to express ourselves and communicate, and with which life expresses itself and communicates to those who know how to listen.

Listening as time, the time of listening, a time that is outside chronological time—a time full of silences, of long pauses, an interior time. Interior listening, listening to ourselves, as a pause, a suspension, as an element that generates listening to others but, in turn, is generated by the listening that others give us. Behind the act of listening there is often a curiosity, a desire, a doubt, an interest; there is always an emotion.

Listening is emotion; it is generated by emotions and stimulates emotions. The emotions of others influence us by means of processes that are strong, direct, not mediated, and intrinsic to the interactions between communicating subjects.

Listening as welcoming and being open to differences, recognizing the value of the other's point of view and interpretation.

Listening as an active verb that involves interpretation, giving meaning to the message and value to those who offer it.

Listening that does not produce answers but formulates questions; listening that is generated by doubt, by uncertainty, which is not insecurity but, on the contrary, the security that every truth is such only if we are aware of its limits and its possible "falsification."

Listening is not easy. It requires a deep awareness and at the same time a suspension of our judgments and above all our prejudices; it requires openness to change. It demands that we have clearly in mind the value of the unknown and that we are able to overcome the sense of emptiness and precariousness that we experience whenever our certainties are questioned.

Listening that takes the individual out of anonymity, that legitimates us, gives us visibility, enriching both those who listen and those who produce the message (and children cannot bear to be anonymous).

Listening as the premise for any learning relationship—learning that is determined by the "learning subject" and takes shape in his or her mind through action and reflection, that becomes knowledge and skill through representation and exchange.

Listening, therefore, as "a listening context," where one learns to listen and narrate, where individuals feel legitimated to represent their theories and offer their own interpretations of a particular question. In representing our theories, we "re-know" or "re-cognize" them, making it possible for our images and intuitions to take shape and evolve through action, emotion, expressiveness, and iconic and symbolic representations (the "hundred languages").

Understanding and awareness are generated through sharing and dialogue.

We represent the world in our minds, and this representation is the fruit of our sensitivity to the way in which the world is interpreted in the minds and in the representations of others. It is here that our sensitivity to listening is highlighted; starting from this sensitivity, we form and communicate our representations of the world based not only on our response to events (self-construction), but also on that which we learn about the world from our communicative exchange with others.

The ability to shift (from one kind of intelligence to another, from one language to another) is not only a potential within the mind of each individual but also involves the tendency to shift across (to interact among) many minds. We enrich our knowledge and our subjectivity thanks to this predisposition to welcoming the representations and theories of others—that is, listening to others and being open to them.

This capacity for listening and reciprocal expectations, which enables communication and dialogue, is a quality of the mind and of the intelligence, particularly in the young child. It is a quality that demands to be understood and supported.

In the metaphorical sense, in fact, children are the greatest listeners of all to the reality that surrounds them. They possess the time of listening, which is not only time *for* listening but a time that is rarefied, curious, suspended, generous—a time full of waiting and expectation.

Children listen to life in all its shapes and colors, and they listen to others (adults and peers). They quickly perceive how the act of listening (observing, but also touching, smelling, tasting, searching) is essential for communication. Children are biologically predisposed to communicate, to exist in relation, to live in relation.

Listening, then, seems to be an innate predisposition that accompanies children from birth, allowing their process of acculturation to develop. The idea of an innate capacity for listening may seem paradoxical but, in effect, the process of acculturation must involve innate motivations and competencies. The newborn child comes into the world with a self that is joyous, expressive, and ready to experiment and explore, using objects and communicating with other people. Right from the beginning, children show a remarkable exuberance, creativity, and inventiveness toward their surroundings, as well as an autonomous and coherent consciousness.

Very early in life, children demonstrate that they have a voice, but above all that they know how to listen and want to be listened to. Sociality is not taught to children: they are social beings. Our task is to support them and live their sociality with them; that is the social quality that our culture has produced. Young children are strongly attracted by the ways, the languages (and thus the codes) that our culture has produced, as well as by other people (children and adults).

It is a difficult path that requires efforts, energies, hard work, and sometimes suffering, but it also offers wonder, amazement, joy, enthusiasm, and passion. It is a path that takes time, time that children have and adults often do not have or do not want to have. This is what a school should be: first and foremost, a context of multiple listening. This context of multiple listening, involving the teachers but also the group of children and each child, all of whom can listen to others and listen to themselves, overturns the teaching-learning relationship. This overturning shifts the focus to learning; that is, to children's self-learning and the learning achieved by the group of children and adults together.

As children represent their mental images to others, they represent them to themselves, developing a more conscious vision (interior listening). Thus, moving from one language to another, from one field of experience to another, and reflecting on these shifts and those of others, children modify and enrich their theories and conceptual maps. But this is true if, and only if, children have the opportunity to make these shifts in a group context—that is, in and with others—and if they have the possibility to listen and be listened to, to express their differences and be receptive to the differences of others.

The task of those who educate is not only to allow the differences to be expressed but to make it possible for them to be negotiated and nurtured through exchange and comparison of ideas. We are talking about differences between individuals but also differences between languages (verbal, graphic, plastic, musical, gestural, etc.), because it is the shifting from one language to another, as well as their reciprocal interaction, that enables the creation and consolidation of concepts and conceptual maps.

Not only does the individual child learn how to learn, but the group becomes conscious of itself as a "teaching place," where the many languages are enriched, multiplied, refined, and generated, but also collide, "contaminate," and hybridize each other, and are renewed.

The concept of "scaffolding," which has characterized the role of the teacher, also assumes new and different methods and meanings. It is the context, the web of reciprocal expectations (more than the teachers themselves) that sustains the individual and group processes. In addition to offering support and cultural mediation (subject matter, instruments, etc.), teachers who know how to observe, document, and interpret the processes that the children undergo autonomously will realize in this context their greatest potential to learn how to teach.

Documentation, therefore, is seen as visible listening, as the construction of traces (through notes, slides, videos, and so on) that not only testify to the children's learning paths and processes, but also make them possible because they are visible. For us this means making visible, and thus possible, the relationships that are the building blocks of knowledge.

Documentation

To ensure listening and being listened to is one of the primary tasks of documentation (producing traces/documents that testify to and make visible the ways of learning of the individuals and the group), as well as to ensure that the group and each individual child have the possibility to observe themselves from an external point of view while they are learning (both during and after the process).

A broad range of documentation (videos, tape recordings, written notes, and so on) produced and used *in process* (that is, during the experience) offers the following advantages:
• It makes visible (though in a partial way, and thus "partisan") the nature of the learning processes and strategies used by each child, and makes the subjective and intersubjective processes a common patrimony.
• It enables reading, revisiting, and assessment in time and in space, and these actions become an integral part of the knowledge-building process. Documentation can modify learning from an epistemological point of view (enabling epistemological assessment and self-assessment, which become an integral part of the process in that they guide and orient the process itself).
• It seems to be essential for metacognitive processes and for the understanding of children and adults.

In relation to recent studies that increasingly highlight the role of memory in the learning and identity-forming processes, we could hypothesize that significant reinforcement can be offered to the memory by the images (photographs and video), the voices, and the notations. Likewise the reflexive aspect (fostered by the "re-cognition" that takes place through use of the findings) and the capacity for concentration and interpretation could benefit from this memory-enhancing material. This is only a supposition, but in my view it deserves to be confronted and discussed.

In this movement, which I would define as a spiral as it weaves together the observation, the interpretation, and the documentation, we can clearly see how none of these actions can actually be separated or removed from the others. Any separation would be artificial and merely for the sake of argument. Rather, I would talk about dominance in the adult's level of awareness and consequently of action. It is impossible, in fact, to document without observing and, obviously, interpreting.

By means of documenting, the thinking—or the interpretation—of the documenter thus becomes material, that is, tangible and capable of being interpreted. The notes, the recordings, the slides and photographs represent fragments of a memory that seems thereby to become "objective." While each fragment is imbued with the subjectivity of the documenter, it is offered to the interpretive subjectivity of others in order to be known or reknown, created and recreated, also as a collective knowledge-building event.

The result is knowledge that is bountiful and enriched by the contributions of

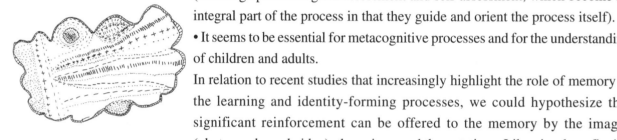

cloud

many. In these fragments (images, words, signs, and drawings) there is the past, that which took place, but there is also the future (or rather what else can happen if…).

We are looking at a new concept of didactics: participatory didactics, didactics as procedures and processes that can be communicated and shared. Visibility, legibility, and shareability become supporting nuclei because they are the basis of communicative effectiveness and didactic effectiveness. Didactics thus becomes more similar to the science of communication than to the traditional pedagogical disciplines.

At this point, a particular aspect emerges that structures the teaching-learning relationship and that in this context is made more visible, more explicit. At the moment of documentation (observation and interpretation), the element of assessment enters the picture immediately, that is, in the context and during the time in which the experience (activity) takes place. It is not sufficient to make an abstract prediction that establishes what is significant—the elements of value necessary for learning to be achieved—before the documentation is actually carried out. It is necessary to interact with the action itself, with that which is revealed, defined, and perceived as truly significant, as the experience unfolds.

Any gap between the prediction and the event (between the inherent meanings and those which the child/children attribute in their action) should be grasped readily and rapidly. The adult's schema of expectation is not prescriptive but orientative. Doubt and uncertainty permeate the context; they are part of the "documenter's context." Herein lies true didactic freedom, of the child as well as the teacher. It lies in this space between the predictable and the unexpected, where the communicative relationship between the children's and teachers' learning processes is constructed. It is in this space that the questions, the dialogue, the comparison of ideas with colleagues are situated, where the meeting on "what to do" takes place and the process of assessment (deciding what to "give value to") is carried out.

The issue, then, is to consider the child as a context for himself or herself and for the others, and to consider the learning process as a process of construction of interactions between the "subject being educated" and the "objects of education" (seen as including knowledge as well as social-affective and axiological models of behavior).

This means that the object of education is seen not as an object but as a "relational place." With this term I underscore the way in which the teacher chooses and proposes the knowledge-building approach (assuming all due

85

responsibility). It is a construction of relationships that are born of a reciprocal curiosity between the subject and the object. This curiosity is sparked by a question that stimulates the subject and the object to "encounter each other," showing what the child knows (understood as theories and desires for knowledge) and the knowledge of the object in terms of its cultural identity. This identity is not limited to the elements that are immediately perceivable, but is also directed toward the cultural elaborations that have been produced around it, and above all those that *can* be produced in this new knowledge-seeking relationship. This re-knowing of the object is not only "historical," that is, reproducing what is culturally known about the object (for example, what we know about a tree in its disciplinary interpretations: biology, architecture, poetry, and so on). It is also a living organism because it comes to life in the vitality, freshness, and unpredictableness of this encounter, where the children can give new identity to the object, creating a relationship for the object and for themselves that is also metaphorical and poetic.

Documentation is this process, which is dialectic, based on affective bonds and also poetic; it not only accompanies the knowledge-building process but in a certain sense impregnates it.

Documentation not only lends itself to interpretation but is itself interpretation. It is a narrative form, both intrapersonal and interpersonal communication, because it offers those who document and those who read the documentation an opportunity for reflection and learning. The reader can be a colleague, a group of colleagues, a child, children, parents, anyone who has participated or wants to participate in this process. The documentation material is open, accessible, usable, and therefore readable. In reality this is not always the case, and above all the process is neither automatic nor easy.

Effective documentation requires extensive experience in documentary reading and writing.

Legibility

Documentation is thus a narrative form. Its force of attraction lies in the wealth of questions, doubts, and reflections that underlie the collection of data and with which it is offered to others—colleagues and children.

These "writings," where different languages are interwoven (graphic, visual, iconic), need to have their own code, their own convention within the group that constructs and uses them—this in order to guarantee, even though partially, the effectiveness of communication.

That is, these writings must be legible, effectively communicative for those

cloud

who were not present in the context, but should also include the "emergent elements" perceived by the documenter. They are three-dimensional writings, not aimed at giving the event objectivity but at expressing the meaning-making effort; that is, to give meaning, to render the significance that each author attributes to the documentation and the questions and problems he or she perceives within a certain event. These writings are not detached from the personal biographical characteristics of the author, and we are thus aware of their bias, but this is considered an element of quality.

The documenter looks at the events that have taken place with a personal view aimed at a deep understanding of them and, at the same time, seeks communicative clarity. This is possible (though it could seem paradoxical) by bringing into the documentation the sense of incompleteness and expectation that can arise when you try to offer others not what you know, but the boundaries of your knowledge; that is, your limits, which derive from the fact that the "object" being narrated is a process and a path of research.

Assessment: A Perspective that Gives Value

What we offer to the children's processes and procedures, and to those which the children and adults together put into action, is a perspective that gives value. Valuing means giving value to this context and implies that certain elements are assumed as values.

Here, I think, is the genesis of assessment, because it allows one to make explicit, visible, and shareable the elements of value (indicators) applied by the documenter in producing the documentation. Assessment is an intrinsic part of documentation and therefore of the entire approach of what we call progettazione (progettazione is defined on page 17). In fact, this approach becomes something more than a prescribed and predefined procedure; it is a procedure that is nurtured by the elements of value that emerge from the process itself.

This makes the documentation particularly valuable to the children themselves, as they can encounter what they have done in the form of a narration, seeing the meaning that the teacher has drawn from their work. In the eyes of the children, this can demonstrate that what they do has value, has meaning. So they discover that they "exist" and can emerge from anonymity and invisibility, seeing that what they say and do is important, is listened to, and is appreciated: it is a value.

It is like having an interface with yourself and with whoever enters into this sort of hypertext. Here the text acts as vector, support, and pretext of the children's personal mental space.

The Teacher's Competency

In this context, it is obvious that the role and competency of the teacher are qualified in a different way from how these elements are defined in an educational environment in which the teacher's job is simply to transmit disciplinary knowledge in the traditional way.

The task is not to find (and teach) a specific series of rules, or to present certain propositions organized into formulas that can be easily learned by others, or to teach a method that can be replicated without modifications.

The teacher's competency is defined in terms more of understandings than of pure knowledge. It indicates a familiarity with critical facts, so as to allow those who possess this familiarity to say what is important and to hypothesize what is suitable for each situation—that is, what is helpful for the learner in a particular situation.

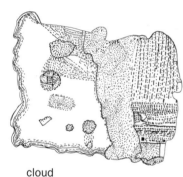

cloud

So what is the secret? There is no secret, no key, if not that of constantly examining our understandings, knowledge, and intuitions, and sharing and comparing them with those of our colleagues. It is not a transferable "science," but rather an understanding, a sensitivity to knowledge. The action and the results of the action, in a situation where only the surface is visible, will be successful in part thanks to the success of the actors—children and teachers— all of whom are responsible, though at different levels, for the learning processes.

Proceeding by trial and error does not debase the didactic paths; indeed, it enriches them on the process level (that is, the process and our awareness of it), as well as on the ethical level.

There is also an element of improvisation, a sort of "playing by ear," an ability to take stock of a situation, to know when to move and when to stay still, that no formula, no general recipe, can replace.

Certainly there are also risks, quite a few in fact: vagueness and superficiality can lead to mistaking a series of images or written notes for documentation which, without the awareness of what one is observing, only creates disorientation and a loss of meaning.

The issue that emerges clearly at this point is the education of the teachers. The teacher's general education must be broad-based and range over many areas of knowledge, not just psychology and pedagogy. A cultured teacher not only has a multidisciplinary background, but possesses the culture of research, of curiosity, of working in a group: the culture of project-based thinking. Above all, we need teachers who feel that they truly belong to and participate in this process, as teachers but most of all as people.

Loris Malaguzzi, architect of the pedagogical and philosophical thinking that permeates the Reggio experience, once said that we need a teacher who is sometimes the director, sometimes the set designer, sometimes the curtain and the backdrop, and sometimes the prompter. A teacher who is both sweet and stern, who is the electrician, who dispenses the paints, and who is even the audience—the audience who watches, sometimes claps, sometimes remains silent, full of emotion, who sometimes judges with skepticism, and at other times applauds with enthusiasm.

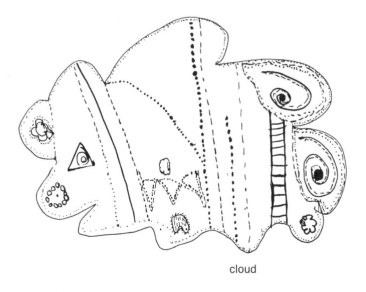

cloud

Protagonists
Katherine, 2 yrs. 8 mos.
Mario, 2 yrs. 6 mos.
and two- and
three-year-old
children
Infant-toddler Center
Bellelli
Teacher
Lucia Colla
Photographs by
Mirella Ruozzi
Marina Ferrari
Text by
Carla Rinaldi

Theatricality

Can play be a context for individual and group learning? It certainly can. Can play be a context for learning even for very young children? Is imitation a fundamental part not only of play but of learning as well? We are convinced that it is, thanks to examples like the one presented here.

These images are part of a much wider-ranging research study conducted by the teachers at the infant-toddler centers whose aim was to test the hypothesis that very young children are able to produce and decode "theatrical alphabets," those conventions and instruments that are typical of drama and theater.

The protagonists are Katherine and Mario and a group of friends who have been attending an infant-toddler center together for the last two years.

Katherine and Mario dance about, wrapping themselves in large tulle veils, lightweight and transparent, which take on shapes in relation to the children's movements. Thanks to the fact that they never lose sight of each other, a subtle dialogue between the two children develops in which the imitation of each other's gestures seems to be more an affectionate declaration than passive repetition.

Their mutual understanding becomes more and more refined, to the point that...

only a glance is needed to decide in unison to wrap themselves in a single veil, thereby creating a sort of "niche" that is an accessory to their game and to their mutual understanding.

The situation, or rather, the enjoyment in that situation, does not go unnoticed by a group of children who are playing in the piazza. They are attracted by this "performance" and they are sensitive to its "spectacularity," to the point that they seem to fan out in the space as if they were the audience.

The two children sense that they have an audience and turn in its direction. Their sensitivity to the audience's reactions is immediately revealed. The audience participates more and more actively. They are so completely involved that...

the two actors welcome the group of spectators into their game. A single group is formed, which creates a new shape and a new project for play.

Though few words are spoken, the mutual understanding is profound. The game is enriched and varied by the inclusion of the new protagonists. All seem to perceive the essence and the rules: transparency, seeing and not seeing, movement, the sound—or better yet, the voices—that accompany the movements. It is easy to create conventions.

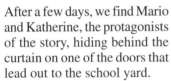

After a few days, we find Mario and Katherine, the protagonists of the story, hiding behind the curtain on one of the doors that lead out to the school yard.

The semitransparent curtain fabric powerfully evokes their previous experience: the two children are re-creating the situation of their initial game.
Is this repetition? Is it re-creation? Is it learning? Perhaps.
At least it seems so to us. In fact,...

Katherine, who is behind the curtain, seems to delight in this chance to resume her game, even though its features are different. Everything is there: her friend, the transparent fabric, but...
something is missing—the audience, those spectators who give meaning to her being the actor, the author-protagonist. The effort made to re-create a situation that is assimilable to the previous one seems to signal not only the pleasure of reproducing a successful situation but also the consolidation of the concept of actor-spectator, elements that are essential to the concept of theater.

Documenting
the Documenter

Laura Rubizzi

From a project by
Vea Vecchi
Laura Rubizzi
Isabella Meninno
School
Diana
Photographs by
Vea Vecchi
Isabella Meninno

In our study on the identity and role of documentation in learning processes, we now shift our focus from the children to the teachers. Although these processes may be less visible, they are no less fascinating than those of children.
• What thought processes orient the teachers as they document?
• Does an even partial awareness of these processes have value for professional growth?

These challenging questions lead us to shift the area of our research to domains of implicit knowledge; we accept the risks this research may pose as well as responsibility for the limits this documentation too may have.

Why should we observe and increase our awareness of the processes that support the teachers' process of documentation? Our hypothesis is that when teachers reflect on and discuss their choices and their actions, their awareness of the proposals they make to the children is significantly heightened. Approaching their work in this way makes them more capable of listening to the children and more willing to introduce changes to their procedures that are more in tune with the children's own strategies. The result is that teachers discover and appreciate the role of sharing ideas in terms of their professional development. We are aware of the value of interpreting reality and thus of the risks of excessively individualistic interpretations. We therefore structure every documentation process in a way that will foster exchange. The process develops within dynamics in which subjectivity and intersubjectivity attempt to establish an ongoing dialogue. Our attention focuses on individual and group learning, which is the constant condition that nurtures the idea of being able to elaborate original theories and didactic approaches that can be continuously updated and changed.

How can we convey such a complex documentation process to others?

We tried different ways, but none seemed sufficiently clear. In the end we chose as an example a discussion meeting with a group of children that lasted a few hours during a project they were working on. We felt this would give us the opportunity to follow and document the generative potentials of comparing the different viewpoints of the teacher-documenters. We have tried to make visible some of the more hidden aspects of the documentation process that nevertheless seem fundamental to the construction of sense and meanings shared by the teachers engaged in documentation.

Introduction to the Documentation Context

A number of years ago we began asking each class of five-year-old children to create a collective work to leave to the school, with the idea of building over

seated figure

time a sort of permanent exhibit of the ideas and competencies of the children in their interactions with the environment. This year the place chosen as the site for their project is one of the inner courtyards of the school. The children's attention is immediately drawn to a log that happens to be there. Their curiosity is stimulated and many questions emerge. Their attention is then drawn to the impressive large tree nearby, and especially to the fact that the tree is a living organism. Looking at the log, one of the girls comments: *Poor thing! Let's make a bridge that joins it to the tree that's alive.* The teachers immediately applaud this magnificent project and suggest that the children try to represent the idea graphically in order to explore it further.

Over the next few days, the children follow up their study of the project, producing three-dimensional models as well as computer generated drawings. The differences between these media enable the children to make conceptual advances and in-depth studies on the nature of the problems their project presents, in terms of the shape of the bridge, its height, length, width, and aesthetic features. The various designs are examined by the children and interpreted by the teachers: **the bridge as a union of vital energy between the living tree and the log represents the principal metaphor of the project and will serve as the guideline for the duration of the project.**

The documentation and comparison of interpretations we will follow here, as they develop, involve Isabella, a young atelierista who started working at the Diana School in September 1999; Vea, who had been the atelierista at the school for thirty years and has now been replaced by Isabella; and Laura, one of the teachers of the five-year-olds who has been working at the Diana School for twenty-six years.

The presence of Isabella, who is in the process of learning about the significant aspects of teaching and documenting, provides all the protagonists with a perfect opportunity to further their professional development. Her questions, uncertainties, and different outlook will provide her colleagues with the opportunity to reflect further on their own work. Becoming aware of the subjective differences, and together developing the meanings that derive from different discussions in order to construct shared communication codes, are essential to fostering dialogue and the pleasure of future exchanges. Over the years, this has been a constant challenge for Vea and Laura as well.

Before meeting with the children, the teachers agree, among other things, that Isabella will conduct the project, Vea will document the project with slides, and Laura, on the sidelines, will intervene only when she senses that Isabella needs help so that the quality of the discussion with and among the children will be enhanced. A tape recorder will serve as the "objective" memory of the

seated figure

group's conversation.

The relatively high number of adults in proportion to the number of children in the group makes sense when it is correlated with the need to offer Isabella, Vea, and Laura an opportunity for professional development. We often choose this kind of organization in small groups in order to offer all the teachers development opportunities that are considered essential.

A detailed, ongoing "storyboard" will make it possible to see the documents produced, the observational tools used, and the interpretations made by the three teachers.

A Brief Sketch of the Protagonists

Isabella, the present atelierista at the Diana School, has been working at the school for eight months; this is her first experience in the field of education. She has a background in the arts, has worked in the fields of fashion and graphic design, and has experience in the use of new technologies.

Vea has a background in the arts and has made a key contribution to the development of the identity of documentation through an uninterrupted thirty-year research experience in the Municipal Infant-toddler Centers and Preschools of Reggio Emilia, in particular at the Diana School.

Laura has a background in education and has been an attentive and committed investigator of young children's learning and knowledge-building processes. Hers is the narrating voice of the storyboard.

These three very different individuals advance in their professional development in a context that is common to all three and in continuous dialogue with each other, while maintaining their different strategies and objectives.

Isabella is seeking her own interpretation of the role of the atelierista and is fascinated and captivated by the children and their extraordinariness. Here she encounters two more experienced teachers and accepts them with respect but dialogues with them in a straightforward, open manner.

A challenge in staff development is to think of ways for new teachers to grow professionally that do not involve necessarily accepting and assuming the more conforming aspects of the situations in which these teachers find themselves. Professional development should not be merely a process of transmitting the "accumulated knowledge" that the school and more experienced teachers can offer. In fact, accepting the new teachers' different points of view, which are often dissimilar and sometimes critical, may revitalize the entire group of teachers and create new thinking strategies capable of questioning even what may seem almost obvious.

Vea and Laura, aware of their competencies and their role as mentors, approach this experience with their usual research inquisitiveness. After many years of working together they have perfected communication codes and developed common project approaches. At the same time, the differences in their individual approaches have also become more apparent, and these differences make each and every exchange more interesting.

With the three teachers, the direct protagonists in this path of knowledge-building are four children:

Caterina, age 6 years 3 months, author of the sculpture idea chosen and developed by the group, unshakable supporter of the group's competencies and careful listener; she contributes ideas and always expresses her points of view.

Luca, age 6 years 3 months, is captivated by project design, hypothesizing and investigating problem-solving strategies. He is inclined to formulate hypotheses constantly, choosing the most feasible and most effective ones. He pushes himself to find optimal organizational solutions that balance risks and goals and is easily infected by the group's optimism.

Ferruccio, age 6 years 1 month, is a "possiblist." He is ironic, logical, yet always ready for narrative digressions. Along with Caterina, he is custodian of the more emotional and meaningful part of the group's project.

Martina, age 5 years 11 months, interprets the group's work primarily as an opportunity for her own individual learning, which she develops at home with her father's help. She rarely speaks during the group discussions, limiting her comments to brief suggestions and reformulations of the problems the group is facing.

The discussion we examine here lasted about one and a half hours and concerned the necessary step the children had to take to transform one of the three-dimensional models they had previously produced into the large-scale bridge that would join the log to the large, living tree. We anticipated that the children would almost certainly try to decide on the measurements of the actual bridge. This would provide a learning opportunity that moved into another domain of knowledge, one that is important and difficult but, in this case, is supported by the children's desire to realize their project.

Project Log

May 13, 2:00 p.m. Laura shares with Isabella some thoughts she feels are important for identifying and understanding, at least partially, the meanings of the proposal that will be made to the children:
• How can we as teachers deal with the problem of measurement within the project the children are working on?
• What does measuring mean to children of this age?
• What previous experience have they had with measuring?
• What might the children and teachers learn?
• Does the school have any previous documentation on this topic that can be consulted?
The experience gained through working on project strategies increases the teachers' ability to anticipate the paths of research the children may undertake, and to hypothesize methods and lines of observation. All this contributes to the teachers' awareness in constructing forecast models which give direction but must also be open to any changes that may be suggested by the actual work with the children.

May 16, 8:30 a.m. Isabella and Laura prepare the courtyard so that it welcomes the children in a more meaningful way: a cozy area with benches for the initial group meeting near the site where the children will build what they have begun to call the "hug-bridge." On hand are the children's project designs and three-dimensional clay model of the bridge (which they had made earlier) so as to assist their memory. Off to the side is an assortment of "intelligent materials" aimed at stimulating thought and action related to taking measurements, if the children should feel the need for them (strings, small bricks, ribbons, measuring sticks and tapes, sticks, wire, wooden boards, and so on).

9:30 a.m. Meeting with the group of children:
Isabella introduces the proposal for that morning: "Ferruccio, Luca, Caterina, Martina, do you remember what we've done so far?"
We will present the first part of this discussion in detail later in the text so that our readers can better understand how we use documentation tools and how we share our impressions.

11:00 a.m. Today's discussion with the children is over. Isabella and Laura have produced some notes, Vea has taken two rolls of slides, the children have a numerical annotation of the "distance" and the "height" of the bridge, and there is also a

98

tape recording of the conversations, which will be transcribed later and which will be an essential element in the interpretation and documentation processes to come.

Isabella's notes taken during the children's conversation

Laura's notes taken during the children's conversation

A first glance at Laura's and Isabella's notes shows that their observational priorities differ. Laura's notes are jotted down, she highlights some of them, and she includes drawings and sketches. Laura also notes some of the children's phrases that she considers significant. She summarizes what she feels are the most meaningful moments of the discussion in order to be able to reconstruct the discussion itself.

Isabella, very involved in leading the group discussion, takes some notes primarily on the problem of measuring, an aspect that both worries and excites her.

The children's notes

Isabella, Laura, and Vea meet in the atelier while their impressions of the experience they have observed are still fresh in their minds. This immediate sharing of interpretations ensures a communicative exchange where the emotional aspect is crucial not only in recalling the experience but also in increasing the number of points of view with which to approach subsequent interpretations and the identification of future proposals (that is, proposals based on interpretations made at this moment).

Vea and Laura, again aware of their role as mentors, leave room for Isabella's interpretations. Vea starts off their meeting by asking some questions that create a context both for the experience they have just observed and for their task of narrating and documenting the experience. Vea, whose approach is to maintain a dialogue and "relaunch" ideas, comments briefly on Isabella's statements. Laura comments on Isabella's considerations and offers her own interpretation and predictions concerning the possible evolution of the project.

11:30-12:30 p.m.

Isabella's comments are lengthy. She gives a detailed reconstruction, from her point of view, of the phases she has observed, in an alternation of images that are complex and, in certain moments, may even have disoriented her. For example, when describing the children's excitement while measuring, she says, "For the children, measuring the bridge means measuring everything, the tree, the trunk, the environment."

Her comments and considerations are penetrating. While describing with admiration some of Laura's comments during the meeting with the children, Isabella says, "You always have to follow two tracks when working with children; you have to let yourself get involved in what's happening but you also have to interpret. Instead, I followed everything… all the little lights turning on…"

Isabella continues to be surprised by the amount of attention even apparently small choices require. Of her own considerations she says, "I think I have to ask myself what's important. I can only see how Laura and Vea consider even the smallest choices so doggedly—some might even find it obsessive. Instead, they're choices that build a big picture for the children…"

How much weight will these comments and rereadings have as the project progresses, and to what extent will they frame Isabella's forecasts of how the project will continue?

Isabella's comments reveal great sensitivity and reawaken in Laura and Vea the sense of amazement and the peak moments that risk getting lost over time after constant practice of careful, structured listening.

Isabella, Vea, and Laura agree to proceed with the comparison of their approaches by first making individual interpretations of the observations they made during the meeting with the children, to arrive at a narration in words and images. This sort of short documentary would underline the idea that the visual language belongs not only to the final documentation of the project but also contributes to giving meaning to and communicating the processes observed during the project itself.

The three teachers agree to have their interpretations ready in two days' time. Each of them will use her personal notes, the slides taken by Vea, and Isabella's transcription of the conversation recorded during the meeting with the group of children.

They also agree to note the criteria and procedures that they will apply because these too, along with the personally produced documents, will be the subject of comparison and discussion.

The documentation usually focuses primarily on the children's learning processes. In this case, as we have said, the focus shifts to the learning processes of the documenters, to their subjectivity as it emerges in comparison with others. This kind of exchange is seen as an opportunity for each teacher to know herself better, to appreciate her own positive traits, and to identify those competencies that need to be developed or strengthened.

In the atelier Isabella transcribes the audiotape of the meeting with the children. She will then photocopy it and give copies to Vea and Laura. For all three teachers, this transcription represents the most objective reference for a second level of interpretation (that is, the narration through words and images) that will be carried out individually and without shared reference schemas other than the objective of producing something that can be circulated, commented on, and discussed.

3:00-5:00 p.m.

If we want the observation of a group of children to be more than just a chronicle of a series of events, we must reconstruct and interpret those observations on different levels, without losing sight of the individuals who make up the group (the children and the teachers), of the group itself, the learning processes, the nature of the participation, or the methodologies produced.

Laura, alone in her classroom, goes over the notes she took during the meeting with the children. She reconstructs in more detail the events she observed and the concepts the children seem to have dealt with, and makes note of possible foci for the continuation of the project.

5:00-5:30 p.m.

She believes that this is a very productive procedure to follow as the project unfolds, providing a sort of written "recent memory" that will be reinforced or modified when rereading the dialogues and consulting any available photographic images. With this approach, the teacher gets used to proceeding by searching for meaning and it becomes possible to generate preliminary hypotheses of what will be "relaunched" to the children.

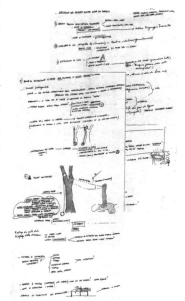

Laura's second set of notes:
a detailed reconstruction of
the events

In their own times and places, Isabella, Laura, and Vea have each produced the documentation of the events they observed. Isabella's transcription of the audiotape and the slides taken by Vea were available to all three. Isabella and Laura also had the notes they took during the meeting with the children.

May 16, 17, 18

101

May 18, 4:00 p.m.   Isabella, Laura, and Vea exchange copies of their verbal and visual narrative hypotheses, including notes on their procedures.

The three teachers have noted the procedures they used chronologically so that the criteria and ways these procedures were adopted for putting together the documentation of the observed episode can be more fully appreciated.

Here were three documentation hypotheses that, although all stemming from a common observational situation and all using the same photographic images and transcriptions of the children's conversation, have some similarities but also considerable differences due to the teachers' different expectations, their different roles, and their subjectivities.

Once again we have evidence that reality is not objective, but is the fruit of interpretations.

Isabella's documentation hypotheses clearly show a sense of wonder, discovery, research, and indefiniteness.

Laura reveals her unswerving attention as an experienced teacher to the individuals who make up the group, to their learning and growth processes.

Vea concentrates on a narration that is meaningful, effective, complex, capable of revealing multiple points of view, and rich with interpretations and new proposals.

The three narrative hypotheses prove to be very interesting even after a preliminary reading. The strategies used by Isabella, Laura, and Vea provide a decisive interpretive lens, as they seem to reveal the processes and relations each developed in order to arrive at her final narration.

The three hypotheses seem to have in common the fact that each teacher has given value to the transcription of the conversation recorded during the meeting with the children; what varies is the interpretive filter through which the conversation is analyzed.

Isabella proceeds by means of a series of readings, the first of which leads her to highlight the moments she feels are "emotionally interesting." Her visual narrative aims at being what she calls "a documentary by concepts." Her process is characterized by concentrating on the written text in order to interpret and understand it and on a visual outline that, as she says, "attempts to match up with the written text to produce a narrative that is comprehensible, simple, and strong." For the moment, this narrative is a series of notes to herself that she will use in the first exchange of interpretations of what took place during the discussion with the children.

In order to achieve the ambitious objective she has set for herself (and it is right to have high ambitions), Isabella will subsequently need many more

102

elaborations and exchanges of opinion. Communication is a very complex constructive process.

Laura seeks out the key procedural elements in the transcription of the group's conversation, in terms of both learning and the development of the relationships among the children and between the children and teachers. Her intense process of interpretation then links these elements to the notes she took during the actual encounter with the children. For logistical reasons, she will not see the slides until later; consequently, Laura works from memory and constructs an outline based on hypothetical images, which she will verify later.

When she does receive the slides, Laura partially revises her hypothesis since the photographic images significantly enrich and integrate the perception of the atmosphere, the emotional aspects, and the spatial interrelationships of the group.

Vea tries to transform the words in the transcription of the children's conversation into visual images, constructing what she defines as "the script of a film that will come later."

She then proceeds by looking at the relations between two "scripts": the one related to the audiotape transcription and the other based on the visual report she has produced (her slides). She selects the images based on what she sees as the "significant emerging elements" and hypothesizes the missing photographic images. The result is a narration where text and images are intensely interpenetrating. She entrusts the evolution of the narration to a "first encounter with an audience outside the project," as sharing ideas with others will modify not only the narration but also the interpretation of some of the moments of the project path.

What elements of a professionally enriching exchange can we expect to find in this sharing of ideas? The true value of this moment lies not so much in deciding on a documentational procedure that all will respect but in the fact that it bears witness to the different mental procedures through which each teacher has tried to generate a hypothesis of documentation. Its extraordinary value lies in perceiving oneself as a distinct individual in comparison and in dialogue, and thus in a position to identify those areas of learning and exchange on which to concentrate. There is also the more articulated and precise perception of how our own thoughts can benefit from and evolve by listening to other points of view. Finally, our exchange leads us to examine the deeper meanings of documentation, thereby updating the idea of documentation itself.

Our brief attempt to give an example of the teachers' work during the documentation process stops here, fresh from an exchange that we extend to the reader, to whom we dedicate a short exercise that we hope will stimulate his or her curiosity and elicit questions.

For obvious reasons of space, we show here (opposite page) only the first page of the notes Isabella took during the children's discussion. This observational technique is frequently used by the teachers at the Diana School because we feel it is useful to subsequent interpretations, circulation, and for sharing ideas and opinions.

The name of each child and the teacher or teachers involved head separate columns on the page; in this case, one of the teachers present is Isabella, the atelierista. The participants' comments are entered in spatial sequence and are numbered. When the chart is completed, each child can be "read" individually, by going down his or her column, and in relation to the group, by reading horizontally. The very first column on the left is for indicating time, including breaks and moments of silence, and the last column on the right is for the teacher's personal interpretations and those of her colleagues. On this chart there are three columns in which to record comments of Laura, Isabella, and Vea. Notes and interpretations of Isabella's observations by Laura and Vea appear on page 107, using the same numbering as Isabella's notes.

To facilitate reading, comments that were actually made on two separate occasions—individually and as a group—have been combined. As the reader, you may approve or disapprove, and add your own interpretations. What usually takes place following this is a discussion, which results in the final interpretation.

Comments on Isabella's Transcription

The document, transcribed and circulated to gather impressions and interpretations, must have the elements that enable this to happen. In Isabella's transcription some of these important elements are missing. Since a camera or video camera is not always used, it is important to take notes not only on what is said but also on the atmosphere; quick drawings and sketches (for example, eyes turned to a child, smiles, yawns, and so on) are very helpful.

Also missing are the starting and stopping times, as well as intermediate times that would help to better understand what is happening (for example, how much time passed between the beginning of the discussion and the taking of the first actual measurement, how long the children remained silent, and so on).

Isabella's notes

Martina	Cate.	Luca	Feno	Laura	Isa

Isabella's notes (translated and typed on the computer)

Martina	Caterina	Luca	Ferruccio	Laura	Isabella	
	2 Nice!	1 Lodi did this one... It looks like a fish. 4 (talking to himself) Here's a ladder...			3 Ferro, Luca, Caterina, Martina... 5 Do you remember what we did?	
			6 We put a man here, sitting on the bridge, a leg came out from this hole...		7 Apart from that, let's take a look... There were our two trees... the big tree...	
		8 It's our little itsy bitsy...			9 ... and the little one. Why was there this bridge?	
		10 Because like this we can put us on it ... some photos	11 No!! We were going to connect them!			
			12 It made a hug.		12 Right, we connected them.	
		13 Caterina said we could attach the two branches; that way they could be friends.			14 Okay. It could be a project we could do.	
		15 No, I don't remember it like that.	16 Yes, we can really make them hug.		17 Is it a project that can be done big?	
		18 Hmm... I don't think so.				
20. Davide's not here.	19 I have an idea!	20 We'll have to get a ladder.	20 As big as that tree!		21 Why can't it be done big, do you think?	
		22 Well, it's sort of too hard.			23 Why is it too hard? What do you think the hardest thing is?	
		24 To make the hug here, we don't have a ladder that goes that high up.			25 Is the hug the hardest thing? I can find a ladder for you.	
		26 As long as it's not ten meters high!	28 I'm a monkey who doesn't know how to climb.	27 Do you need a ladder?	27 A ladder? Ten meters! We'll show you that everything is possible!...	
		29 This tree is old and it's full of spider webs.	31 There.	30 Where do we put the ladder?	31 What do you have to look at now with the ladder?	
		32 We have to see if it's really tall.			33 Luca's climbing up because he said it's hard to make the hug. Luca has to check and not just climb up. Is it hard? What's it like?	
		34 Kind of big.			35 Is the hug like it should be?	
		36 Real big!	37 I know, I know how!		38 Luca said that this hug has to be really big... what does it mean to be "big"?	
		39 It has to be a huge hole!				

Critical notes and interpretations
by Laura and Vea
on the first page of Isabella's observations

Preliminary note
The context is missing: Where are the children?
What are they doing?

1 What looks like a fish? The element is missing.

3 Good to repeat the names of the group members: it makes
them feel like individuals in a group.

8 Appreciate the interventions that recall and communicate the
important meaning (the metaphor) of the project.

10 Idea that gives strength to the group and communicates to
everyone who the authors of the project are. Bridge and children
are united in the project.

11 Underscore again Caterina's initial idea. The children
continue to hold onto the meaning of the project. Has the
metaphor already been transformed into a structural hypothesis?

17 Good question, but introduces a difficult problem in too
direct a way. Maybe it could have been formulated like this:
"How can we connect these two tree friends with a bridge-
hug?" The question recalls the concepts just expressed by the
children and, even though it doesn't modify the problem they
have to confront, it frames the problem in a less distant and
more acceptable way.

18 First doubt that emerges in the group about the real
construction possibilities.

19 What is Caterina's idea? If someone has an idea is it always
better to hear what it is?

21 Isabella's question gives a pessimistic perspective to Luca's
legitimate doubt, and could convince the children that it really is
too difficult a project to realize.

20 The roles the children have in the group in this phase begin
to emerge: Ferruccio, the "possiblist,"
22 Luca, the skeptic.

23 Good intervention by Isabella.

26 Luca's concern about the height appears (then climbing the
ladder makes it visible).

27 Laura becomes a practical support of the children's
indications. In
30 this way the ideas don't run the risk of getting dispersed.

32 The first measurement hypothesized is by using the body.

34 First hypotheses on the dimensions of the embrace (when
the bridge
36 will be hooked to the large tree).

40 Why aren't the two girls getting involved? It's a good idea
for the teacher to ask herself this question and look for a way to
encourage them to participate without letting their role be
characterized by the long time that goes by in silence.

Visual Essay

It might be of interest to see how we construct the final narrative when photographs or slides are available.

Let's see how the observation chart, once it has been interpreted, is transformed into a narrative in order to share it with others. This narrative will be commented on by the children, families, and our colleagues, and will invite further reflection and interpretation. The visual narrative does not follow the events by means of a series of captions, but progresses via meaningful syntheses.

Although the introduction to the problem of the bridge appears earlier in this text, we feel it may be of interest to the reader to see how the subject is introduced as a whole.

At this point the documentary is still a working tool which requires some photographs that were not taken during the discussion itself; these will be taken later. A broader exchange of ideas with other colleagues and pedagogistas is also needed.

The Embrace
Height and Distance

* the asterisks indicate slides to be taken

Over the last few years, we have developed the awareness and the custom of leaving a collective work in the school environment. This work contributes to building over time a sort of permanent exhibit of the ideas and competencies of children in relating to the environment. This year the children identified one of the school's two inner courtyards as the project space.

* slide of inner courtyard taken from the outside looking inside to better show its relation to the school

Immediately on entering this small space,

the children's attention focuses on...

a log that happens to be there.

* slide of the log

Poor thing!... (other comments not heard that lead to): *Let's make a bridge that connects it to the tree!* (and further comments)

The teachers ask the children to try to visualize this initial, wonderful project idea.

* slide of some of the preliminary
drawings with brief interpretations

Ferruccio's drawing

Caterina's drawing

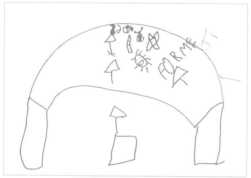

Luca's drawing

Martina's drawing

The bridge as a union of vital energy between the living tree and the log represents the principal metaphor of the project. It is necessary always to bear it in mind and use it as the guideline for the entire project path.

The moment documented here reflects a discussion that lasted about an hour and a half (presented here are only the first fifteen minutes) dealing with the necessary passage from the graphic and plastic models previously produced to the full-scale realization of the bridge.

We anticipated that this passage would lead the children almost inevitably to dealing with problems of measuring. We are always pleased when a project involves a number of very different problems from different domains of knowledge, and when these are dealt with by the children for a good reason.

Although many measuring instruments are available in the classroom, this group of children had never before faced this problem, except perhaps indirectly, and certainly had never used a measuring stick or tape.

The courtyard as it waits for what might happen.

Laura has prepared materials that could be used for measuring and has put them to one side. There is a wide variety of materials, carefully thought out to allow for different hypotheses and experiments.

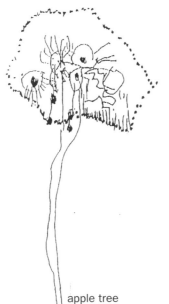

We will see whether the children realize that these materials are there, and if and how they use them.

apple tree

111

As soon as they enter the courtyard, Luca and Ferruccio are drawn to the model of the bridge done on the computer. All four children will repeatedly turn to the models of the bridge they prepared previously (drawings, clay models, computerized models). It is interesting to understand better the conceptual relationships the children manage to construct between the models and the actual bridge, and how they will make use of them.

The children are invited to sit down. Laura and Isabella are present.

Isabella: "Ferruccio, Luca, Caterina, Martina, do you remember what we talked about before? What do we have to do to continue our work and build the bridge?"

By calling each child by name Isabella reconfirms the identity of the individuals in the group, and by asking questions she redirects the children to an ongoing path. Together, she and the children begin to tell their story.

Isabella: "Here are our two trees. A big one…"

Luca: *...and the little one... Let's put our pictures on them.*

This idea gives the group strength and communicates to everyone who the authors of the project are. The bridge and the children are united in the project.

Ferruccio: *We connected them, they were hugging.*

Ferruccio underlines Caterina's original idea. During this entire first approach the children maintain a clear sense of their project. Is the metaphor on its way to becoming a structural hypothesis?

* close-up of Isabella

Isabella asks: "Could we build this bridge, make it life-size?"

While the question is valid, it does introduce a difficult problem far too directly. Perhaps the question should have been formulated as: How could we connect these two tree-friends with a bridge-hug? This question would thus use the concepts the children had just expressed, and even though it would not change the problem they have to deal with, that problem would be introduced in a way that is in harmony with the children. This would facilitate the passage from metaphor to structural hypothesis.

The idea of an embrace is particularly important because that is what has generated the children's project. The idea emerged spontaneously from their feelings of tenderness and solidarity toward the log. **It is important never to lose the essential sense and meaning of what one is doing. The children's and adults' actions and forms are constructed within this sense of the embrace.**

During the project path the children have intuitions that escape our notice during the "live action" of their work. We glimpse these intuitions only later, when we read and interpret what has taken place. We must not avoid asking ourselves to what extent our not listening to the children's ideas may have led the children away from the problem and even at times disoriented them.

Being quick to listen, however, is by no means simple. We can make it more careful by capturing and reflecting beforehand on the principal concepts, as in this case—where right from the start we captured in the children's words the profound meaning of a structure/bridge that is generated by the solidarity of the embrace between the log and the tree.

Luca: *We should get a ladder… we've got to see if it's really high or not.* Immediately afterward: *Well, it's a little too hard.*

The children's first approach to measuring is physical and puts height and difficulty in relation to each other.

Here Isabella intervenes with a well-pitched question: "Can you try and tell me what's hard about it?"

She helps Luca and the other children articulate and visualize the complex operation they will have to perform. For the moment, the difficulties are expressed as the need for a ladder and the danger connected to the height. As for the rest, we will see what happens.

Luca: *As long as the ladder isn't ten meters high!*

One of the roles that Luca will have that morning—that of the skeptic—begins to emerge.

Ferruccio, instead, will be the "possiblist," and Caterina will alternate moments of silence with moments when she will single-mindedly support the desire to build the bridge. Martina has the most elusive personality in the group; she is very quiet, almost absent. Her interest will be sparked only during the exploration and discovery of the measuring stick. She will extend and continue developing this interest at home and will question and challenge her father for never having told her about measuring sticks or taught her how to use one.

Are children's roles within the group generally stable or do they change in the course of a project? What other roles do they take on? Do their roles change based on the topic at hand?

We ask ourselves these questions in all situations, not just in this particular case. Although we may have our opinions and impressions on the matter, it is important to continue to verify them in other situations and contexts.

Luca and Ferruccio are constantly playing the protagonist roles, albeit in different ways. Caterina is sometimes attentive, and Martina often seems absent. In these cases the teacher must seek out the reasons and try to get anyone who seems distant more involved. This is not easy. Children have their own personalities and approaches, and it is unfair to constantly hold back someone with an approach like Luca's. What is more, with his intelligent impetuousness, he often contributes to giving direction to the work and carrying it forward. Isabella also tends to rush headlong and is carried away by Luca and by the fear of losing the direction he is giving to the project. She speaks a lot, too much perhaps, but it is not always easy to maintain self-control. Even after many years of experience we still find it hard.

Isabella should have perhaps been more aware of the girls' silences and their expressions. Sometimes we are aware of these things but it is not easy to find a balance that still supports the vitality and creativity of the whole group. We must also accept the fact that there will be alternating moments. If the difficult ones last for some time, however, as in this case, it is necessary to try different ways of involving everyone. Once again, this is not easy to do.

Talking about the size of the embrace (the point where the bridge encircles the tree trunk), Luca defines it as "very big, an enormous hole" and to confirm where the embrace takes place…

(The brief narration that follows comes from another page of Isabella's notes; we include it here in order to complete our account of Luca's thoughts.)

…he turns to the clay model: *That's what it says in the clay.* The children seem to be aware that the models contain information and memory concerning how to build the bridge. We say "seem" because we will see that at other times the children appear to completely lose sight of the indications the models provide or to no longer consider them important.

The children continue talking about the "hug": Caterina defines it as "enormous," and Martina, who finally speaks, uses a metaphor to describe it—"a belt," she calls it.

Although the discussion with the children lasted an hour and a half, our account here only deals with the way it began. Another discussion is needed to solve the problem of measuring.

After numerous discussions and design variations, the bridge is now under construction.

Conversation with a Group of Teachers

Amelia Gambetti

This conversation took place at the Villetta School during one of the professional development sessions attended by a number of teachers who have been working at the school for many years and teachers who have only recently started their experience there. Like other conversations, it was part of a professional development project whose objective, among many others, was to analyze the problem areas that were emerging from the daily experience of these new teachers. Terms such as theory, practice, professional development, observation, documentation, strategies, projects, collaboration, and many others came up repeatedly during the conversation and became concepts within which new content started to develop.

The voices of the participants followed one another, alternated with one another, and at times overlapped, seeming to need more space in which to be heard. At times the thoughts that emerged were echoed, as if to find confirmation in different ways or to strengthen a reflection that has been enriched by the opinion of someone else.

This seesaw of dialogues and different points of view is part of a long-term knowledge-building process that leaves open the possibility of revising one's thinking within a situation that is in a constant state of flux, in a search for new identities.

The first question in this conversation stemmed from discussions held during earlier sessions, which had led the teachers to look for more appropriate definitions of their roles based on a careful analysis of the complexity of their work.

Discussion group

116

Amelia Gambetti - 50 years old, has been the Coordinator of Reggio Children since 1996 and Liaison for Consultancy in Schools in different countries all over the world. She was a teacher at the Villetta School for twenty-five years.
Since 1992 she has been collaborating with universities and schools mainly in the United States for the research and study of the experience of the Reggio Emilia Municipal Infant-toddler Centers and Preschools.

Simona Laiacona - 22 years old, is a substitute teacher at the Villetta School, currently teaching in the five-year-olds' class.
After receiving her secondary school diploma in science and education, she became a substitute teacher on a yearly contract in the Reggio Emilia Municipal Preschools, where she has been working for three years.

Orietta Montepietra - 27 years old, has been working at the Villetta School since 1994; she currently teaches in the three-year-olds' class.
After receiving her secondary school diploma in education, she has been a substitute teacher on a yearly contract in the Reggio Emilia Municipal Preschools for about four years.

Diletta Tirelli - 30 years old, has been working at the Villetta School since 1993 and currently teaches in the five-year-olds' class.*
After receiving her secondary school diploma in education, she worked for about two years in a municipal infant-toddler center before going on to work in the preschools.

Teresa Bucci - 31 years old, currently works at the Villetta School as a support teacher in the four-year-olds' classroom. Like Simona, she is a substitute teacher with a yearly contract.

Giovanni Piazza - 47 years old, has been working as the atelierista at the Villetta School since 1973. He started his teaching experience here after receiving his secondary school diploma in visual arts.

* Current class assignments refer to the 1999-2000 school year. For further information on school and staff organization, see Appendix D.

Barbara Martelli - 26 years old, has a degree in pedagogy and works as a substitute teacher on a yearly contract at the Villetta School, currently in the three-year-olds' class. She worked for a number of years as a substitute teacher in other schools in the Emilia-Romagna region.

Paola Barchi - 40 years old, has been working at the Villetta School since 1987; she currently teaches in the five-year-olds' classroom.
After receiving her secondary school diploma in education, she worked as a substitute teacher in the Reggio Emilia Preschools and Infant-toddler Centers for about seven years and was subsequently hired on a permanent contract.

117

Amelia: In the Reggio Municipal Infant-toddler Centers and Preschools, the concept of "being in a state of permanent research" is being increasingly developed. We like to define our work, the way we are immersed in our work as teachers, as a way of permanently "researching/searching for something"; and I think the way we evolve within various experiences is also part of the long-standing process of building our own identity. In view of this, how have you begun to understand the meaning of the statement that teachers can be considered "pedagogical researchers"? What discoveries have you made and what difficulties have you encountered during this process?

Simona: I'm not sure of the extent to which I am able to grasp the profound meaning of the term "pedagogical researcher." Thinking about myself and also my first experience here, yes, I think in the first few days I felt I was a researcher, but more in the sense of someone who was searching for solutions, even immediate ones. I was looking for something, and especially for someone who would say to me straightaway, "Do this, do that" or "Look, this is how we do things here." I could see that the educators worked a lot in the daily life in the school, so I used to ask myself how you could reconcile so much action with the time needed for observation and reflection. I realized, perhaps wrongly, that I needed something that could be used immediately. During my studies at school, I had understood that that's how it would work.

Amelia: What does all this mean to you? Can you give some examples, and tell us in more detail what you mean by "something that could be used immediately"?

Simona: I was expecting to be told what to do and why, I expected some guidelines that would give me specific instructions.

Orietta: Did you also expect someone to teach you what you had to do?

Simona: In some way, I did. The first few times I participated in the morning group assembly, for example, where all the children meet together (which I had already seen in other schools), I didn't know where to start or how to interact with a large group of children. So I was expecting Diletta, the other teacher in the class, to say to me, "Look, this is how you should do it," as if there were a formula. Since I was quite new to this type of situation, I wanted someone to tell me what to do straightaway.

Amelia: But what kind of relationship did you have with Diletta before you started teaching?

Simona: I arrived at the Villetta School on September 1, when the children were already there, so there wasn't really time for much communication between us. I came to school one day before the children arrived, but the classroom was being

GIULIA

Villetta School

118

organized and some things were being completed so that, frankly, there was no time to stop and explain. You had to understand and act at the same time, in the context of what was going on.

Amelia: Were there times, though, almost immediately afterward, in which people could discuss and share with you what the day was like at school?

Simona: Yes, but it wasn't enough, because there were still a lot of situations to take care of. It wasn't just the game of finding out who was at school and who was at home, or lunch time, or cleaning up the classroom, it was the whole complexity of the experience I had in front of me. Just to give you an example, in the morning, when we and the children were dividing into medium and small groups, I didn't know what to do. I wasn't sure whether I had to follow a single group or walk around the groups. I felt that I didn't know how to organize myself or how to organize my thoughts and actions.

Amelia: So would you have liked someone to tell you what you had to do?

Simona: Yes, I felt that I wanted and needed it, because I didn't want to be seen as incompetent—even if my incompetence was due to my not knowing what had to be done, rather than to my unwillingness to do things. I am always a little bit intimidated in any situation, it's part of my personality. I don't want people to think that I can't do certain things because I don't want to do them; if I don't know how to do them it's because I don't know them.

Amelia: You seem to me to be afraid of how other people might judge you. Is that right?

Simona: Yes, always. I like other people to see that I can do things, but I think this can belong to everybody. I worry that other people may not understand that you need time, even a long time. But often, because work situations are constantly going on, we can't be given this time.

Amelia: Going back to your experience in this new context, did the passing of time make a decisive difference?

Simona: Yes, I realized—and this is my own assessment—that later in the daily life of school, and also when I was involved in other situations, whenever I set myself the goal of documenting and doing small investigations with the children, I felt more confident. Perhaps by acting and doing things myself, I no longer needed someone to say to me, "Look, this is where you have to start" or "Do this, do that." Maybe all I needed was input and then I would face the situation in my own way, as I had seen it done and as I felt like doing it myself. I have no doubt in my mind that doing things and working in the field were important to me.

Amelia: I want to go back to the original question: What strategy did you find helpful in discovering your attitude to be one of "permanent research"?

Simona: As we were speaking just now, I was considering the extent to which I've had to assess myself, and as a result have had to become more aware of what was happening. I think that being aware of things helps you to focus on the problems, because it obviously gives you a certain kind of perspective: you are aware, and as a result you have to make choices, therefore you have to learn to make choices. So you keep going on and the experiences begin to take shape. I think these reflections are an important aspect of self-assessment and of the ability to review what you do and why you do it, in a meta-cognitive way. If I was feeling like a "floating soul" during the first few days in the classroom, a few days later I was becoming more aware of what was happening. Maybe this "floating" feeling is also part of being in a condition of research. Perhaps that's just how you are when you are researching. You approach everything with different levels of awareness and then you go back to it with practical reflections. In my view, daily practice and reflection are definitely essential: they allow me to internalize the things I do.

Amelia: Did the images and knowledge of the Reggio experience you already had help you in any way?

Simona: I felt that my knowledge was superficial, and then, when I realized that the philosophy of the Reggio schools was part of a daily practice of constantly elaborating contents, it wasn't easy to make connections between what I already knew and the work I was doing at school.

Amelia: And what about the difficulties? Could you talk about the first difficulties you have encountered in this process?

Simona: As I said before, the difficulty of not finding answers to everything immediately was a serious problem. It was based in part on my own expectations, perhaps, but it was also a difficulty because I couldn't find everything right away. Maybe I didn't have enough time to exchange thoughts with Diletta. I was still thinking in terms of sitting at the table, with her doing the talking while I would be writing, and of her giving directions for me to follow and put into practice. Another difficulty was finding the courage to ask people in the school other than my classroom colleague Diletta for explanations.

Amelia: Can you explain more clearly what you mean by the difficulty of finding the courage to ask other people in the school for explanations?

Simona: I didn't feel up to it and wasn't able to interpret my unease. I couldn't feel the solidarity of the group. I think this was because I was worried about being judged, and maybe I felt I was bothering people. One of my biggest difficulties was my fear of encountering any possible misunderstandings. Also, what could I have asked? I felt I didn't know where to start. I had a long list of

stairs

120

questions. I wanted to know this and that and more; I wanted to know everything.

Paola: What about the procedures? More specifically, which and how many things were you curious about?

Simona: I remember something Diletta told me on the first day I arrived at the Villetta School. She said, "Observe Paola very closely because Paola is a very good teacher; I learned a lot from her." So I thought that observing the way my colleagues with more experience went about their work could certainly help me, because I realized there was no single theory that could explain to me how to operate in practice. So I observed, I tried to understand, and I started to build relationships.

Amelia: This seems to me to be an excellent strategy. I've applied it on other occasions too and I continue to apply it to my work: I observe others a great deal because I think I can learn an enormous amount from the things I am able to see. Yet it's also true that, in a sense, there's something reciprocal in observation. I find it helpful to feel that I'm being observed; it makes me feel valued, or rather, it makes it easier for me to capture the valuable aspects of my actions.

Orietta: The way I experience the action of observing is as a more immediate way of learning and perhaps a more reflective one. You look at how the other person is doing something, you internalize it, make it your own, and put it into practice, not only according to general procedural attitudes but also according to your own interpretations.

Amelia: Don't you all think that these processes that we call observation and documentation of particular situations were already under way within yourselves?

Simona: In my case, perhaps they were. I was looking at everything from the panels on the wall, to my colleagues, to the children, to the physical spaces. Perhaps I wasn't always aware of doing this, because actually, at the beginning, I used to ask myself, "Why is this done this way?" or "Why is the furniture arranged this way?" And my curiosity kept growing.

Amelia: I think what you're saying is really important, because it suggests that the role of observation is not just when you have a video camera, a tape recorder, or some other tool in your hands. It's as if there were another tool of documentation that consists of the way in which we experience our actions and the way we learn to ask ourselves questions—which is itself already part of the concept of learning. I think that when we are aware of the situation we are experiencing, and are choosing the things we observe, we are already documenting. You were observing yourself in a new stage in your life; therefore you were interpreting, giving answers, and trying to find situations that you

A meeting is organized for the new teachers to reflect and exchange thoughts on the first few days of school with the children.

A few days later, the teachers meet to examine documentation material from the school archives regarding the "settling in" period. The teachers who were directly involved in the experience comment on this material.

could analyze. This way, you were reflecting; and I'm sure you were writing a lot as well.

Simona: Yes, it's true. I was writing a lot and felt the need to write as a way of leaving traces of what was happening and what I was seeing. I remember I had my own diary, in which I noted down sentences, thoughts, comments, and ideas that came to me and that I would then share with my colleagues.

Paola: If I think back to my first experiences here, one very important thing to me was to have questions to ask. I used to find it difficult to ask questions and to find questions to ask. Then, with time, it became much easier for me to think of questions. So even asking yourself questions, finding questions that might have seemed to me to be the right ones, or that could help me to find a strategy to identify some of the answers, even this wasn't such a straightforward step.

Amelia: If you were to share something with your colleagues in the United States that might be helpful to them, what kind of importance would you give the role of observation?

Simona: I would give it a great deal of importance. I'm thinking of observation and also observing the other teacher. There were also a lot of other things that were helpful to me and might be helpful to others, like participating in the professional development sessions or in specific professional development events and initiatives like the showing of videos, even though I didn't find these in particular very helpful. I remember meetings we had in which we were shown a video or a slide documentary with the teachers explaining it. It was something quite unusual for me and I didn't feel particularly involved in it. I felt more like a spectator.

Amelia: In your opinion would it have been more helpful to you if it had been done in a different way? You said you were shown a slide documentary or a video and the teachers were explaining them. Do you think there might have been a different way of showing the documentaries that would have been more helpful to you?

Simona: Just yesterday I was looking through the notes I took during the showing of a documentary. We discussed a lot of complex concepts such as generative questions, for example, hypotheses for projects, documentation, participation. Maybe the important thing for me would have been to have the opportunity to ask more questions while the documentaries were being shown, but especially to have some clarifications straightaway.

Amelia: I agree with you. Based on my own experience both in Reggio and the United States, questions have always helped me a lot, the questions I asked and those that others asked me. In my more recent experiences in the United

States, for example, the questions that teachers asked enabled me to understand the way they were interpreting and understanding, what their thoughts and understandings were "lingering" on. I think that from the questions that others ask you, you improve your understanding of who you are, what you are doing, and why you are doing it. Therefore it really does become an occasion of reciprocal exchange. In this respect, I'd like to emphasize how important the questions raised by new teachers and their comments really are: their perspective has not yet entered our understanding, but it does bring in a particular understanding.

Another important occasion in our experience that I believe contributes significantly to our professional development is when we organize a visual document such as a slide show or a video. Indeed, I think that making a slide show, a video, or a publication means having the opportunity to construct a sort of "reflective space" that stands between ourselves and our action. A space where, to an extent, we can "invite" other people's contributions and comments. This is why a documentary or a publication is also an unfinished experience.

Teresa: Did you find the production of documentaries to be a milestone for yourself as well? When did you start producing them in Reggio?

Amelia: It's not so easy to recall experiences that go back such a long time without any supporting documentation, but I seem to remember we started right from the very beginning, precisely because I have no clear idea of a definite beginning. I have so many precious memories of my first experiences with Loris Malaguzzi and my colleagues. We spent entire afternoons examining in detail the children's drawings, photographs, and conversations. I recall the great efforts we made together to try to interpret different situations without ever taking anything for granted.

I remember how demanding Loris Malaguzzi was, but also the profound respect he showed for the teachers' opinions. He always required us to make a great effort, but the satisfaction we accomplished gave us a new image of the work we were doing, which also involved achievements, fun, the pleasure of doing things, the joy of learning, and discovering new worlds.

Barbara: Is the strategy of producing slide shows or videos or publications as a tool for professional development also used by foreign experiences that take their inspiration from the Reggio approach to pedagogy—say, those in northern Europe, Sweden, the United States, and Albania?

Amelia: I think it's a very widely used strategy. When, for example, I work in a school abroad for a period of time, after I've established a relationship with the teachers, I often ask them to put together a documentary research project. Instead of talking about what they did in the school using only the verbal language, I ask them to do so by means of a short video or short slide shows, so that they can narrate their experiences using different languages. Otherwise I ask them to take me to visit the environment in their schools and to present to me the things they've done that are visible inside the spaces through different types of documents. I've noticed how this kind of work gives the teachers greater opportunities to allow new identities within themselves to emerge. It also seems to me that my own contribution to their experiences becomes more articulate and allows problems to emerge more forcefully. I know that other colleagues of mine also use these strategies in their work.

Barbara: I find what you are saying and the procedures you describe very interesting. Going back to the aspect of making a video, not so much the construction stage but the final product, I remember that at first I used to watch them a little passively, because I didn't know what to observe. Looking at something is one thing, but observing, capturing something specific rather than the whole thing is quite different. I don't know if I'm making myself clear, but I wanted to point out that during those experiences, more than having questions I found I was reflecting on things. For example, watching the documentary about a day at school, I realized the extent to which I was taking for granted the children's arrival at the school, the transition time, the morning group assembly, lunchtime, and so on. I didn't have any questions then and there, but later, after reflecting for a while, I thought more deeply, for example, about the role the teacher might have. I reflected on this and then asked myself: In some cases, on certain specific occasions, what could I have done? I had great admiration for the teachers' capabilities, I admired the children's potentials and competencies and was amused by them. But until I tried myself, I didn't understand how I should be proceeding.

Amelia: Do you think it would be important to have time to look at these kinds of documents over and over again?

Barbara: Yes, this would help in reflecting more deeply on the experience. I think having time to reflect is very important to me. Just now I was referring to the video documentary, but personally I think it's extremely important to reflect, and consequently having the time to do so is very important too. The need for the time to reflect, to formulate questions, to understand and develop ideas, to consolidate, all this makes me feel that the time factor certainly seems to be very significant in learning processes. And I mean time in every respect—even the time to communicate, for example.

Teresa: Going back to my own experience, I remember that I was really being involved in everything right from the beginning. Indeed, I'd say I was overwhelmed from the first few days.

The new coteachers view and discuss documentation produced at the school in previous years.

Amelia: Why do you say overwhelmed?

Teresa: Overwhelmed… perhaps because I got here when school had already started. It was October 12, so everything was already in motion; a range of initiatives, activities, work in progress… Then I arrived, and I remember that my colleagues did explain things, but that was never enough for me. It seemed that a lot of things were taken for granted, as if I was supposed to know them already. But even if I did know them, I didn't know how to experience them, making them part of my own life in the school; I had to learn them day by day. Not to mention my first encounter with all the children! I was attracted to them, excited by them, but I was also scared of them, in a way … I was kind of afraid… My relationship with each child taken individually was more than enjoyable and rich, but coping with all of them together… Reflecting on all that now suggests to me that the main thing you have to do is look for the things you need to learn, the things you need to know, what you need to be able to do, what your approach should be.

Amelia: But more than anything else, it's important to know that these are not things that you know just once and for all. What is important is redefined in each particular situation. That's why, and I emphasize this again, a young teacher's perspective is helpful to us: it's an opportunity to reappraise what really is important. What did you try to do, for example?

Teresa: I had a tendency to observe everything. It was difficult to choose and therefore I felt more and more the need to exchange views with others. I think it's only by exchanging views with others that you can gain a better understanding of what you should be observing.

Amelia: So it was the time for communication that you felt you were lacking; and as you were saying before, it was this attitude of taking things for granted that contributed to your difficulties.

Frankly, I realize how many mistakes I made, too, when I was relating to others without giving enough weight to this problem of taking things for granted. We who work in Reggio, especially when we have a great deal of experience behind us, run the risk of really taking a lot of things for granted. Sometimes, even the language we use to express our thoughts is filled with an inherent complexity and is extremely elaborate. When I was here in Reggio, working at the Villetta School, I used to do that too. But when I went to the United States I reflected on this aspect and became more self-critical. I asked myself more often than before why I was saying some things, where they were coming from, and from what context they had emerged. "Taking things for granted," even in its positive value of implying group agreement, can sometimes become an obstacle to communication. If one of the principal objectives, when you are relating to others, is to be in touch with them, then you have to find various strategies to do so. If you take things for granted and the other person simply keeps quiet because he or she, not understanding what you mean, doesn't have the courage to speak, then that person ends up thinking that you are more intelligent than him or her, more knowledgeable, and so on. I don't think continuing in this way gets you anywhere.

Teresa: I agree with you, but then with me it's also a question of my personality. I'm really afraid to ask even simple questions. But if I were to go back now, I wouldn't do what I did then. I'd ask more questions because I realized that, in the end, I lost out by not asking them. I see now that the less you ask questions, the less you have answers back, and then your problems stay with you and grow bigger. You are also left with many doubts, but maybe this is a good thing, too.

Amelia: Do you think it would have been helpful to you if you'd had somebody else watching you during your own learning processes, someone who would give you immediate feedback on what you were doing and ask you to give reasons for what was happening?

Simona: It would have helped, for sure. Maybe the fact of being observed, being "documented" in a way, would have made me feel embarrassed; it would probably also have held me back a bit. But it would have made me reflect, too, on what I was doing, or rather, what we were doing. It's true that we observe the children, and it's just as true that they also observe us. Quite wrongly, I was more afraid of being observed by the adults than by the children, but as time went by, I learned to want children to observe me. Sometimes talking to your colleagues is not enough. Then you find that the atelierista or another colleague with more experience can help you, particularly someone who's had the opportunity of reflecting on what you've been doing. There have been times when I would tell myself over and over that I was ignorant.

Amelia: You mean in the sense that you didn't know things and were ignorant of them.

Simona: In the sense that I was also ignorant of the thoughts of others. Perhaps I didn't understand them. But I'd like to say something more about observation and feeling observed. If I think about what happened, I realize that, to an extent, I was aware of the fact that I was being observed. Whether intentionally or not, someone would always be observing me. The children were observing me first of all. It would have been helpful for me to have a person by my side who, on observing me, could intervene by saying things like, "You know, you're doing this wrong" or "You shouldn't be acting this way in this situation."

Giovanni: Is that how you perceived the person who was observing you? Was it

126

so that he or she could say whether or not you had gone wrong?

Simona: Yes, that was probably what I expected and what I probably felt I needed at the time.

Giovanni: To me, this context of observation implies that the other person observes you not to pass judgment but to help you identify and examine the causes and effects of some of the problem areas arising from a particular situation.

Orietta: Talking about examining the problems in a particular situation, I would add my own reflection here: being observed helped me a lot. Perhaps I was helped by having someone in my classroom who was newer to the school than I was, and where I was the "point of reference." I remember that the first thing I said both to Barbara (her coteacher during the 1998-1999 school year) last year and to Ramona (her coteacher in the 1999-2000 school year) this year was, "You should often ask me things because I may take them for granted." So the fact that they would ask me "Why are we doing this?" gave me the opportunity to go back and together with them reconstruct the way things had evolved, doing things the way we were talking about earlier. It gave me the opportunity to understand the reasons for things and to build a mutual understanding.

Amelia: I very much identify with this kind of approach as well. That's what I did when I was in Washington, D.C. (Amelia consulted with the Model Early Learning Center of Washington, D.C. from 1993 to 1996) and found I was beginning to become more aware of the reasons why I was acting the way I was, and aware of the questions that emerged. This was an extremely important step for me. It's exactly what you were referring to earlier: this kind of situation is extremely helpful. I think it helps you to grow and it helps the other person to understand what he or she is doing and be aware of it. Going back to the issue of professional development, is there anything else we can add? Can you describe your experiences—the gratifications, challenges, and difficulties you experienced when documenting the children's learning processes, but also from your own learning process?

Simona: At the beginning, when Giovanni and I were observing the same group of children in the atelier and he used to share his reflections with me, it seemed that I didn't have anything of my own to share with him. That was because I couldn't express myself and I used to say to myself, "it seems as if I have been observing something else entirely." I was there with my eyes, looking at these children moving around, I would write down their conversation, for example, but I wasn't able to interact with them or to make any comments. Most of all, it seemed that Giovanni and

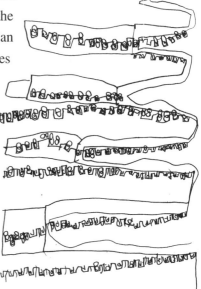

stairs

127

I were observing different things!

Amelia: Why do you think that was?

Simona: Because I wasn't able to see. I was only seeing the things I was capable of seeing.

Amelia: Do you think that Giovanni is capable of seeing things? Why do you think that is?

Simona: Yes, I think he is, because he has a lot of experience and he's also had many opportunities to reflect with others. I think Giovanni is capable of supporting the children's actions, getting them involved and making them feel that they are taking an active part in whatever they are doing.

Amelia: From your point of view, why do you think this happens?

Simona: Maybe because Giovanni has a model in mind, or perhaps because he can adapt his contribution concerning the situation using his past experiences. Perhaps he has a mental map of how to act, based on the things he's observing, which he's relating to his previous experiences.

Amelia: So you think he has a map. Can you elaborate on this?

Simona: I think he has several cognitive maps that can be adapted to the different contexts and that derive from his experience. I've also noticed that Giovanni has the ability to follow other people's thoughts without steering them in a particular direction. It's like sustaining the other person's action based on a prior intuition of how the situation might evolve, in order to be aware of what will be important to observe later on.

When I was first observing and documenting, I had the impression that I was missing everything. I found it difficult to write quickly, and then, at a later stage, I was given a camera. When I was taking photographs I was missing the dialogue, which was a terrible thing for me because I thought I was missing everything. To me, missing one of the children's words meant missing everything, so I used to write an enormous amount and my documenting was

In the atelier, Simona documents the construction of a robot in paper by a group of three girls, with Giovanni present.

She transcribes what she observed during the development of the project.

Simona and Giovanni compare their interpretations.

limited to transcribing the children's verbal dialogues. Then I placed the tape recorder next to me and I had sheets of paper with different types of observation grids. I had to follow the children and I wanted to follow the relationships they were building, the ways in which the children were moving inside the group. I had a lot of things to deal with all at the same time, and I couldn't do it because I wasn't able to have all the tools that I had intended to use under my control. I think I was capturing neither the children's hypotheses nor the strategies they were using, nor was I able to see whether they were influencing one another. Perhaps I was registering and not documenting. I could see that both the adults and the children were adopting certain strategies, but I wasn't able to keep up with the timing of their actions.

Giovanni: With respect to the children, the competencies they were demonstrating through their strategies, and the construction of their theories, to what extent do you think all this can be related to your image of the child at the time?

Simona: Very much. Yes, I was familiar with the theories related to the image of the child, but that wasn't enough. It was as if I was never able to see enough.

Amelia: Did you not credit the child with so many competencies?

Simona: I don't think I did. Obviously, without knowing it, I had a strong stereotype image of the child as an "empty vessel to be filled"—in the same way that I had a stereotype image of the adult as someone who, rather than sustaining action, would steer it in a certain direction, guiding and leading the other person to where he or she (the adult) wanted it to go.

Orietta: Which, unfortunately, is what we were taught at school as professional development. As you know, a major debate is going on, not only in Italy, about the quality of professional development today.

Simona: Yes, unfortunately that's been our school experience. It was rather lacking in content, analysis, and ability to identify and examine the causes and effects of the problems you encounter in teaching.

Curious about the observation documents, the children ask the teachers to explain them.

Teresa: My experience was somewhat different from Simona's. I worked mainly with just one child, a child with special needs. I used strategies that were somewhat different, I daresay more spontaneous, that I thought were more suited to the particular situation.

Amelia: What do you mean by "more spontaneous" and "more suited to the situation"?

Teresa: I was referring to strategies that were more immediate. I was finding immediate answers to the situation in hand.

Diletta: It seems to me that you had to analyze the situation and then you had to make choices.

Teresa: Yes, I realized that I had to apply certain observation strategies in order to understand what was happening. I had to make a choice and then act. Thinking about that now, perhaps I was too absorbed in the situation. But I was documenting, I was making choices from the multitude of events and gestures to be documented.

Giovanni: I think she's constructing a set of parameters to refer to. She may not always have been aware of it, but she was drawing them up, meaning that she was evaluating and making choices.

Paola: I think that within these processes a constant activity of self-assessment and assessment is going on.

Teresa: And my self-assessments were often negative, both those about myself and about the expectations I had of the child concerned.

Amelia: Did you feel inadequate perhaps?

Teresa: I certainly didn't feel I was up to the situation, because I felt that in the majority of cases my expectations were also based on certain prejudices.

Amelia: It seems to me that you were harsh and almost ruthless judges of yourselves!

Orietta: Yes, it's true. Talking about this, I'm thinking of an example that may be banal, but in the context of the family, when a parent says to you, "Look, you shouldn't do certain things because…" this leads you to rebel, to want to decide for yourself because you don't accept other people telling you what you do, even if it's your parents. The "other" person, with his or her behavior, will always be there for you to refer to, but still, you need to have a certain independence of judgment and of thought that you acquire over time and through your own experiences.

Amelia: I like to think I need the other person because I believe that other person can suggest a different point of view.

Giovanni: It seems to me to be very important because acknowledging differences and the need to be open to the thoughts of others are essential elements in order to have a future. We need to have a future that, through difference, is capable of welcoming the potentials that other people bring. This is something that applies to children, it applies to adults, and it should apply to the context.

Amelia: I was wondering to what extent people who have experience, this kind of experience, are capable of listening when new people come into the school; to what extent they put themselves in a condition or a situation of listening; to what extent they know how to listen to what the other person brings in and know how to learn from the other person. I think there's a lot to learn from people who are new to the experience, precisely owing to the fact of their being new. Even at Reggio Children, when I work with my young colleague Paola, listening to her views helps me enormously to understand my own view better. It helps me to understand how fossilized I can be about certain issues; how I may be wrong about them because I'm not flexible enough in taking the situation on board; and how I carry within myself evaluations that are sometimes presumptuous and at other times stereotyped. Having a long experience can carry some of its own risks. The problem I'm raising here is the extent to which we are able to put into practice the concept of listening—and I put myself in the shoes of those who have more experience—listening to the other person and not seeing him or her simply as a "weak link" that you have to "train." It may happen, just as it may happen in relation to the children, that you can't and aren't able to listen.

window

Paola: Though observation, in a sense, is a way of listening. If I think about my own experience as a teacher, I found it very helpful when someone was looking at me and observing me. Then later, discussing things with that person, I'd understand things that I hadn't seen before, so the following time I was encouraged to observe the details more closely. Of course, sometimes I became discouraged; but I used my frustration as a resource, because I would set myself the task of trying to think about things in more depth.

Giovanni: I think this question of feeling evaluated belongs to the nature of the relationship. It's not only the new person who is in a situation of disparity, but the other person too, who possibly for the first time has to set about building a relationship with another person. So we can say that it's the possibility of finding the right balance in the mutual relationship; and this isn't easy. Even with my own long experience, I think it's something that still needs to be reinforced.

Amelia: I'm wondering to what extent, for a person who's just beginning to teach, the fact of being with someone who has twenty-five years of experience and feeling a disparity or a difference resulting from the fact that one person has experience and the other doesn't, can create obstacles in mutual understanding.

Giovanni: It's certainly a significant factor that should be taken into consideration. Also, to this difference in experience you still have to add other differences, which can be personal differences or related to people's backgrounds.

Amelia: I was wondering, though, to what extent the other person, meaning the one who has more experience, is able to convey the idea that he or she is also undergoing a process, and that experience acquires greater value if one has the ability to keep oneself alive within the process and within change.

Giovanni: I think this was a problem for me, because I wasn't able to show Orietta that the process I was undergoing was in perfect synergy with her own. While she was interacting with the children, I was observing the relationship between her and the children so that we could discuss it later. We had shared this approach beforehand. Obviously sharing something like this at the beginning isn't enough, you also have to put it into practice during the experience in an interactive way. I wasn't only documenting the things that the children were doing, I was also documenting the relationship between her and the children, which was going to be the subject of our discussion. We did discuss it later, and at that point my lack of immediate interaction with her at the time led to a less positive appreciation of my presence during the work. I think that being openly interactive with the other person is essential during the process itself and is crucial when two people work together.

Paola: But it's a different kind of experience when two people are together, as Simona and I were in the mini-atelier the first time the children built a bridge, for example, and we had agreed to use two different types of documentation strategies in order to compare them in the end. We wanted to compare her type of documentation with mine, to understand what it might offer in terms of interpreting what had happened. As the work progressed, we had to find times in which, every now and then, we would look at each other and understand whether we had to stop or go on. I remember that in some situations we didn't know what to do.

Diletta: All of this also requires a high degree of complicity, exchanges, comparisons, and reciprocity—which you only acquire over time and with experience, all within the overall context of a collaborative approach.

Amelia: In a lively educational community such as ours, what has it meant to you and what does it mean to be part of a group, a group of people who are learning together?

Simona: First of all, it's a way of really making you feel that you're part of a group: it's a way of feeling that you share things with others, and that others perceive you as being part of the group and are willing to help you. That way you overcome the problems together and you feel more accepted. There's something that school, and perhaps life itself, hadn't helped me to understand, and that is the importance of making mistakes: learning to use mistakes as a resource, the importance of exchanging views with others and finding strategies and solutions together. If I had to start over again today, I wouldn't be afraid any more of a situation like the one I experienced. If there wasn't anyone there to help me deal with it, I would accept the situation, I'd ask for help and support, I would understand the situation and see it more positively.

Orietta: I would also consider from a more open point of view the fact of being observed by a critical eye, and therefore the open possibility of being interpreted negatively, too. I would see this now as something that could help me to grow. I've realized how all this can help you in the search for your own identity, both your professional and your personal identity.

Paola: I, too, believe that being part of a learning group helps you in the constant search for your own identity. The critical perspective of others offers further building elements for the complexity of the situation.

Diletta: I agree with you because when you understand and live through these kinds of experiences positively, you also understand that you are being given a certain amount of didactic freedom. You have the opportunity to learn, while knowing that you can rely on others and no longer need to be afraid of their judgment. I think this applies to parents, too.

Giovanni: I think this is really important if we consider families as being part of the learning group as well. Have there been any occasions, in your admittedly short experience, when in your exchanges with the parents you have felt that the groups of parents represent a group learning situation?

Orietta: Yes, there have been, because parents give you a picture of things that have their own history, their own idea of family-based experience in relation to the children, and you have your own, as a more or less experienced teacher. In my view, the family is part of the learning group because it's complementary; it completes your perspective, or it helps you broaden your horizons from the factors you are familiar with as a teacher and offers other points of view.

Amelia: And is this how you've felt about the situation with the families right from the beginning?

Orietta: In some cases I did, but at other times I also experienced it as a test, meaning that I saw the parents as people to whom you had to give a report. At times I perceived it almost like an...interference, something else to have to cope with, and then I felt myself inadequate for the role I was responsible for. At the beginning I perceived mostly my lacks, of which there seemed to be an awful lot, and all very obvious, too. I thought I was noticing some almost inquisitive looks by the parents; I was conscious of them and also felt

One of the methods of professional exchange among teachers with different levels of experience is to document the teacher who is interacting with and documenting the children. Orietta and Giovanni decide to document how the children design and produce a message for their friends and to present their documentation during the class meeting with the families.

Orietta and the children prepare the materials for making the message.

Giovanni observes and documents the words and gestures of the children and the teacher, making written notes and taking photographs.

uncomfortable because the opinion of the parents was important to me.

Teresa: I was afraid of their judgment, especially since my role was a bit more marginal, in the sense that I was a support teacher. So the parents didn't relate to me directly. At times, in fact, I also felt a bit excluded by the parents, and seen by them as more of an external figure, and therefore a little more like an outsider whose presence might be almost unimportant.

I think at the beginning the parents had to get to know what my role in the class was, what kind of relationship I had with the other two teachers and with the children. These were all things that had been explained to the families, but I think that the parents wanted to see and understand them by themselves through the actual work of the school. I also felt I was being observed. During my time of getting to know the new experience in the school, I also had to take this factor into account, and it really wasn't easy.

However, over the course of time, we did find some adjustment mechanisms that helped us to get to know and respect one another, and this is true of the parents, the children, and my colleagues.

Simona: I think that the time you spend within the evolving experience gives value to your work and that of others, and acts as a complement in creating a deep sense of belonging to what you do. It also helps you to understand the reasons why you do things and gives you a greater deal of awareness.

Now that I am more able to distance myself, emotionally as well, from my early experience, I am able to appreciate all its inherent value and richness. I feel that I have a positive baggage of experience that will help me to approach new experiences in a way that is more constructive and open both to myself and to others. I feel that my personal and professional development has been enriched also by the obstacles I've had to overcome, the mistakes I've made and have realized I made. The important thing is not to feel discouraged, but

The next day, Orietta and Giovanni compare the documents they have produced in order to share them with their colleagues during the weekly staff development meeting.

The observations compiled by Orietta and Giovanni are examined by their colleagues, and this exchange enriches the material with new points of view.

Brief summaries of the observations are given to the parents, so that they feel involved and can add their own interpretations.

to learn to see problems with greater optimism. This helps you to grow and gives you more strength to be able to deal with your work and with your life.

These conversations then continued in the course of the school year and left significant traces on our learning processes and our personal and professional development.

Realizing the importance of building one's experience within the daily life of the school, through ongoing sharing and exchange with others, has underscored once again how essential it is for us to learn to take on responsibilities, with a constant effort to analyze and develop. This also helps us not to give up in the face of difficulties, and is an important message for the new teachers as well.

This shared experience, this process of constant dialogue with others, made up of exchanges and sharing of ideas and opinions, negotiations, agreements, and disagreements, has given new value to the context of our personal and professional lives, enriching our different personalities with new elements. It has meant documenting our ongoing learning processes as well as constantly "documenting" our own lives. It has also meant thinking about documentation as an opportunity to define the quality of our work and our development; as an act we owe to ourselves and which is necessary for us as teachers and people; as an act we owe to the children and the parents.

We hope that this wealth of knowledge will not be dissipated but will stay with us as our experiences evolve, helping us never to lose sight of the values of collaboration and learning as individuals in a group who see ongoing research as an indispensable part of their work.

School as a Place of Group Learning for Parents

Paola Cagliari
Claudia Giudici

In the framework of the themes developed in this book, we consider the school-family relationship to be particularly important as a context that can foster children's individual and group learning. In this chapter we describe briefly the theories and meanings that provide the background for this relationship, which is an essential feature of the educational project of the municipal early childhood institutions of Reggio Emilia. Some of the processes and experiences offered to the parents as opportunities to learn and to deepen their understandings can also be found in other chapters of the book.

In Italian schools, the relationship between school and family is generally referred to with the term "participation," though the theories, experiences, and projects encompassed by this single term may be very different. The experience of Reggio Emilia represents one of the possible approaches.

The educational project of the Infant-toddler Centers and Preschools of Reggio Emilia is by definition a participation-based project that finds its true educational meaning in the participation of all concerned. This means that everyone—children, teachers, and parents—is involved in sharing ideas, dialogue, a sense of common purpose, and communication as a value. Rather than separation or contrast, these encounters foster both dialogue between different subjects (different roles, different ideas, different cultures) and negotiation toward building together. Rather than being an experience where the competencies of some negate the competencies of others, there is a recognition that everyone—children, teachers, and parents—is an active subject in the educational relationship, each contributing complementary and necessary knowledge.
Carla Rinaldi states:
"Participation is an educational strategy that characterizes our way of being and doing school. Participation involves the children, the families, and the teachers and is viewed not only as 'taking part' in something but even more as being a part; that is, the essence and substance of a common identity, a 'we' to which we give life by participating. Thus, in our experience, education and participation are fused together: the 'what' (education) and the 'how' (participation) become the form and substance of a single process of construction."

In the Reggio Emilia experience, therefore, participation does not indicate simply the involvement of families in the life of the school. Rather, it is a value, an identifying feature of the entire experience, a way of viewing those involved in the educational process and the role of the school.

The subjects of participation, then, prior even to the parents, are the children, who are considered to be active constructors of their own learning and producers of original points of view concerning the world. If the school truly values and practices participation, then the children's sharing of their points of view with other children and adults can translate into a culture of childhood that is deeply embedded in the school itself as well as in the broader social fabric.

The subjects of participation also include all the school staff. The teachers, in particular, do not merely execute programs established by others but participate actively in the construction of the knowledge-building processes of each child and each group of children, as well as their own; that is, they are learning to teach. All this takes place through listening and research conducted within a collegial framework.

Participation, in fact, is based on the idea that reality is not objective, that culture is a constantly evolving product of society, that individual knowledge is only partial, and that in order to construct a project, especially an educational project, everyone's point of view is relevant in dialogue with those of others, within a framework of shared values. The idea of participation is founded on these concepts; so, too, is democracy, in our opinion.

Therefore, if we want to have a school based on participation, we must create spaces, contexts, and times when all subjects—children, teachers, and parents—can find opportunities to speak and be listened to. This first and necessary level can already be found in many Italian schools. But if participation is to assume a role of active and democratic construction in the educational project of a school and a community, this first level is not enough.

Each child and adult has a different way of participating, of being an active part, because each individual is different.

"To participate" is a verb that can be conjugated in both the singular and the plural. Each person can participate as an individual subject who singly makes his or her contribution and singly takes in the information and contributions provided by the others. But individual participation that is, and will always remain, a characteristic of the participation of everyone, takes on further meaning if the school presents itself as a community—in relation to the wider community of the city—which has a broader-based project strategy.

An infant-toddler center or preschool that aspires to be a real place of education must maintain close contact with social and cultural issues, ideas, contexts, and lifestyles, all of which are constantly changing, in order to be able to read, interpret, and produce updated versions of practices and values, and to develop cultural and political proposals. This should be done with an approach that, as Reggio pedagogistas Lanzi and Soncini state, "keeps together the great cultural, political, and philosophical currents, the values that look toward the future, and the particularity of daily educational practice."

This aim can only be achieved by adopting the value and practice of participation as we have thus far defined it; that is, by actively engaging all the children, teachers, and parents in a community dimension that involves reading and interpreting change together.

Participation therefore defines the infant-toddler center or preschool as a social and political place and thus an educational place in the fullest sense. However, this is not a given, so to speak, a "natural," intrinsic part of being a school. It is a philosophical choice, a choice based on values, which the experience in Reggio Emilia has always tried to implement in terms of didactics as well as professional development and family participation.

But are parents competent "participants"? Usually, schools do not consider them so, because they do not see themselves as social and political places and therefore do not recognize the competencies of parents as citizens. Furthermore, by concentrating their attention on teaching the various subjects, what schools consider to be important is mainly specialized knowledge that, for the most part, parents do not have.

What do we mean by competency? In one sense, it is a recognition of value that schools must give to parents, as well as to children and teachers. This recognition—again a choice based on values—is an acknowledgment of the citizen's right to engage in the discussion of social issues that concern everyone. Parents are therefore competent because they have and develop their own experiences, points of view, interpretations, and ideas, which are articulated in implicit or explicit theories and are the fruit of their experience as both parents and citizens.

In another sense, competency is a process that is nurtured and enriched precisely by the participation processes; these processes must therefore have competency as their goal.

The images in this chapter, accompanied by brief captions, illustrate some possible occasions of participation by the families, but they are not exhaustive in terms of the complexity and variety of situations, moments, and learning processes and strategies that shape the experience of participation. Even if it were possible and desirable to compile a complete index of all the events included in the participation process, we feel this would not give the reader a fuller sense of the parents' participation. Indeed, participation is not a model that can be reproduced, and above all it is not a series of sequential events. It is an experience and a process whose contents and strategies are interconnected and interdependent and which generate unique and original paths that develop in strict relation to the identity of the individual protagonists and of the groups to which they belong.

When there is real dialogue in the group, a group identity will emerge that makes room for the individual ideas, thoughts, expectations, proposals, desires, and rights of all its members. These subjectivities are enhanced through research and the identification of proposals that bring together these elements in such a way that all can recognize themselves and feel that they have participated.

Concerning this last point, the example of "Parents and Robotics" is a good illustration of a process in which parents, children, and teachers, all with their individual competencies and cognizant of their own roles, collaborate in the construction of a unique and original research context within which each person has the opportunity to develop his or her own learning.

Reading the title of this chapter, some may object to the idea that being a learning place for parents should be one of the aims of school. Others, however, may ask why school, with its own pedagogical knowledge that has been tried and tested in practice, does not teach parents to be better parents. These are both valid concerns, even if they come from opposite perspectives. Our answer to the first, in light of our educational project, is that if we use the term learning, as many educational experiences do, to mean the result of a teaching strategy based on the transmission of knowledge, behavior, and competencies that are the same for all, then this is a well-founded concern. In this chapter though (as in the chapters dedicated to children), we put forward an idea of adult learning as research that takes place in the relationship between the individual and the community, leading to the consensual creation of change and of a culture that is new because it is generated by authentic democratic processes.

Council members discuss the election process for the new Community-Early Childhood Council.

The election commission organizes the election of the new Council...

and the parents vote for the candidates during the Christmas party.

This argument also partly answers the second concern. Yet we also need to add that if we think of education as a relationship that is shaped by the identity of the subjects involved and their interactions, influenced by the contexts within which they occur, a relationship in which each subject educates and is educated at the same time, then the role of parents, just as that of teachers, cannot be based on certainties or models that are the same for all and can be transmitted through teaching. If school adopts this perspective, then the goal cannot be to teach parents the procedures to follow in order to become better parents, but rather to construct public spaces within which to produce shared reflections, enabling each person's self-reflection to circulate and increase.

Parents and staff designing and building furnishings and structures for the school interior and grounds.

Parents on the Council and representatives of the editorial board of the newsletter "La Mongolfiera" (Hot-Air Balloon) meet to write the article "Educating toward Community" published in the June 2000 edition.

The newsletter published by the Community-Early Childhood Councils.

Parents and school staff preparing the Christmas party.

Before the incoming children begin attending the infant-toddler center or preschool, the parents and teachers prepare the environment so that each child and all the children feel awaited and welcomed.

Children, parents, and staff celebrate the end of the school year.

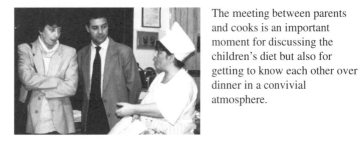

The meeting between parents and cooks is an important moment for discussing the children's diet but also for getting to know each other over dinner in a convivial atmosphere.

A trip to the beach enables parents and children to have an unforgettable experience together.

Parents meeting to view a project carried out by the children and teachers.

Parents, children, staff, and other community members demonstrate in favor of a national law guaranteeing increased funding to the infant-toddler centers.

Protagonists
Parents, teachers, and
children of the five- and
six-year-olds' class
Teachers
Angela Barozzi
Paola Barchi
Giovanni Piazza
School
Villetta
Photographs by
Giovanni Piazza
Paola Barchi
Text by
Angela Barozzi
Paola Barchi

Parents and Robotics

This episode, which is a fragment of a broader research project, tells how a group of adults, made up of parents and teachers, chose to be actively engaged participants in the processes experienced by children when approaching new technologies.

The school is a place where ideas and desires can be encountered and exchanged: a context of individual and group research where the meanings of life that children, parents, and teachers are constructing from their different perspectives can be interwoven.

The rapid transformations brought about by new technologies, affecting society in general and the relationships between people, have created a situation of reciprocal learning for the three elements of the school community—children, parents, and teachers—simultaneously and for the first time. It is a dynamic and evolving situation marked by a willingness to learn how to learn together.

Domenico (Ilaria's father): I believe that it's important for these tools to be available to the children, but I think it's equally important for them while they are at school to continue to experience working in the kitchen, working with materials such as clay, paints, and so on, in addition to experiencing new technologies.

Giacomo (Manuel's father): In fact, we talk about technology using our own parameters as a reference, and these are related to our own experiences. But to our children, is technology actually technology or is it a form of life? What can we do about this? How can we understand more clearly what it is that our children are investigating?

Primi incontri dei bambini con oggetti costruiti con il LEGOMINDSTORMS

"secondo me questo robot è come un insetto con le antenne per ascoltare i rumori...come quelle delle farfalle che le usano per ascoltare le musiche nel cielo e per danzare...loro sentono anche il vento" Anna Claudia

"On macchinina alle 2 macchinine gli dici di andare sempre dritto e di fare comparire lo stesso numero?" Nicola

"Forse si possono fare nel computer i programmi per questi robots..." Francesco
"Con ON si accende il motore, che sono 2 i motori" Luca
"Ci vuoleun numero che faccia capire alle macchine quanto tempo devono andare...quando il tempo è finito si devono fermare" Nicola

At our first class meeting, we give the parents a brief summary of the elements that have emerged from the children's discussions. We try to highlight the problem areas that came to light from the children's encounters with cybernetic objects (robots; self-propelled cybernetic vehicles such as cars, cranes, bulldozers, and other remote-controlled objects; small computers) within the daily contexts of play and investigation.

We sense that the parents are at once fascinated and worried about the issue of how one relates to technology.

Luciano (Athina's father): I think the fears that we have as adults are linked to our lack of knowledge about the innovations that these new technologies introduce into our lives. But to our children these are "normal" encounters and experiences which they approach in a more natural way than we do. Perhaps we, too, should learn how to use them more naturally.

At the end of the meeting, which was marked by lively discussion, it is decided that a working group should be set up to study the subject in more depth and to provide an opportunity for parents to continue to exchange and compare their views on the subject.

Seven parents (two mothers and five fathers) decide to participate in the study group together with the teachers from the class.

A few days later, the school receives a new software program with a programming interface that is easier for the children to interpret and that can broaden the opportunities for play and investigation. In fact, one morning, while the children are playing with the new robot and the new program...

Luca: *I think those things there on the screen are robots that are racing each other. It looks like there's a track on the screen.*
Francesco: *It's true; it looks like the Grand Prix track! But how can you build it? I wish we could have one ourselves.*

The group rallies around the idea with enthusiasm:
Why don't we ask Giovanni?... No, we could ask our dads... or even our moms!

The idea proposed by the children (a track for robot racing) is welcomed by the parents' group. The group's intent is to study the robot and to design and construct a track that can satisfy the wish expressed by the children.

The children's approach to the materials has a determining influence: the parents are struck by the children's capacity to come to grips with the robots by making use of their previous experiences, the errors made and progressively overcome.

Luciano: You see how they managed to get the robot to move? It's amazing to see their thoughts about the old track evolving!

Giacomo: I don't understand very much about robots, but it seems to me to be important that the children should talk about and use their mistakes to advance their knowledge. Even if our adult experience helps to support us, error is important in our work, too!

It seems that the relational dynamics within the group of adults, while different from those of the children, are nevertheless not too distinct from them.

Luciano: I actually work with information technology and I also like robots. I'm very curious to try them.

Giacomo: That's great! It's a good thing we like different things. If I can understand the things we're doing, then the children will also understand them, for sure.

Domenico: Well, we'll do our best to learn, too. I've just bought a new computer but I don't know how to use it.

The parents decide to break into two subgroups, according to each person's self-professed abilities: one group is to draw the graphic layout for the track; the other is to build the wooden structure for supporting the track.

145

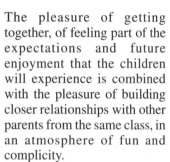

The pleasure of getting together, of feeling part of the expectations and future enjoyment that the children will experience is combined with the pleasure of building closer relationships with other parents from the same class, in an atmosphere of fun and complicity.

After three working evenings, the structure takes shape and the members of the group show their satisfaction through the way they evaluate their work, at times with a sense of irony, as well as by their recognition of having acquired new skills.

Everything is ready. The group gets together to share and test the hardware and software solutions they tried to find together.

The next day, the work they have done will be presented to the children.

When the children and the parents meet, the learning that they have constructed in their respective groups is compared. They have mutual expectations: the children are trying to find new ways in which the robots can behave, while Luciano is concentrating on the look on the children's faces and the questions they ask to find confirmation that the work done by the parents meets the requirements and expectations expressed by the children.

The parents in the group are aware that their research not only is useful to the children and to themselves, but also can be shared with the other parents. On this basis, a class meeting is organized where all the other parents can partake in the work done by the group, the discoveries they made, and the joy and sense of fun that are experienced when creating something together.

The class meeting of all the parents thus becomes a community learning context that allows the joint construction of meanings, the sharing of values, and the identification of possible new opportunities for the children and parents to relaunch the original questions.

The Courage of Utopia

Carla Rinaldi

At the end of this first part of the book, I propose to offer the reader some reflections which I hope will strengthen the reasons that lead us to regard this research as an important stride in our experience, as well as a possible contribution to the international debate on the meanings and role of schools, teachers, and teaching in contemporary society.

The first reflection was suggested to me by rereading some excerpts from the writings of Maria Montessori. This is what she wrote at the beginning of the twentieth century:

"...always starting from the children, with the ability to welcome them as they are, freed from the thousand different labels with which we now presume to identify them..."

"...to shift the action of the school from teaching to learning, not only with words but with tangible deeds, fostering children's constructive and collaborative behavior and the teacher's presence as a helper who is always available but never looming or intrusive; that which the children are able to do together today, they will be able to do on their own tomorrow..."

"...to construct, together with the children, too, an educational learning environment by arranging spaces, furnishings, materials, tools, educational projects, encounters, collaborations, discussions, and exchanges."

I have asked myself and I ask you: What else or what more could we say to ourselves and to those who look at and listen to us with interest and curiosity? What else and what more can we offer the child and the children that is not already contained in these words of Maria Montessori? Much has been written, analyzed in detail, enriched, and evaluated, starting from these works by Maria Montessori and later writings.

But the context in which Maria Montessori worked was different, as were her images. A rich body of research, carried out in various new fields of learning and knowledge, has now enabled us to talk about scaffolding, group learning experiences, interdisciplinary approaches, expressive qualities and languages, and about reciprocity between learning and teaching.

I am afraid, however—and I would very much like to be wrong about this— that too little has changed in the way that schools are and do things in their everyday activities, to the extent that in many school situations (in Italy and

the city of Reggio Emilia

148

throughout the world) Maria Montessori's words run the risk of being a goal that remains to be achieved. The reasons for this are manifold, and we could enumerate a few areas here, such as political, cultural, and labor issues.

One reason that seems to me to be crucial, however, and is hardly ever taken into account, is that discussions about schools, learning, and teaching have continued to be conducted only through the verbal language; that is, with spoken and written words. Generations of teachers have continued to undergo their initial preparation and in-service professional development without ever having reflected on what is known about learning and its relationship with contexts, and moreover forgoing the search for new ways and new languages to enable them to live, share, narrate, and articulate learning events.

Adopting these approaches, these languages, and this "infectiousness" between different languages could lead to the opening of new horizons (as has happened in other disciplines) and to children and teachers acquiring new leading roles. Promoting teachers from simply executing predefined programs to becoming authors of pedagogical paths and processes could contribute, at least in the field of pedagogy, to overcoming the arrogant idea of constantly separating theory from practice, and culture from practical fields.

The persistence of this idea, which means that teachers continue to be defined as "practitioners," is an absurdity that needs to be overcome; it is the result of a misunderstanding and of an "intellectualist" and mistaken concept of research, pedagogy, and education. Being able to reflect on and engage in discourse about the ways in which children and adults gain knowledge (thus enriching humanity, theirs as well as ours) is a great possibility and a necessity that schools, up to now, have not been able to or wanted to offer themselves.

The possibility of doing this, of overcoming the barrier and the limits imposed by using only one language (verbal), means having access to the extraordinary enrichment that derives from the integrated and interconnected use of multiple languages. Nowadays, this has become not only a hope but a necessity and an indispensable choice. The places where one can engage in research about learning should be extended to include schools and should allow teachers and students to reflect daily on their learning methods and on how knowledge is gained.

To be sure, I am referring to documentation (such as we have developed and presented), as a visible trace and procedure that supports learning and teaching, making them reciprocal in that they become visible and sharable. I believe *this* has been the important contribution made by the Reggio experience to national and international pedagogy (and to other fields as well), and it can become even more important in the future.

However, I believe we have to go even further. I am convinced, as I said earlier, that the effect of documentation (documents, notes, slides, and recordings) is not limited to making visible that which *is*, but on the contrary, by making an experience visible, documentation enables the experience to exist and thus makes it sharable and open to the "possibles" (possible interpretations, multiple dialogues among children and adults). Therefore, I believe that narrating the learning process requires the use of verbal and visual languages not only in a narrative and analytical way, but also in a poetic, metaphorical, musical, physical, and dramatic sense.

In other words, in order to make a learning experience possible—and therefore to make it a conscious form of learning that can also be narrated—processes and language should be closely interwoven, so as to support each other reciprocally and to support the quality of the learning experience itself. What we actually have to document (and therefore bring into existence) is the "emotionally moving" sense of the search for the meanings of life that children and adults undertake together—a poetic sense that metaphorical, analogical, and poetic language can produce and thereby express in its holistic fullness.

Another condition that I believe has inhibited the beliefs about learning dear to Montessori, but also to Dewey, Piaget, Vygotsky, Bruner, and many others—even to the point of stifling them—is the fact of denying schools and school environments access to the concept of research. We are well aware of what is meant by "scientific research" and of the current debate concerning the so-called hard and soft sciences, and the experimental as opposed to the historical sciences. But we believe that the concept of research, or indeed, a *new* concept of research that is more contemporary and alive, might emerge if we legitimize the use of this term to refer to the capacity to describe the cognitive tension that is experienced whenever real processes of learning and knowledge acquisition occur. Research, in this sense, is used to describe the paths of individuals and groups in the direction of new universes of possibility.

Research as the disclosure and the revelation of an event.

Research as art: research exists, as it does in art, within the search for the being, the essence, and the sense of things.

The research and the experiences that are still unknown provide the kernel of the potential interior reorganization through which we gain proof of the changing world and the changes that we ourselves produce in the world by interacting with it. The basis of research is not only to have alternative orientations as a starting point, but also to construct new orientations as the research evolves.

Why should research be undertaken in a group? Among the many reasons that appear in this work, there is one I would particularly like to underscore: research embodies some very strong emotional aspects that underlie each individual's commitment, increase in awareness, personal search for meaning, and the affective relationships inherent in a reflective stance that is consciously adopted. In short, learning involves the learner's emotions. Groups are undoubtedly ideal structures for being receptive to learners' personal needs, such as worries, doubts, and desires, but they are also an unrivaled tool for the solution of social problems.

John Dewey states that children's school experience should have a high degree of continuity with the life of the adult world. I venture to say that in this context the experience of school, if constructed around the values and meanings expressed here thus far, could contribute to renewing the democratic qualities of the broader cultural and social context. It could (and should) contribute to a definition of a "democratic context" as one that is capable of facing up to the challenges presented and imposed by globalization. For the future, school *must* have a decisive influence on the present; otherwise the message and the very identity of school will not survive.

We have used the terms research and research work with these meanings in mind, in an attempt to describe the vital force that can bring together children and adults inside and outside school. We need to create a culture of research.

I am convinced that this "attitude of research" is the only feasible existential and ethical approach within a cultural, social, and political situation that is subject to changes, ruptures, and to positive but also risky mixings of ethnic groups and cultures. We are talking about the value of research, but also about the search for values.

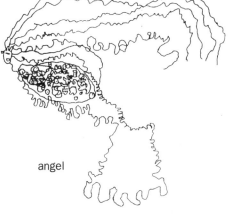

angel

151

RE
PZ

Looking Closely at the Group: Notes on Pedagogical Research

In this part of the book we offer visual and written documentation completed during our collaborative research into the learning of groups of young children and adults. The following four chapters present the core of our joint research. But first a word about methodology—how we arrived at our ideas about making individual and group learning visible—is in order.

The ideas in these chapters emerge from a process that Reggio educators call pedagogical research. As we saw in the first part of this book, pedagogical research begins with teachers' classroom experiences with children. Reggio teachers observe children throughout the school day: in moments of play and activities that are planned and organized by the children themselves, as well as during longer, more complex projects in which children and teachers work on topics not only for an extensive period of time but also from different points of view. Both these situations offer children and teachers an enormous variety of themes and problems to investigate. This is why the teachers of the Diana and Villetta preschools, along with the Project Zero researchers, considered it opportune to use these contexts in generating the visual essays and propositions that follow.

Often children work in small-group projects with one classroom teacher and the atelierista, while another teacher observes, sometimes supports, and coordinates the activities of other children who are usually working in groups around the room. Throughout the day the teacher and the atelierista share ideas about what they are seeing, making decisions about whether or not to intervene and how to sustain children's motivation and support their learning. This daily exchange is fundamental to shaping and adjusting the research path and determining what will be documented and how. As we have seen, teachers document children's words and actions through a variety of means such as notes, photographs, videotapes, and sketches. Almost always, a tape recorder is running. The tape will be listened to at the end of the day and either wholly or partially transcribed. Teachers read the transcripts together several times in order to understand and interpret what took place. They also look at photographs as soon

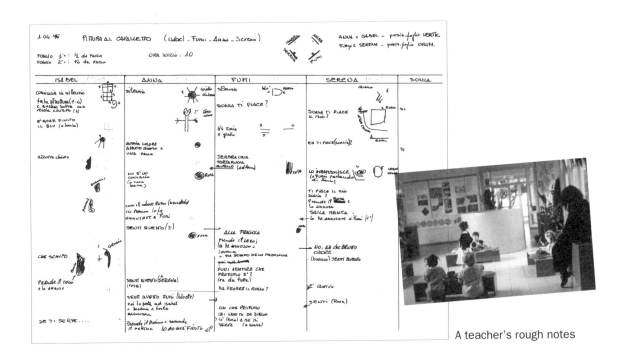

A teacher's rough notes

as possible, so that they can consider other hypotheses and directions for the research. Based on this review, the teachers generate hypotheses that will structure the next day's experience.

The pedagogical research process is continuous. Reggio teachers are constantly modifying their hypotheses, predictions, and interpretations as the children's projects develop. They communicate their data daily to other teachers, children, and parents. They use multiple languages to make their research visible: transcriptions of children's conversations, slides and photographs, documentation panels on the classroom walls of children's work at varying stages of development, and formal and informal presentations to other groups of teachers.

The declarations, stories, and propositions reported in the next chapters were generated by Reggio educators at the Diana and Villetta preschools who reflected together in roundtable discussions on their experiences with group learning. From their observations and documentation, the teachers identified important "recurring elements," which they then shared with the Project Zero team for discussion and reflection, together examining these elements in more depth and expanding on them. The Reggio team examined some of these ideas more closely in the classroom. During the project work, Reggio educators used the propositions to structure their observations and their documentation of group learning. They confirmed some aspects, modified others, and strengthened still others. This process is ongoing: teachers continue to generate new hypotheses, investigate them in their classrooms, and look for additional examples of group learning.

At the same time, the Project Zero researchers reflected on the propositions, considered them in light of other research about group learning, and solicited feedback from colleagues. Drafts were exchanged across the ocean, and through this process some common understandings were reached. How each organization articulates these understandings differs. In "The Curiosity to Understand" Vea Vecchi begins with a series of declarations about learning in groups that are supported by documentation. She focuses on a number of projects from the Diana School where ideas about individual and group learning are explored in depth. In "The City of Reggio Emilia" and "The Fax," Giovanni Piazza and his colleagues at the Villetta School present more expansive examples of documentation of the type found in the ministories. The theories of Piazza and his colleagues about learning groups are embedded within these visual essays. In "Form, Function, and Understanding in Learning Groups" Mara Krechevsky draws on the documentation shared by Vecchi and Piazza, along with examples from the ministories and other sources, to explore a set of propositions about individual and group learning. We believe that the various styles and multiple languages used in this part of the book allow us to share our collective understandings more effectively.

ice cream cones

The Curiosity
to Understand

Vea Vecchi

Here we have one of the *matrices* of our work as teachers: the documentation of the individual and group strategies of the girls and boys who attend our schools.

The documentation in this chapter and the two that follow comes from projects that differ in terms of subject matter and scale, some presenting mere fragments of experiences and some taken from long-term projects carried out at the Diana and Villetta preschools. We present these materials to further clarify and more fully substantiate the meaning we attribute to documentation, how we use it, and how it orients the way we proceed with the children, as well as for its contribution to our professional development and the modification of our pedagogical theories.

Through the episodes recounted here (with written texts and photographs), we offer the reader the genesis of some of our current interpretations and affirmations, providing other points of view and material for further study and discussion.

The particular contribution of the Diana and Villetta preschools to the research carried out in conjunction with Project Zero has been to offer our observations and documentation of work carried out in the field for the interpretations of others.

We are aware of the many significant studies and writings related to the subject at hand, but we feel that the material we offer, which can stimulate further confirmations, denials, and reflections, emerges from a particular *matrix*: that is, **teachers who view observation and documentation as fundamental to the educational and knowledge-building processes, those of the children as well as their own.** In this lesser-known approach, learning is viewed with *ways of looking* that can provide a particular and perhaps unusual framework for studying the material collected. (The chapter entitled "Documentation and Assessment: What Is the Relationship?" offers some reflections that explain this aspect more fully.)

The teacher's job is a difficult one, requiring continuous and clear-sighted self-assessment, along with a good measure of the sense of relativity, irony, and fun.

Children's learning strategies have always been a main focus of our work, along with professional development (teachers and pedagogistas), relationships with the families, and in-depth study and communication of the educational theories that we follow.

As a very brief history in this regard, starting in the 1970s, the educational approach of the Diana School, along with most of the other municipal preschools in Reggio Emilia, placed attention on the whole group of children in each class (twenty-five children). We were engaged in studying and re-elaborating within our own context the most avant-garde didactic theories of the time—those of Freinet, Piaget, Vygotsky, Dewey, and so on—along with the discoveries, conceptual aspects, and experiences of the visual arts (which at that time were considered by traditional pedagogy to be far removed from preschool education). It was a period of experimentation and discovery of children's enormous competencies, which led to the first version of the exhibit "The Hundred Languages of Children" in 1981.

In the mid-1980s, our curiosity to understand the children's strategies better led to observational and documentational *excavations* focused on small groups of children (investigations that we call "probes," represented in the book *Shoe and Meter* published by Reggio Children). Subsequently, in the early 1990s, we began to document children's individual strategies, which we believe offer evidence that the creativity of many children can be encountered more easily in the processes than in the results.

Based on a wealth of such experiences, in the mid-1990s we returned to the whole-class group, looking at it with greater awareness and sensitivity. We were searching for the individual identities that form small, fluid groups (which in turn constitute the whole-class group), with particular attention to the relational modes (cognitive, expressive, and social) between the different individuals.

The research in conjunction with Project Zero began at this point in our educational history. The many questions posed by the Project Zero researchers, and our extensive discussions, in a certain way *compelled* us to revisit our history, to understand it better, to describe it with greater clarity, to examine certain parts in more depth, and to give direction to the continuation of our work and further studies.

Another preliminary reflection has to do with the visual documentation (mainly photographic) that has always been a part of our experience. Its principal aim is to allow us to see and understand better the children and ourselves, as well as to enable others to do the same, so that we can continue to see, reflect, interpret, and understand over time that which took place. We can then use the resulting conceptualizations to verify, modify, and further develop our basic theories.

The significance and use of this observational approach and photographic documentation cannot be fully understood if viewed only in terms of pedagogical tradition; they should also be seen in relation to the artistic processes, where communication is often constructed using language that is metaphorical and poetic.

Our frequent use of aesthetic language and thought may have caused some misunderstandings within certain areas of the pedagogical world, where this way of observing and communicating may be seen as a superficial advertising-style "gloss" on the Reggio educational product, far removed from the scientific seriousness of true research conducted using only the verbal language. But we have always believed that beauty, joy, humor, and poetry are an integral and important part of knowledge-building, and thus that learning should be experienced in daily life through multiple languages (verbal, written, musical, visual, dance, and so on) and it can and should be narrated by means of many languages.

The documentary process is the path along which we have proceeded together with the children for many years. When, as frequently happens, we are asked the question "How often do you use documentation with the children?" we reply, "Always." This is our attempt to explain documentation as a system for approaching problems and a strategy for moving ahead with our work.

Thinking about documentation only in terms of the final visible part is a theoretical and conceptual error that hampers comprehension of the overall approach and of the relationships that are created between the individual child, the group of children, the teachers, and the subject at hand.

It is easy to imagine the extent to which the presence of the atelier and the atelierista in the school has contributed to this type of documentation, which becomes tangible in the daily life of the school. However, it would be difficult to measure the relative *weight* of this contribution, in that the mere combination of atelier and pedagogy does not suffice. The process of dialogue between the expressive languages and the pedagogical languages in the schools of Reggio Emilia comprises many cultural, pedagogical, artistic, and political identities, many events, and many choices made.

The fact remains, however, that Loris Malaguzzi had an extraordinary educational intuition when he developed the idea of an organizational structure that involves a group of teachers from different educational backgrounds, working in a context of continuous dialogue among themselves, with other groups, with the families, and with the community at large.

Another important insight was that of not limiting the teachers' professional development to the field of pedagogy, but extending it to the general culture, with particular attention to philosophy, science, art, and neurobiology.

Given the above considerations, we feel that it will be more effective to communicate part of the research conducted with Project Zero in the schools using both of the languages that we use on a daily basis (written and visual). What follows is a good exercise in parallel and synthetic languages.

We will not cover all the strategies of groups of children engaged in learning together that we have seen over the years, and which have been the source of our discussions and exchange of ideas with the Project Zero researchers, but only some that we feel are particularly interesting today in terms of orienting the continuation of the research in our daily work.

One aspect particularly interesting to us has been discovering with greater clarity than in the past **how much one learns to *learn* in a group when the group work is carried out with a high level of awareness**.

This declaration could easily be seen as obvious, but it becomes something more if we underscore the term *awareness*, which is permeated with extensive observation, documentation, and interpretation.

The writing of these visual essays is based on the research, interpretation, and discussion of the staff of the Diana School: Marina Castagnetti, Sonia Cipolla, Tiziana Filippini, Isabella Meninno, Marina Mori, Evelina Reverberi, Laura Rubizzi, Paola Strozzi and Vea Vecchi; and of the Project Zero-Reggio Children research team. Special thanks to Tiziana Filippini, Claudia Giudici, and Carla Rinaldi for their helpful suggestions.

161

Social Individualism

Episode from the project
"The Beautiful Wall,"
a collective ceramic
sculpture
Authors
Five- and six-year-old
children
Teachers
Marina Mori
Paola Strozzi
Vea Vecchi
Photographs by
Vea Vecchi

Without losing sight of the final objective of a project, children often implement a series of strategies aimed at maintaining group cohesion, in a conscious act of intelligent "social individualism." What we mean by this is that children seem to be aware of the positive gains, including individual ones, that can derive from the success of the whole group: gains in terms of effort (to which children are very sensitive) and gains in the quality of social relations and friendships (to which they are even more sensitive).

In the course of their work, children make use of a sort of "code of good manners" for group work, a mixture of formal rules that the group seems to follow and that are seen as effective for reaching the objective. So effective, in fact, that the more children's research advances, the more the term "good manners" seems to us to be too ephemeral, and the actions related to this behavior seem to be inseparable from the process and concept of learning in a group.

To illustrate this, we offer a brief excerpt from a project in which children are creating a ceramic sculpture for a wall of the inner courtyard of the school.

162

Selection of the final design for a ceramic sculpture

One of the most arduous phases of a collectively produced visual representation (painting, sculpture, and so on) is always the construction of the final designs ("designs" meaning the trials that prepare and precede the final collective product).

Children's drawings reduced using the photocopier, and a sheet that simulates the wall where the ceramic sculptures will be placed. The children choose the drawings and put them together as they wish.

Six children (three boys and three girls) have previously worked in pairs to prepare a collage design, one per pair, so now they have three different designs. Choosing the one that contains the best ideas for the ceramic sculpture that will be produced by all the children of the class is a particularly delicate moment.*
The children have the problem clearly in mind: there is only one wall, so there has to be only one final design.
A sort of pulsing begins to take place in the group, the bodies come closer together,

becoming almost a single body with lots of heads, arms, and legs. This union, so physically declared, seems to anticipate the need, but also the solidarity required, to choose one design and eliminate the other two. Children typically want to preserve everything; in this case exclusion seems almost too painful. So first Daniele and then Chiara propose hypotheses that overcome the problem of choosing by elimination.

* Prior to the final "The Beautiful Wall" project, moments in which all the children of the class were involved alternated with others (like the episode described here) where primarily one group was involved. The decision to have this alternation was suggested by the way the project actually proceeded.

Here we present only Chiara's hypothesis, because it is the one adopted in the end.

Chiara says: *I have an idea. Let's make a new design all together. Everybody puts in a piece and asks the others if they agree. That way, we're all even in the end.*

In order to realize Chiara's idea, the children arrange themselves in a line. Each one in turn selects one of the cut-out drawings of animals and plants that will make up the collage design; the child then places it on the simulated wall...

and asks whether the other group members agree.

Then the child goes back to the end of the line, waiting for his or her next turn.

We think this is a slow and boring ritual, and express our perplexity to the children. They agree with us but continue unperturbed, explaining that with this system all of them would have their own work on the wall and all would be able to say whether or not they agree with the decisions of the others.

Children have a strong sense of justice, and if they understand and share the meanings of this, then they are prepared to submit to a great many rules.

Equally strong is the desire to identify themselves individually in a group product.

The completed design

Children show pride and excitement in constructing something together in a group, but also show the desire to leave a recognizable individual trace. Subsequent to the episode reported here, we have found confirmation of this in many other situations, just as we have seen many attempts to search for solutions that keep these two aspects together. These solutions generally emerge when the children are about five and a half, following a long experience of being together. This does not mean that the same desire does not exist at an earlier age, and it can certainly be glimpsed in many situations. For younger children, the difficulty is finding solutions that are clearly argued and equally clearly shared (or perhaps it is only our nearsightedness that keeps us from noticing or realizing what is happening). Episodes such as the one described here are also useful in helping us to *see* a bit better and to be more aware and respectful of the paths that we follow together with the children.

Within this network of relationships and collective concerns, are individual intelligence and invention diminished or enhanced? Are they trapped by the self-regulation established by the group or do they acquire greater flexibility and fluidity? These are only two of the many questions we asked, and they can provide one of the many sources for discussion.

Our impression is that the group situation offers an enriching condition, particularly when it is accompanied by recognition and utilization of the different individual identities and abilities. This situation helps to develop many of the characteristics of intelligence: argumentation and explaining, negotiation, the capacity to consider multiple possibilities of the same problem, and the ability to use other points of view as a resource.

The Size of Work Groups that Enables Communication

Excerpt from the
documentary "A Day
in the Life of the
Four-year-olds"
Teachers
Marina Mori
Paola Strozzi
Project coauthor
Vea Vecchi
Photographs by
Vea Vecchi

The size of work groups is a subject that has been extensively discussed and written about; perhaps it has been less common to relate the findings of these investigations to the organization of the activities and life of the school in general.

From the moment they arrive at school in the morning, the children await each other, tell each other about things, plan their day and the roles they will have. The groups that form rarely exceed three or four children. Only the boys sometimes form larger groups.

To what extent are the didactic methodologies proposed by the teachers able to *calibrate* themselves in this regard? To what extent are we able to make the intuitions regarding our observations and pronouncements concrete?

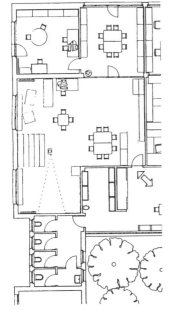

The numerical thresholds that enable communication to flow, indicated autonomously by the children, should be kept in mind in our approach to the various multidisciplinary activities and, in general, in all the organized moments of school life.

In our school, groups of children are engaged simultaneously in different activities. The groups rarely exceed six children; they may reach eight if permitted by the subject at hand.

In a class of twenty-five children aged five to six, there are about six groups working at the same time, some with a teacher, others by themselves. For the autonomous groups, the teacher has previously made hypotheses about the material to place at the children's disposal, material that enables interesting explorations and experiences even without the presence of an adult.

For the three-year-olds, the organization is naturally slightly different (in general we have three groups, one of which is very small). Over time and with extended experience, the children construct the relationships and methods for working and learning together.

167

Episode from the project
"The Beautiful Wall,"
a collective ceramic
sculpture
Authors
Five- and six-year-old
children
Teachers
Marina Mori
Paola Strozzi
Vea Vecchi
Photographs by
Vea Vecchi

When we talk about a group, we are actually talking about individuals who come together and split up into small units of two or three subjects.

In the past, we often made the mistake of observing and documenting a group as a cohesive unit. Even though there is a common objective and the children's desire is for everyone to participate (as we attempted to show in the first episode reported), the group does not often follow a single *rhythm* (cognitive, relational, empathetic, and so on); rather, a number of contemporaneous rhythms tend to be established. We look now at an episode from the project mentioned before (the collective ceramic sculpture), which at this point has advanced to the production phase. The children are making animals and plants out of clay.

Six children (three girls and three boys) seated around a table are deciding and agreeing among themselves and with the teacher which subjects to make out of clay. While they are discussing, some of the children move around the table, and the initial single discussion becomes two intersecting and contemporaneous discussions between the group of girls and the group of boys.

It often happens that boys and girls, even though they get along well together, divide into separate groups of their own accord. When asked why, the children give responses such as:

Caterina: *Usually the boys and the girls don't think in a different way and they talk pretty much the same way. But sometimes the girls choose each other because they're friends; being friends is important, it helps in the group. Otherwise, sometimes the girls don't talk.*

Federico: *You have to work hard in the group, and if you're friends you work better. If you make a mistake, nobody says anything about it and you start over again.*

Armando: *I like working with the girls better, because they're nice; they talk politely, they're not loud.*

168

In this particular episode, the children organize themselves autonomously into three working subgroups. The three boys decide to make a scorpion together, each one assigned a different part: Daniele, who is good with clay and a bit impatient, will make the head and the body; Alessio, a good and persevering modeler, will make the legs because there are lots of them and they're a bit difficult; Davide, who's good at speaking but decidedly less adept at constructing, is assigned the stinger.

When a project is engaging and the children participate willingly, they go beyond the phase where they simply seem to *content themselves* with the result (quite a common phase). They know how to make good use of the different skills of the members of the group in order to achieve a good result.

The atmosphere is lively and amused. If one of the boys abandons the work, he is immediately scolded, but construction errors are easily forgiven. Time is given to redo the work, and there is always a friend in the group who intervenes to make adjustments and help with any difficulties that may arise.

The scorpion is completed. The boys have consulted a book with photographs of the arachnid, which they found on their own in the library. Seeking and using tools to achieve a good result is a positive and intelligent sign of learning.

This is a method often used by the teachers as well. We have a number of books with photographs of animals taken from different points of view, where the use of the macro lens and new technologies enable unusual visual elaborations, which make an important contribution to the children's mental images and understandings.

169

The three girls, following quite a long negotiation session, decide that Laura and Caterina will make a big tree together.

> Laura: *We already have an idea about how to do it!*
> Caterina: *It's getting real skinny!*
> Daniele (glancing over from the nearby table where he is working on the scorpion): *The problem's going to be making it stand up!*

Chiara has chosen to make a frog by herself; it's an animal which she is very fond of and with which she seems to have a particular empathy.

She is a very sociable girl, but sometimes she really enjoys working alone. (Since she is particularly skillful in building with clay, perhaps she is afraid that collective work will lower the aesthetic quality of the product, or else she is simply happier to work along her own path.) **The group is therefore composed of three subgroups, but the attention between them will remain vigilant, constant, and interconnected for the entire duration of the activities**.

The frog's eyes are the starting element of Chiara's sculpture. The perceptual structure she applies in building the animal is to work from a map of attraction that is significant to her; that is, the eyes are the identifying element of the frog, so that's where she begins.

Chiara and the frog study each other.

Every now and then, the girls give each other their opinions and advice, some of which are friendly remarks that help to maintain a pleasant context; others stimulate comparisons with other points of view regarding the work at hand.

The finished frog. It's beautiful. Chiara has used the book of photographs too, following the example of her companions—or rather, advised by them to do so. As we can clearly see by looking at their sculptures, the children do not remain imprisoned within sterile copies. The photographs are used for remembering the subject better and grasping its identity when it is not possible to have it in front of you or when you are not particularly familiar with it. The photographic images used for reference provide further representational hypotheses for the children's mental imagery.

Flexibility of the groups

The large clay tree requires a good deal of time and work, and at a certain point Laura and Caterina, neither of whom is particularly persevering, decide to ask for help from Elisa and Daria, two girls who are skillful in working with clay.

What does it mean to move in and out of a project at different stages while it is being carried out? What does it mean in this particular case for Elisa and Daria?

The children in the class are always familiar with the various projects going on, and being called in to help is a sign of acknowledged skill. Perhaps the framework of meaning around what the "helper" is doing is less clear, but different levels of participation in a project are always present and accepted, even sporadic participation.

It often happens that the initial group loses or acquires members as the work progresses.

The groups are open to size changes brought about by the natural course of events and by the characteristics of the participants.

Naturally, the entry of new members with their own individualities modifies the rhythm of the group and its organization.

Self-organization

Quite often, as in this case, we see children confronting complex representations by choosing a sort of "assembly line" method of organization with distribution of fixed tasks:

Elisa, you do all the branches, I'll put them together and attach them to the tree. Daria, you make the leaves and Caterina will stick them on... (and so on).

We have found this type of task assignment for making a single subject more often in groups of girls, but fearing generalizations, we immediately add that it can also happen in groups of boys.

In any case, there are some types of self-organization that are more commonly seen in groups of boys or groups of girls.

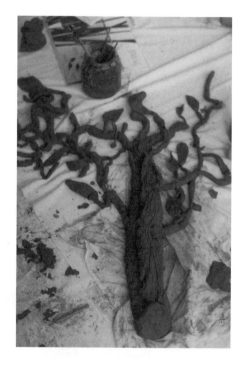

The finished tree. In this case, the girls have used a tree that they could see outside the window as their reference. Using a live model is another strategy often proposed by the teachers because we consider it to be very effective for gaining knowledge and creating empathetic relationships with the subject being depicted. Laura has made the clay branches using a construction strategy that is not very economical, the same used in another sculpture she made about a month ago.

When we compare the documentation of the construction strategies of the same children, collected at different moments and in different contexts, we realize that children have a great memory for constructive schemas that have shown to be effective in previous work (because of the result achieved and the appreciation received), and they tend to use them again. After re-using a previous strategy, even though it was not the most economical, the children often arrive at a new one.

172

Verbal language

One element that we have often seen in work groups is a particular use of the verbal language, which is employed for the purposes described below (these are just a few examples):

- Asking for approval: *Do you like it?*
- Giving approval: *It's nice. That's good.*
- Asking for opinions: *Do you agree? What do you think?*
  (awareness, therefore, of the possibility of different points of view)
- Expressing one's point of view: *I have an idea…*
- Asking for help: *How do I make this leg?*
- Intervening to help: *I'll explain it to you. Look how I did mine.*
- Projecting possibilities using the plural: *We can do this. Come on, let's do this.*
- Seeking negotiation immediately following a little dispute: *Let's do it some like I say and some like you say.*
- Particularly with girls, a sort of seductive language is often used: *Oh, you're so good!*
- Names are often used (Daria, Anna) to attract the attention of other group members.

(Naturally, the language also varies in relation to age. The examples given here come from groups of children aged four and a half to six.)

Different time frames

Generally, the subgroups do not have the same time frames because each moves with a sort of relational musicality and approach to the work that is different, but we feel it is right for the teacher to allow these different rhythms.
Girls often need more time than boys, precisely because of the different ways of relating among themselves and with the work they are doing.

Self-assessment and group assessment

When all the subgroups have finished for the day (the work often continues the next day), we usually bring all the initial groups back together and ask them to comment on their work and that of the others. This applies not only to the visible result but also to the entire construction process, where the children can revisit the phases or moments they consider to be the most important or most interesting. This revisiting is sometimes done with the aid of the products the children have made (drawings or other objects), and sometimes by means of the teacher's notes, or by viewing the videotape recordings (though this happens more rarely).
When possible (and the new digital technologies have made this more frequent), the children also use the photographic images in the moment of revisiting.
As we feel that this revisiting is a very important issue for the subject of our research, later in the chapter we present an episode in which it stands out more clearly.

Protagonists
Five- and six-year-old
children
Photographs by
Vea Vecchi

There are many projects that the children carry out in a completely autonomous way. We only come to know of a few of these, but we are certain that many of them happen without our ever being aware of them.

What we offer here is a brief episode among those we have glimpsed, one which leads us to assume the existence of an elaborate and *bustling* social network that the children pursue with great interest and tenacity.

It is a normal occurrence for some children to migrate from the work they are doing and approach other groups, offering opinions and advice. At other times, certain children are called in specifically because they are recognized as being skilled in a particular area. This happens frequently in activities involving languages such as writing.

Armando wants to write a love letter to Caterina, but he doesn't know all the letters yet. He asks for help from another boy, Michele, who can already write autonomously.
Here is how the teaching takes place:

Armando dictates to Michele what he wants to write. Michele holds Armando's head and uses it like a video camera, directing his friend's eyes on the computer keyboard, pointing letter by letter to those he needs for composing the words and sentences he wants to write.

Caterina, seated next to them, listens to the message and immediately writes her reply, as she is partially autonomous in writing.

Immediately afterward, we see Armando copying out by hand the computer written message. Somewhat surprised, we ask him why he's doing this. He replies: *Because HE wrote that one* (indicating the computer), *and I'M writing this one.*

The great wisdom of a learning process.

Armando's message

CATI I LOVE YOU A LOT BECAUSE YOU'RE PRETTY AND NICE. ARMI GANAPINI

Caterina's reply

ARMANDO TOMORROW I'M GOING TO MAKE A PICTURE FOR YOU I'M GLAD YOU ALWAYS PLAY WITH ME. CATERINA

This episode confirms, among other things, that peers are excellent teachers. On a number of occasions, we have made use of the children's own teaching strategies (naturally avoiding ones like using the head as a pointer) because of their effectiveness.

Armando's desire for Caterina to be his *special* friend is very strong, and evidently he sees writing as a skill that can win her over, so he organizes or participates in various projects where writing is an important part of the communication…
such as the one that took place shortly afterward.

When we divide into work groups, all the spaces of the school are occupied, including those outside the classroom.

A group of children is working with a teacher in the space just outside the entrance to the classroom.

Another group of children, including Armando, having completed their morning's work, are playing nearby and making a lot of noise. After asking them several times to lower their voices, to no avail, the teacher loses her patience and sends them back into the classroom, where all the other children are engaged in various activities.

The classroom door is closed, thus allowing the groups inside and those outside to work in peace.

At a certain point, the door opens and a boy from the group that was scolded comes out and, quickly and silently, tapes a sheet of paper onto the door, then goes back into the classroom and closes the door. The same scene and the same gesture are repeated three times, each time by another child from the group, one of whom is Armando.

The teacher, initially absorbed in the work she's doing, doesn't pay much attention to the event, but then she becomes curious. Approaching the door, she sees that the three pieces of paper are messages addressed to her, shown here on the right.

How could we not appreciate this small protest project carried out by the group?

The episode then continues with further explanations between the teacher and the children.

Three months have passed, and Armando continues to write love letters to Caterina, now by himself. What's more, writing has become Armando's preferred method of communication with his teachers. Almost every day, in fact, Sonia and Laura (the teachers) receive messages from Armando with comments or requests. They received the one shown at the right on the last day of school.

We can certainly confirm that in learning, motivation is always the fundamental element of success.

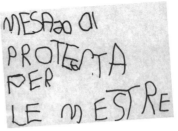

PROTEST MESSAGE FOR THE TEACHERS

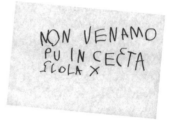

WE ARE NOT COMING BACK TO THIS SCHOOL ANY MORE

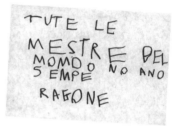

ALL THE TEACHERS IN THE WORLD AREN'T ALWAYS RIGHT

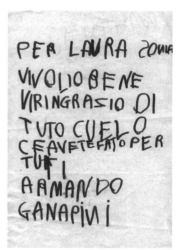

TO LAURA AND SONIA WE LOVE YOU THANK YOU FOR EVERYTHING YOU HAVE DONE FOR ALL OF US

Group Formation
How the children choose each other autonomously

Photographs by
Vea Vecchi

An error in evaluation we have made a number of times in the past was to declare the cognitive advancement of a group when actually the understanding and advancement were of just one or two members of the group. This erroneous assessment can easily happen if the processes of the individuals and the group are not documented contemporaneously. There are aspects of knowing how to learn as an individual and as a group that have elements in common. Some are different, such as the pauses, the moments of listening and of "contagion," the reconversion of the other person's ideas, and so on. In order to grasp these elements, the teachers need to be aware of their own theories and have experience in documenting.

The individual characteristics present in a group are an important basis for making the group a learning group. This issue is treated more extensively by the Project Zero researchers in "Form, Function, and Understanding in Learning Groups"; in the ministry on page 322 we can *listen* to how the children choose each other in the formation of groups.

The list of criteria is long, and it changes over time. The attentive teacher knows that, when she proposes the composition of a group, if she wants to ensure that it works well, she has to negotiate with the children's desires. She also knows that no matter how "correct" her predictions are, they are never certain. Other factors have to be introduced, which are established in each situation with the actual children and in relation to the context in which they are living and working.

We have little faith in models that seek to regulate; it is good to be familiar with them but we have to distrust rules that are too fixed. We need to be sufficiently lucid and open-minded to verify whether they work or not. What is important is the teacher's awareness and desire to place the children in group situations that can increase the possibilities for the understanding of the various individuals and of the group as a whole. Some children, for similar or different reasons, have difficulty constructing the verbal and body language of being and working in a group. Not being able to cooperate with the others can become frustrating and tiresome. In our experience and in some of the documentation we have clearly seen that many of these children, who are sometimes incorrectly defined as difficult, when playing or working with their peers have movements and body gestures, and particularly verbal language, that do not attract and engage the others in a common project. There seems to be a discrepancy between their desire to socialize and their lack of gestural and verbal competency to satisfy this desire. This often leads to arguments and excessive aggressiveness that distance their peers and increasingly cast them in a negative way.

These children should be given the opportunity to experiment with and exercise their social relations and learning; perhaps the more we know about the processes involved (learning and cooperation), the more we can help those children who have difficulty putting them into practice.

177

From a brief investigation of cooperative construction carried out with all the five- and six-year-old children divided into groups of boys only, girls only, and mixed boys and girls
Teachers
Sonia Cipolla
Laura Rubizzi
Project coauthor and consultancy
Vea Vecchi
Photographs by
Vea Vecchi

Almost all of the episodes we narrate in this chapter are representative of good collaborative abilities and therefore run the risk of portraying the children of Reggio Emilia as having a sort of innate gift for cooperation that could make the work of the school seem almost irrelevant.

Though the city of Reggio Emilia has deep roots of cooperative culture and organization, and though sociability is a very strong desire in children and something they continuously and autonomously practice, the attitudes and processes involved in working on projects together and collaborating are not a given.

Effective learning benefits from organized collaborative situations which, though varying in form, are repeated over time. Teachers must be prepared to evaluate whether the proposals they make to the children, the methodologies used, and the organization of the work guarantee possibilities for individual and cooperative learning.

If skills of collaboration and negotiation are deemed to be important in a given society, then school is perhaps one of the places where they can most easily be explored, developed, and practiced.

The episodes that follow involve constructing with clay. In these episodes it is clear that attitudes of collaboration and negotiation cannot be taken for granted. When children have many opportunities to experiment with these skills, they arrive at using them naturally in ways that are increasingly highly evolved and gratifying.

This is the second time in this chapter that clay appears as the material used, so we were doubtful whether to include the following episodes. But as both these episodes provide effective examples of the affirmations we have made, we believe this justifies our taking the risk that they could give a distorted picture regarding the variety of materials and languages used in the school (which are naturally many more than are indicated here).

The episodes we describe have to do with two analogous sculptures made by the same children one week apart.

The first proposal is made to eight children (four boys and four girls) seated around two different tables, asking them to make a mirror simulation in clay of the context in which they find themselves at that moment; that is, a single table with four children seated around it who are constructing a table with four children seated around it.

The proposal is one that *compels* the children to seek cooperative strategies, and falls within the sphere of a series of opportunities offered to the children to develop, experiment with, and consolidate the concept of group work.

The children are amused by the proposal and immediately accept the game of reproducing themselves and their present situation.

Both groups, however, have difficulty finding a collaborative strategy immediately.

Despite the fact that the teacher reminds them of the proposal several times to make sure it is clear, the boys proceed individually. Each one builds a table and a chair situated on a clay floor, probably for reasons of greater stability. Ferruccio begins, followed by the other three. Later, on Ferruccio's suggestion, the four portions of floor are joined (and the boys are very pleased about this), thus forming a single floor with four tables and four chairs on it.

The initial idea of the mirror situation is only truly implemented after Ferruccio's discovery that in the classroom where they are working there are actually four tables. Having constructed four clay tables, the boys decide that they really are recreating the actual situation. Only at this point do they accept to choose one of the tables they have constructed, around which they can place the four chairs in which they are seated. Following some discussion they choose the largest one.

Final sculpture of the boys' group

The girls' group, at first, partially reproduces the pattern of their boy counterparts, with each girl building a table and one chair so that in the end they have four tables and four chairs.

Unlike the boys, however, following a quick check on the work done, the girls immediately accept the initial idea of the mirror representation. Without difficulty, they choose the largest of their four clay tables.

What they do not accept, however, is using the chairs they have already constructed, and they decide to make new ones. They do this very meticulously, adjusting the size of the chairs and the table as they go along.

When the teacher asks them why they eliminated the first chairs, they reply:

These are better for sitting on.

Because they have to be right for the table.

And if some other kids come, there'll be enough chairs for everyone.

Final sculpture of the girls' group

At the end of every project, it is useful and necessary for the teachers to note some of their reflections, even if only briefly. In this case, some of ours were:

• Both groups (boys and girls) confirm to us the extent to which a meaningful context for the work is important and motivating.

• They also confirm the extent to which the choices made in cooperative organization show a preference, when possible, for solutions that do not require elimination but democratically preserve and use the individual work of all those involved.

• A doubt: To what extent did our decision to place on the table a block of clay and a work base for each child encourage individual work? The context and the materials that accompany a proposal are much more important elements than we generally think, and should therefore be carefully considered.

We should keep this clearly in mind (though we frequently forget) so that we can make our proposals and actions more in tune with the children's strategies, thus allowing them a greater degree of freedom and creativity.

After about a week, we decide to propose an analogous theme and observe to what extent the past experience has been useful to us and to the children.

We make this new proposal with certain adjustments suggested to us by the children's previous experience. It often happens in the course of our work that suggestions made by the children orient how we proceed.

Before starting the new project, we ask the children to look at the sculptures previously made and try to remember what took place.

The girls primarily remember the problems of stability of the objects they made: *The chair fell down, it kept falling down.*
If we make the legs fat, it won't fall down.

The boys, looking at their own work, have no doubts: *This is our classroom.*
They continue, remembering with pleasure and amusement the construction of the floor, then:
It was Giuseppe who won, you know. We put ourselves at his table because it was just the right length.
Nobody wins really—it wasn't a bicycle race, you know!
But first we argued because everybody wanted their own table, then I was the first one to pick Giuseppe's table.
Yeah, but it's not very nice because if one guy wins and the other one doesn't want to lose, then he's sad because he lost, really.
Teacher: But if the work that all four of you did in the end is really good, then all four of you have won.
Yeah that's right. This work is almost great, and we had fun doing it together.
Teacher: Your idea to put the table with you sitting around it in the classroom along with the other tables and chairs gave us teachers an idea, too. Why don't you, with all your friends, make everything there is in the classroom? That way it will be a real model of your classroom.

The idea is approved, communicated to the other classmates, and a project begins that involves all the children in the class. It is a small investigation that enables us to document the children's cooperative strategies and to place the children in contexts where they can hone their skills in the organization and negotiation of working in a group.

This investigation is still under way, so we do not have the final summaries, but we can follow the two previous groups and document what happens, in the hope that the children will be able to make use of their past experience, just as we strive to do.

We know, however, that we needn't be too certain, because children are often unpredictable and leave us in a state of bewilderment. We need to be very flexible and optimistic regarding their abilities, and ours.

Boys' group   The boys decide to make the two tables pushed together and the chairs that are in the mini-atelier.
They're two real close together that touch each other.

This time the children find the material to be used (clay, work bases, wooden tools, and so on) on a bench and are invited to take what they need.

As in the previous experience, the boys start building right away without making any prior verbal agreements. We wait before intervening. After a short while, Ferruccio says: *And now I'm going to make two good tables. Everybody has to make two tables.*
Teacher: If everybody makes two tables, then how many tables will we have in the mini-atelier?
Six... No, eight.
Teacher: There are only two tables in the mini-atelier...
Michele: *Then we'll pick mine.*
Giuseppe: *I'll pick mine.*
Ferruccio: *I'll make one table, Michele* (who's sitting next to him) *one table, and you* (Giuseppe and Davide sitting nearby) *make the chairs.*
Giuseppe: *No, wait a minute. We'll make the tables and you make the chairs.*

The dispute continues with other attempts at distribution, where constructing the tables continues to be the element of prestige, perhaps because in the previous experience it was the object of contention and of selection, or perhaps because the one who nominated himself to build the tables was Ferruccio, who's considered to be something of a leader.
Giuseppe: *Well, I want to give you another example: Ferruccio makes one table and Michele who's next to him makes two chairs; I make one table and Davide who's next to me makes two more chairs. That way we have exactly what's in the mini-atelier.*
Giuseppe's hypothesis works perfectly for the construction objective but not for the desire of each boy to make a table, so the discussion continues. We hope they will be able to come to an agreement. In any case, with respect to the previous experience, even though the situation is conflictual, the boys are searching for a way to organize their work.

182

 libr秘

Teacher: Why doesn't anybody want to make the chairs?
Ferruccio: *Because they're really easy to do.*
Teacher: Do you remember when you made the other sculpture and you said that it wasn't a race and that you made something together that was really nice? If you can agree on things, it's much better.

Giuseppe: *Because if Michele wants to make the table it's no good; we're arguing and we're wasting a lot of time. So we have to decide if we agree like I said.*

Michele: *No, I don't agree.*
Ferruccio: *Come on, we have to decide.*

Michele: *Okay, let's do this. First we'll do the chairs, then we'll think about the tables... maybe we could do like the other time: we can make four tables and then we'll pick two of them.*

The problem is thus shelved for the time being. We will see whether and how they resolve it.

The boys are now building the chairs, and then start making the figures of themselves seated.

Ferruccio: *Look how I bent my foot.*

He has given his foot the same curvature as the entire seated figure.

Michele, turning to the teacher: *Sonia, later you all choose my table, okay?*

He makes a big "S" with the clay (the initial of his last name) and puts it at the base of his chair, thus marking the identity of his sculpture.

The others like this idea, too, so each one makes his own initials and puts them next to the chair he has constructed.

Ferruccio, Michele: *We're tired. We don't want to work any more.*

Davide: *So who's going to do the tables? I'll make one.*

Teacher: Davide is making one table. There are three of you. Who's going to make the other one?

Michele: *One can make the top of the table, one can make two legs, and the other one can make the other two legs.*

The problem seems to be resolved, though there remains the issue of the different size of the two tables, as well as that of the legs for the same table which, being constructed by two different boys, are different.

Ferruccio: *I make the legs short and then you make them the right length.*

And then later, Ferruccio: *Hey you guys, we made the chairs too high. The people's legs sitting down won't go under the table.*

Michele: *Well, even if they don't go under, it doesn't matter. We're not going to do them again.*

Finally the sculpture is finished. Given the time taken and the efforts the boys have made to agree, the teacher accepts their composition without further comment.

The teacher asks the boys to comment on their work and then begins a discussion with them by asking the questions:

When everybody wants to do the same thing, how do you decide? How can you make an agreement? What do you do if nobody changes his mind?

She thinks that dealing with the problem in the abstract may help the children accept the problem of negotiation with more clear-sightedness.

Girls' group We propose the same theme to the girls that was undertaken by the boys: the two tables of the mini-atelier with chairs and children seated, in order to better observe the similarities and differences.
Benedetta: *Should we make us sitting down and writing messages?*
Her suggestion puts their task in a more meaningful context.

They begin to work, taking the material they want to use from the bench, as the boys did.

Sarah: *I want to make sheets of paper out of clay and pens for writing the messages.*
Benedetta: *I want to do the table.*
Caterina: *Me too.*
Jennifer: *I want to do the children and the pens.*
Benedetta: *I have an idea. Jenni can make the sheets, Sarah the pens, me and Caterina the tables.*
Caterina: *Yes, good idea.*
Unlike the boys, the girls immediately distribute the tasks.
While they work in a fairly relaxed atmosphere, each one is attentive to and vigilant over what the others are doing, as they always are.
Caterina: *Benedetta, your table really sort of looks like a cake with candles on it.*
Sarah: *Jenni, you're making the sheets too big; they don't fit on the table.*
Jennifer, in silence, destroys her clay sheet of paper and makes a smaller one.

Benedetta, who is still making the legs of her table, at a certain point takes two and moves them farther apart.
Teacher: Why did you move them?
Benedetta: *That table there* (the one Caterina has already finished) *is big, so I have to make mine bigger, too.*
Teacher: Are the two tables in the mini-atelier the same or different?
Caterina: *They're exactly the same, but I only know how to do it like this.*
The teacher's words often serve simply as a counterpoint for further clarifying an intuition or a thought already expressed by the children.

Benedetta has moved the legs of her table too far apart; the space between them is too wide, and when she tries to put the clay table top on the legs, it slumps.

Caterina notices from a distance and comes to help her friend

by placing another leg in the middle of the space.

But the clay top continues to bend.

Caterina: *I know what you can do. You put the legs closer together or you make them fatter.*
Teacher: Good idea.

Caterina returns to her table and constructs another clay top the same size as the other one and measures it carefully.

Then she places the top on the four legs of Benedetta's table that have been spaced appropriately. Caterina and Benedetta continue to work together on constructing Benedetta's table.

Before finishing the work, they encounter the measurement problem two more times: for the chairs, which have to be "right" for the tables, and for the seated figures, whose legs are too short so their feet do not reach the floor. The latter problem is easily resolved by lengthening the legs.

It takes more time, however, to understand that in order to lower the chairs that are too high, the best system is not to squash them downward with your hands, but to remove a piece of clay from the legs.

We should always remember that for the children nothing is taken for granted. They are exploring everything, and every new context renews the experimentation.

Here the collaboration between the girls seems to be much greater than that of the boys, but we must be very cautious not to make overly confident generalizations.

The finished sculpture

About a month later, during the construction of a clay model for a ceramic bridge to be placed in the inner courtyard, it was the boys (some of whom were present in the previously described episodes) who became the organizers of the work among the six participants present.

In that particular instance we documented quite advanced collaborative skills for both the girls and the boys.

We like to think that the repeated cooperative opportunities and greater attention on our part as teachers have begun to show their effectiveness.

From a project called
"A Games Manual for the
Three-year-olds"
Authors
Five- and six-year-old
children
Teachers
Evelina Reverberi
Paola Strozzi
*Project coauthor
and consultancy*
Vea Vecchi
Photographs by
Vea Vecchi

When talking about group learning, there may be a misapprehension that it only occurs when the group cooperates in the construction of the same product. In our opinion, a learning group must be defined as such even when the product and process are individual but are generated and constructed within the network of relationships, self-assessment, and assessment carried out by the group and in the group.

We present below a brief look at some individual processes, a full description of which is given in what we call a research and study notebook (a small photocopied book with images, which gives an overview of the whole experience). Here the graphic representation of children playing Ring-around-the-Rosy begins with the production of individual works, which the children then go on to compare with the products of their groupmates. These works evolve quite quickly into a group cultural product while remaining individual products.

We often like to explore even traditional subjects such as drawing in order to discover the invisible content which is often concealed in the products we normally come across. It is a kind of investigation of "very low-definition truth," as Ruggero Pierantoni has described the critique and perception of everyday matters and events.

Effort and pleasure

In comparison to the past, a great many images are available to children today, many of which come from TV—images that are beautiful or ugly, inventions that are intelligent, standard, or stereotyped.

Having exposure to many images does not necessarily mean having the ability to draw better. Perhaps there is a greater distance between mental images and the level of graphic ability linked to biological age; children seem to find it harder than they did in the past to accept a graphic result so far removed from the representations of reality that they see and that contribute to constructing their imagery of the world.

Equally, children find it hard to accept that better representational skills, and consequently greater satisfaction with their products, are gained by drawing more and accepting that they have to put themselves to the test again and again when drawing the same subject. In order to evolve, the graphic language, like all other languages, needs opportunities for expression, trials, and practice. Children's accepted time lag between desiring an object and attaining it has probably become shorter.

It is difficult to predict what role drawing will have in the future. Perhaps it will be replaced by other forms of expression or, alternatively, it may even become a language that is more precious than it is today. We believe it would be a pity to lose a language so rich in expressive potential and conceptual content; therefore, we try to ensure that the children maintain an active desire to draw and do not turn away from drawing because of excessive frustration.

As teachers we believe it is important never to separate the two conceptual aspects—that is, the strictly expessive and the cognitive. Though we are aware that a visual representation is made up of many facets, we are prepared to support the child in a representational process that sometimes favors one part over the other.

The episode described below is a fragment of a situation that highlights the effort of learning, but also the pleasure the children derive from seeing their own competencies grow.

The effort and determination that are always required in learning situations are more acceptable to children when they are aimed at a clear and shared objective or when they are applied to interesting situations, but above all when they are associated with pleasure and gratification.

Over the years, we have collected a great many observations and documentation materials that provide evidence of how children even at three years of age pose problems to themselves about the three-dimensional quality of the images they have drawn. They use various graphic strategies to answer the questions raised, such as using both sides of the paper for the same object or resorting to three-dimensional techniques.

 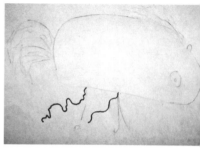

Federica (age three years, two months) announces her wish to draw a running horse. Once her drawing is completed, she looks at it and comments aloud: *A horse has four legs.* She turns over the sheet and draws two more running legs.

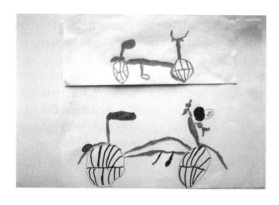 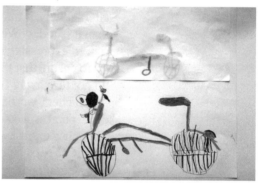

Elisa and Valeria (both five years, six months) draw two bicycles on separate occasions and both find similar solutions for representing them three-dimensionally.

Elisa turns over the sheet and draws the second pedal.

After finishing her drawing, Valeria comments: *"A bicycle has two sides!"* She goes to the window, turns over the sheet, and traces the whole drawing of the bicycle on the blank side of the paper.

We choose to support these types of research efforts because we think they are very interesting. We try to engage other children in thinking about the problems raised, not by suggesting models or solutions, but by identifying occasions that could more forcefully highlight the problems that the children are investigating on their own. The episode described below (the longest of all those appearing in this chapter) also falls within this context.

Project Hypotheses

Before embarking on work with the children, we always jot down some notes and hypotheses on the project we are going to undertake, as tools for initial orientation and reflection and as a basis for discussions with our colleagues. We set out below the initial stages of the project, written by the teachers, as we believe these are important for understanding the strategies we use to approach new projects.

1 **Initial delimitation of the field of investigation and identification of the theme to be proposed to the children**
Noticing the children's independent research on representing three-dimensional subjects using a two-dimensional medium such as drawing, we try to find a project design that can support their investigation, disseminate it, and allow new questions to emerge.
We identify a series of graphic themes as initial opportunities to bring out more forcefully the problems of representation in relation to different contexts, such as a soccer match, the game of Capture the Flag, and so on.

2 **Identification of a meaningful context within which to place the project**
We decide to suggest to the children that they produce a manual of games and associated rules, including illustrations, that can be left as a memory to the three-year-old children who will be joining the school the following year.

3 **Initial questions to be considered regarding the identified theme**
To what extent will the children to whom we make the proposal have a prior idea about the graphic and conceptual difficulties they will encounter?
Can asking them to make predictions about their drawings be helpful to the children as a way of *focusing* on possible problems, and thus enable them to face these problems with a greater degree of awareness?

4 Preliminary lines of observations related to the children's verbal hypotheses

What difficulties will the children perceive in the proposal?
- Drawing the human figure?
- The different points of view from which the figures will have to be drawn in order to make the representation clear?
- The difficulty of producing a two-dimensional representation of a three-dimensional subject?

How many children participate in this game of anticipating hypotheses?
What kind of verbalizations do they formulate?
What are the other children's level and quality of listening to these verbalizations and what do they contribute to them or actively discuss?

In the morning assembly where the whole class gathers together, the children appear to be interested in the proposal of explaining a number of games and the related rules to the younger children. They suggest using very direct forms of communication (which can be achieved with minimal effort), such as coming to the school in person to explain the games verbally, or getting someone to record them with a video camera as they play the game and subsequently showing the recordings to the three-year-olds.

After a process of negotiation between children and teachers, the proposed solutions, which are all intelligent suggestions, are eventually narrowed down to two: one is communication by video recordings and one is a manual with written texts and drawings.

The first game that the children propose to describe is Ring-around-the-Rosy, as they consider it to be particularly suited to three-year-old children.

5 Ring-around-the-Rosy: Identity of the game

"A children's singing game in which players dance around in a circle and at a given signal squat." (Merriam-Webster's Collegiate Dictionary, 10th Edition, 1994)

"…as if children's Ring-around-the-Rosy did not mean going around nothing, as if with their circling action they were going around a space that, though it may contain nothing, is nevertheless delimited and made to become *something*, thanks to that circling action." This is what the philosophers Alessandro Dal Lago and Pier Aldo Rovatti wrote in their manual *Per gioco*.

This *going around* is an ancient game that, we think, is played in various ways by almost all the children in the world. Yet it is also a complex representational situation, since the representation has to account for the rotation of the human figure (front, back, and profile) placed within a circumscribed space delimited by the children holding hands. Our culture defines this space as perspectival (even if this is stating the obvious, we should always remember that perspective is not an objective situation but a cultural interpretation).

While we are aware of the manifold metaphorical and philosophical interpretations that may be attributed to the Ring-around-the-Rosy game, our intention in this case is to use it primarily as a well-known context, frequently *inhabited* by children, which has the capacity to highlight the research problems and possible solutions involved in representing figures at different perceptual levels.

6 **Method of the proposal**
Various graphic materials, sheets of paper of different sizes. The proposal was made to all the children in the class, leaving complete freedom in the choice of group formation.

Lines of observation
- What kinds of group formations do the children choose and why?
- To what extent do the problems that were expressed when the children made their verbal hypotheses re-emerge at the moment of graphic representation? In what way do they do so? Do they resolve them silently or by asking questions? To whom do they address their questions?
- What dialogues are taking place? What cross-influences emerge?

7 **Self-assessment and assessment**
Ask groups of four to five children to comment on the drawings produced and the relationship between their verbal predictions and their drawings. The groups are formed by taking into account the degree of communicative harmony between the members and the different graphic solutions used. The intention is to underline and clarify the value of the children's constructive processes.

Lines of observation
- What aspects do the children emphasize most?
- What kind of verbal language do they use to do this?
- Do the children have any preferred graphic solutions? If so, which and why?
- Do the authors abandon or defend the solutions that are least appreciated? What kinds of arguments do they use? Are these solutions being stored, to re-emerge perhaps in other situations?

These approaches made up the initial framework of the project outlined by the teachers; henceforth the focus will be on the work done with the children.

The Ring-around-the-Rosy Game

Though this project was conducted with all the children from the same class, our narrative deals with only part of the story. This episode concentrates on the graphic representations of the Ring-around-the-Rosy game produced by three children: Giulia (four years, ten months), Leonardo (five years, six months), and Giovanni (five years, seven months). The epidsode is emblematic of the individual learning that is constructed within and with the contribution of the group.

The children play Ring-around-the-Rosy, talk about "Ring-around-the-Rosys," predict the way in which they can be represented graphically, and then draw them.
We will begin by putting together the verbal predictions and the individual drawings of the three children who are the protagonists of the story.

Giovanni: *Drawing a Ring-around-the-Rosy is easy! Because you draw some kids with their faces in front and then... not all of them with their faces, but also with their backs.*
Giovanni seems to have clear ideas about what to do: he identifies the need to draw children from various points of view.

This is the Ring-around-the-Rosy that Giovanni drew after making a verbal prediction of the representation. He comments on his drawing as follows:
I drew a different kind of Ring-around-the-Rosy, with the kids with their heads in front.
Giovanni seems to *make light of his error* by giving a definition of "difference" that can include many things, even a Ring-around-the-Rosy in a straight line.

Leonardo: *I think it's easy to draw a Ring-around-the-Rosy of kids because you draw a round shape like this* (he traces it in the air), *then the kids… then… it's done!*

To Leonardo, the circle seems to be the guiding shape of the whole representation.

Once his drawing is completed, to his great satisfaction, Leonardo comments on it like this:

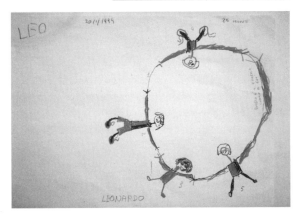

Look what a great Ring-around-the-Rosy! There's an arm here that's a little longer, but otherwise it wouldn't reach!

In his drawing, Leonardo followed the schema that he had previously hypothesized verbally, drawing the circle first and then drawing four children on it.

When the children have completed their drawings, they are called on in groups to comment on their own Ring-around-the-Rosy and those of the other members of their group. The groups are formed partly following the children's own suggestions and partly under the guidance of the teachers, who take into account the different strategies adopted by the children, both in the way they define the problems and in the search for different ways to resolve them.

The children begin to make their first comments, and then turn to Giulia:
What about your drawing, Giulia? Will you show it to us?
Giulia (leaning her elbows and forearms on her drawing):
No, okay, I know I got it wrong, I made a line, not a circle of children… it's hard!

The teacher's assessment is not as harsh as Giulia's, since in her drawing she set the children on a diagonal line across the page. From this layout we glean that she has been asking herself some intelligent questions and playing with ideas intelligently to convey the spatial situation of the Ring-around-the-Rosy through her drawing.

The teacher elicits comments on all the drawings.
Giulia: *Well, they're not really Ring-around-the-Rosys but we did the best we could.*

195

Giovanni: (laughing) **Why don't we all stand like the kids in our drawings?**

Giovanni's idea, which turns around the usual approach of interpreting reality through drawing, appears to us to be excellent; in this way, even the *trip-ups* of the representation can become elements of fun in order to advance thinking. It is an intelligent idea, brimming with questions, trials, and fun. The teachers pick up the idea and later relaunch it to all the children in the class, group by group.

Here we will follow only the work of two of the children we have already introduced.

Giulia: *I want six kids because I drew six!*

She examines her drawing at length and appears to be wondering how to get her classmates to stand in the strange diagonal position she has drawn.

She solves the problem by positioning the children's heads in a diagonal position with her hands.

She also carefully positions her friends' hands and feet in order to make them accurately match the Ring-around-the-Rosy she drew.

Open your arms out, your hands aren't exactly holding each other tight, they're only touching.

Leonardo also calls out the number of classmates he has drawn in his picture (four). Lying down in the position drawn by Leonardo sets off an outburst of general hilarity.

Giovanni says: *In Leonardo's picture he's looking at the kids from above, he's up there and we're down here lying on the floor.*

We are going to see how Leonardo mentally stores the point of view used by Giovanni to *interpret* the situation, and uses it on a later occasion. Very often it is other people who, with their comments and interpretations, make us more conscious of the choices we make.

Leonardo: *To make it into a real Ring-around-the-Rosy we need everyone to stand up!*

One of the most amusing moments is when the children move from lying down to standing up, as requested by Leonardo.

The children do stand up, but they find themselves with their shoulders facing each other in an improbable Ring-around-the-Rosy back to front.

Leonardo: *No, this isn't right. This Ring-around-the-Rosy is kind of small and a little silly. The backs are turned toward the other backs, but the bodies have to face the other bodies.*

Giulia: *But the picture is always still. How can you make the Ring-around-the-Rosy so that it shows?*

Giovanni: *Come on guys, let's try to do a Ring-around-the-Rosy for Giulia, then we can see what we look like, like a photo!.*

Through his words, Giovanni seems to be positioning himself from an external point of view in order to get an overall view of the situation. It is important to know how to move through space with your thoughts.

Giovanni: **There are some kids that you only see their backs. I can see Giulia's back, she's looking at Giorgio's face; Leonardo's side (profile), who's looking at Matteo's face.**

Some statements can be seen as generators of thoughts that *enlighten* the mind. Giovanni's is one of these: backs and fronts, then profiles and fronts of human figures who are looking at each other and are positioned in a relational space. This relational situation will become an important aspect of the experience that other children will take up and use as guidance.

Ring-around-the-Rosy 2

At this point, we suggest that the children make a second individual graphic representation of the Ring-around-the-Rosy, and place them in mixed-gender groups of four to six children. The groups are proposed based on the interpretations the teachers made during the first Ring-around-the-Rosy experience. We continue our focus on Giulia, Leonardo, and Giovanni.

Giulia seems to be the most perplexed: *I'm going to do the kid from the back because you need...*

She gets up from the table and holds out her arms to look like the figure she has drawn, thinking and expressing her thoughts aloud. *Okay... I have to draw some kids who are standing like I am right now. I made this girl with her back turned...* (she holds her arms out in front of her). *But what about the others, how do I get them to look like they're standing up? I don't know how to draw the kids from this side.*

Giovanni: *Giulia, you have to draw the profile...*

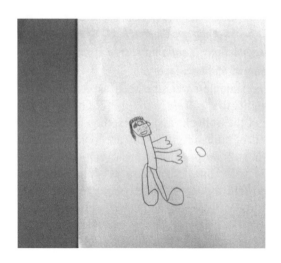

He shows Giulia the first figure he has drawn. The strategic position of the figure is worth noting: the arms are stretched out in front, ready to link up with another figure seen from a front view and one seen from behind. The figure shown in profile is a structural peg of Giovanni's Ring-around-the-Rosy.

This is the profile. Giulia, it's better to draw the profile first because otherwise you keep going on and on and then you can't tell what's going on any more!

This may be what happened to him in his first drawing (the Ring-around-the-Rosy in a line).

Leonardo: *I know how you draw a Ring-around-the-Rosy of kids. First you draw a circle, like a Ring-around-the-Rosy... then you need a kid who's standing outside and looking at it...*

Leonardo's initial schema that we saw earlier is still very strong and seems not to have been undermined by the real-life trials of the Ring-around-the-Rosy or by his classmate's comments. Or, if it has been undermined, since a graphic model is a conceptual schema, it will need time to be modified. At times we may notice that the schema we are using is not appropriate, but we do not know how to modify it.

Giovanni: *Hey Leonardo, you can only see your kids from the front! Because the ones you see from the back are always there, always!*
Leonardo: *Okay, then I'll put some hair on this one, this one, and this one.*

Leonardo takes a pencil and covers up the faces of the figures in the foreground.

In this second Ring-around-the-Rosy all the children have chosen to use pencils, a choice that probably shows an awareness of the difficulties involved and therefore of the possibility of modifying the drawing. Error and modification are integral parts of research and learning. It is necessary to accept them as such intelligently and without worrying about them.
Leonardo: *This is okay because... look: this kid is looking at this one, then this one's looking at this one, this one's looking at this one... there, it's done!* Then, as a final comment on his drawing, he adds: *You can see these kids from above, like this.* He stands

up and raises a hand, almost as if he were defining a point of view from as high as possible: *... and from the top they look like they're lying on the ground!*
In interpreting and commenting on his drawing, Leonardo uses two interpretive *readings* that were made earlier by Giovanni: one child who, in the relational space of the Ring-around-the-Rosy, is looking at the face of another child; and the point of view from above.
Here we can see quite clearly how, during the process of learning, continuous loans of knowledge, hypotheses, and points of view are being made among the children.

This drawing by Giulia shows three figures seen from behind.
Giulia is still a prisoner of her dilemma. She has understood that it is necessary to draw the children's backs, a conviction that has been strengthened by the dialogue taking place in the meantime between Giovanni and Leonardo. As a result of this, she has added two more girls, who can be seen from behind, but she is still not satisfied.

Turning to Giovanni, Giulia says: *How did you do the ones on the other side* (the children facing the front)*?*
Giovanni (pointing at Giulia's three figures seen from the back one by one): **Giulia, I have an idea! Who are these kids looking at? Who's this one looking at? You have to put in the ones on the other side**, *otherwise they're not looking at anything*.

Giovanni: *Just look at this, we're doing a real Ring-around-the-Rosy. Guys, come here, let's do a Ring-around-the-Rosy! Okay, I'm looking at Giorgio for a while, then Leonardo for a while, Giorgio's looking at Leonardo, Leonardo's looking at Giorgio, then we go around, and for you who are looking at us, everything changes.*

Leonardo: *Now, Giulia, I'll explain the profile to you... look at me! See? It's like a little line that goes all the way down, like this.*

Finally reassured, Giulia then draws two figures from a side view, but the problem persists: *Yes, but now where am I going to put the other heads? Can I draw some more faces?*
Giovanni: *You can see a little bit of the front... not all of it, but you can see it... there's a little bit of room here in the middle to put in the kids who are looking at these ones!*

Giovanni: *Look at my drawing!*

After a few more hesitations, and casting a sidelong glance at Giovanni's drawing on the table every now and then, Giulia completes her drawing.

The rotation of the figure seems to have been understood, though perhaps not the representation of space yet, since the foreground and background figures appear to be compressed almost on a single baseline.

Self-assessment and Assessment

We suggest to the children that they revisit in groups the work that they have done. It is not just a matter of narrating their actions, but of re-thinking the process they worked through, the difficulties they encountered, the doubts, the solutions, and the issues that are still unresolved. This is a difficult process but it seems to us to be important (and we often do it) for developing an attitude of self-reflection about the things we do and our own strategies, supporting and at the same time fueling the processes through which we gain understanding.

The groups have been formed by taking particular account of the diversity of solutions identified by the children in the second representation of Ring-around-the-Rosy.
The children are looking at both the drawings each one has made.
Teacher: Shall we try and compare the solutions you found? And, if you can, try to explain the changes you made from the first to the second drawing.

These encounters can sometimes seem rather harsh, but assessment is a precious human measuring tool, especially if it takes place within *balanced* situations, among peers, and in a shared context. The evaluations are certainly not easy, since a number of different but equally legitimate points of view come up against one another. First, the point of view of the author of the drawing, who has a certain mental image and is aware that his or her representation is a mediation between what he or she thinks and is able to do, and then the points of view of classmates who often read the situation and the representation in a different way, undermining the mediation reached by the author.

What the children generally appreciate is the awareness they gain of the way their thinking has evolved. This is an important process that elicits a movement toward the possible—what Vygotsky calls the "zone of proximal development," in which the learners advance their understanding.
The teacher's role at this point is precisely to highlight this advancement, however small it may be. The child ought to emerge from these encounters as a *winner*.

Davide's drawings

Giulia: *Davide, your Ring-around-the-Rosy is great! The second drawing is a lot more Ring-around-the-Rosy!*
Davide: *Yes, I think my second one is really good, too, but maybe I need to change the shape of the circle... I should have drawn lots of Ring-around-the-Rosys with different shapes, because when we move in a real Ring-around-the-Rosy, the shape changes, and it doesn't always stay the same round shape!*

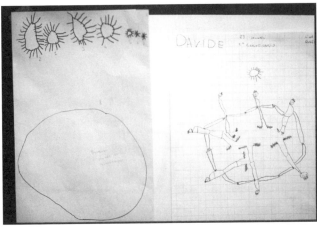

1   2

Davide: *If we do this, though* (he lifts the sheet of paper and makes it circle around), *it looks like it's going around.*
The child may not be an expert at drawing, but he has understood very well that the identity and the fun of playing Ring-around-the-Rosy lie in that very circling-around movement.
Right from the very first verbal hypotheses, Davide expressed the impossibility of drawing a Ring-around-the-Rosy of children because it could never really go around. Yet during his work he never gave up trying to find a solution to this problem. Conveying a sense of motion graphically is a very interesting problem; we address it in our follow-up to the project.

Giovanni's drawings

1

2

Giovanni: *Oh, it's always good for me to do experiments!*

Giovanni: *See that line? That was my first Ring-around-the-Rosy!*
I did it like that because it was easier. Then, when we tried to do a Ring-around-the-Rosy out there, I understood a lot of things, and then as soon as I got the sheet of paper...
(Giovanni is speaking very slowly, as he often does when he is talking about a situation he has experienced, and he always seems to be describing something he is breaking down into sequences.)
I didn't start drawing right away... I stopped for a while... then I started to think... I thought about a Ring-around-the-Rosy... think and think again. (Conscious of everyone's silence and attention, Giovanni exaggerates his narrative style somewhat.) *A Ring-around-the-Rosy came into my mind... oh, it's just that it's like I was seeing it! So, copying from my mind, I got the Ring-around-the-Rosy right! I started from this one who's turned to his side... if I started doing the one from behind, everything disappeared from my mind... instead, I did the one on his profile with two hands like this* (held out) *who was just ready to hold hands with two other kids. The second one I did was one from behind, then this other one from the front... then on and on like that!*

Giulia's drawings

Giulia begins to explain directly from her second drawing.

The first thing I found out was that you really had to have the kids from the back. Then, for these (the profiles) *I already knew how to do them because I had already drawn some kids standing like that. But I didn't know that you had to have them in a Ring-around-the-Rosy just here on one side and on the other side. Giovanni explained it to me. Then we tried it out a few times and I understood that you had to have them. The hardest thing was to do these ones that you can see from the front. There wasn't any room left... so I made them small.*

We think there is little need to add further comments and interpretations since, as this case shows, children are able to engage in self-reflection about their own processes with surprising clarity.

This is a valuable ability that requires frequent occasions for reflection, comparing ideas, and practicing your skills.

Relaunching the Problems

The subsequent steps of our work with the children are guided by our interpretations of the processes we observed and documented.

In the experience we just described, the children's understanding of some of the concepts, such as the rotation of the human figure in relation to different points of view, is certainly advanced, but it needs further opportunities in order to become consolidated. By contrast, the problem of representing space still seems to be unresolved, while the representation of movement is interesting, even though it is still embryonic. The continuation of the work thus has to reckon with these aspects.

Teachers need to have the ability to be in touch with the children's strategies and problems and to play that famous "ping-pong match" with them, as described so wonderfully in the metaphor often used by Loris Malaguzzi to explain the teachers' role.

In this case, we suggest a representation of another game: "Red Light, Green Light,"* which, in comparison with Ring-around-the-Rosy, draws attention to an expanded space where the figures are clearly on different planes in relation to the observer.

* The game begins with one child facing the wall with his or her back to the other players. The child says "Green light" and starts to count. The others, all starting from the same place, have to move quickly toward the wall against which the counting child is facing. When the child at the wall decides to turn around, he or she calls out "Red light," and the children who are running have to stop short. If the child at the wall catches a glimpse of anyone moving, that person is sent back to the starting point.

We think that recording the children with a video camera may provide a sort of *moving photograph*, according to the suggestions made by Giovanni and Davide.
The teacher takes particular care to record from different points of view, including one from the top of a ladder...

to allow the children, in groups, to then discuss their viewings from the various perspectives.

The discussions and viewings continue, and the game is simulated with a scale model.

207

Representations of the "Red Light, Green Light" game

Giovanni's drawing reconfirms his understanding of both the rotation of the figures and the space. Indicating the figure at the top of the sheet, he comments: *I made it smaller because it's the one farthest away.*

In order to illustrate the whole scene of the game, he uses a representational technique that architects call "axonometric projection," which presents a perspective from above. It is a very advanced point of view, which gives a strong narrative sense of the situation.

In Leonardo's drawing, space is indicated by three perceptual levels: the closest part of the foreground is the atelier wall, then there is the dress-up play structure in the middle of the piazza where the child who is counting is standing, then the entrance door in the background. The game is taking place between the atelier and the dress-up play structure.

Leonardo: *The kid who's counting has just turned around and everyone has to stand absolutely still, otherwise they pay for it.*

Leonardo also seems to have understood the rotation of the figures as well as the representation of the space.

In her drawing, Giulia intelligently places herself at the viewing point that enables her to draw the backs of all the figures, this being a new representational discovery that she uses most successfully. The way she arranges the figures across the space of the sheet leads us to suppose that she is engaged in spatial research that has gone beyond the stage where all the subjects are drawn on a single baseline (often coinciding with the bottom of the sheet), typical for children of this age.

208

All three of the children's drawings are made with the sheets of paper situated vertically, indicating the point of view from which each child is observing the scene. Above all, this technique shows that the children are making optimal use of the spatial opportunities offered by the sheet to allow multiple representational planes.

Further occasions are subsequently provided with other subjects in situations of play and movement represented graphically as well as with three-dimensional materials; for example, children sitting around a table playing dominoes, a soccer match, Capture the Flag, Hide-and-Seek, and so on.

The documentation of the events, the comparison of the various drawings made over time by the same child, the recordings of the children's words and exchanges, and the dialogue among the adults, are all precious materials that allow a wider assessment to be made than one that simply focuses on the finished products (in this case, drawings). In particular, it becomes a friendly sort of evaluation that engages both children and teachers in self-assessment and assessment efforts that evolve over the course of the work they have performed together, and that do not make a fixed judgment but open the way to new possibilities.

Note: The compilation of the games manual did go ahead but it never reached the planned goal of publication, owing in part to the unforeseen initiation of other interesting projects.

During an assembly of all the children and teachers, it was decided that two other projects should be completed:

• the charter of home and school rules (a publication that originated from a discussion held by the children about the meanings, interpretations, and construction of rules, and from a direct dialogue and negotiation with the parents);

• the creation of a stage curtain for an important theater in the city of Reggio Emilia (the Ariosto).

Final Documentation

All the material produced in this experience was transformed into a slide documentary that was:

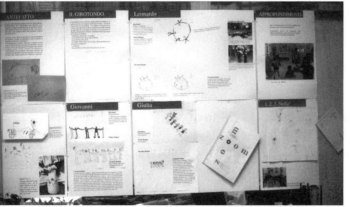

• presented to and discussed with the children, the parents, and teachers from other schools;

• organized into documentation panels on the wall arranged by summaries of the main stages: a prologue explaining the origins of the project, a theoretical presentation, examples from some of the children, and a research and study notebook reporting on the whole progression of the work.

This type of notebook can be photocopied at low cost and easily circulated in order to collect different opinions and other valuable interpretations that add to or are different from the ones we made.
All the documentation materials, in whatever form, should have the capability of being easily disseminated in order to elicit comparisons of ideas and interpretations.

The main problems presented by this kind of work are actually quite simple and are founded on a number of beliefs:

• that imagination and creativity are not separate from cognitive aspects;

• that knowledge is an adventure that should be experienced through personal and group-based research, taking place with different time frames, depending on individual and group-based rhythms;

• that the quality of the processes can construct a type of knowledge that is more capable of fostering creativity and interaction with different problems and languages (disciplines);

• that understanding can be fostered by the reflective thinking generated by in-process documentation and the constant comparison of ideas with others;

• that teachers should be careful not to let day-to-day practice and didactic activities betray the theories stated;

• that it is necessary for teachers to continue to learn; therefore, documentation materials such as these (or of a different kind) give us an opportunity to understand a little more about the children's and our own thinking strategies, and allow us to engage in something as important as exchanging thoughts and ideas with others.

Learning Indicators*   Are there any elements of assessment that can help us understand whether a group has learned and, if so, at what level? This is one of the many interesting questions that we have been asked by our Project Zero friends.

After some initial philosophical and psychological resistance to accepting assessment parameters that are formal and not context-based, we thought it would be inappropriate for us not to deal with this aspect of final assessment. While we remain convinced that many of the assessment processes are enacted during the work itself, we have nevertheless identified some elements that we believe to be representative of a learning process: the use of a certain type of verbal language, the construction of hypotheses, the formulation of theories, strategies of action, and so on. These elements were suggested to us in part from our readings, but most of all by our experience of field observations accumulated over time. We organized these elements by category and in long lists (no doubt excessively long), resulting in the construction of tables of indicators that we regard as being useful for assessing children's work as well as our own.

In order to establish the validity of these indicators, we then attempted to apply them to different themes and processes.

It is difficult to give an example, since these tables would be virtually incomprehensible without written or oral explanations. In addition, we need to have further trials, summaries, discussions, and exchanges of opinion about them. Nevertheless, we feel we can say that the indicators we have identified are for the most part useful for analyzing a learning process and for providing an overall assessment of that process. Most of all, they help us as teachers to build a mental map of *lines of observation* (situations to be noted) that orient and support the observations as the work proceeds. As indicators, they provide sensitive and pertinent elements for interpretation of the documentation produced, increasing our awareness in our daily work with the children.

They are therefore working tools that are certainly interesting, even if we still think that the most formative process for the teacher is the one we have adopted; that is, identifying certain indicators, discussing them with the other teachers, and verifying them. A reference list can certainly provide orientation, as long as we do not adhere to it so strictly that we become its prisoners and abandon our curiosity about children or our attitude of listening and research, which we feel are the real indicators of a good teacher.

* See also Proposition VII in the chapter "Form, Function, and Understanding in Learning Groups."

Falsification of Indicators

It is self-evident that there are subjects and processes for which indicators are hardly applicable, such as those that are mostly connected to processes of deep expressive force (which do not involve simply problem solving), as well as those in which attitudes and concepts are primarily *sown* in the hope that they will germinate in time.

Understanding the growth structure of a small leaf, for example—capturing not only its visible, formal structure, but also the rhythmic growth constituted by its pulse of life (and death), and approaching it as a living organism—means constructing a form of knowledge alternative to formal school-based learning (which is normally the most widely represented). It is a form of knowledge that is constructed through watchful and intense relationships—the very relationships that we hope to foster. In our opinion, it is this kind of learning that makes a difference, to both the children and the teachers and, more generally, to the culture.

This means an approach that involves constant attention to the quality of relationships and is thus difficult to verify by means of indicators, even sophisticated ones. In a sense, the language of relationships is one that we need to know how to speak ourselves in order to listen to it, to understand and assess it.

It is also a challenge, one which is not easy to assess, that we have faced together with the children day by day for many years.

cranes

The Fax
Ideas, theories, and constructions on the journey of a fax between Reggio Emilia and Washington, D.C.

Giovanni Piazza
Paola Barchi

Protagonists
Five- and six-year-old
children of the Villetta
School of Reggio Emilia
and the Model Early
Learning Center of
Washington, D.C.
Teachers
Paola Barchi
Silvana Cucchi
Giovanni Piazza
Jennifer Azzariti
Wendy Baldwin
Sonya Shopthaugh
From a project by
Amelia Gambetti
Giovanni Piazza
Carla Rinaldi
Photographs by
Giovanni Piazza
Jennifer Azzariti
Sonya Shopthaugh

The idea for long-distance communication between two schools in such different contexts as the Model Early Learning Center of Washington, D.C. and the Villetta School of Reggio Emilia came from the five- and six-year-old children following a discussion with Amelia Gambetti, who had been a teacher at the Villetta for many years and was now working at the MELC. On a return visit to Reggio, she brought the children at the Villetta a lot of news about the American children and their school.

The desire of the children and teachers to keep in touch with Amelia and their curiosity about the experiences of the American children led to the idea of initiating a correspondence between the children and teachers of the two schools.

The idea of being able to communicate over such enormous distances, to share interests, thoughts, and experiences, and to build new friendships created a great deal of enthusiasm that spread among the children, teachers, and parents of the class, and the whole school.

After numerous messages, gifts, cassettes, and videos had been sent back and forth, leaving traces of the differences between the two cultures, a suspicion began to emerge in our reflections; that is, that the ten days of waiting time for a reply to a message would produce a progressive weakening of the communicative expectations.

In the children's words, we saw a strong need to communicate by more rapid means.

But how could we do it?

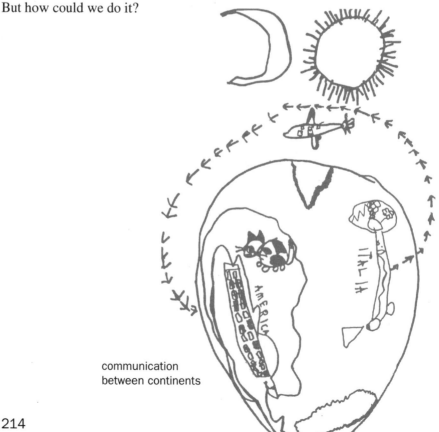

communication
between continents

Pen pals

View of Reggio Emilia

View of Washington, D.C.

Children at the Villetta School

Children at the MELC
in Washington, D.C.

Hypotheses on rapid communication

Alessandra: *Did you know that we still haven't gotten a letter back from our American friends?*

Roberta: *It goes a long way, and when something has to go so far it takes a lot of time. If you go to America, you sure don't get there in five minutes! It takes a whole lot of time!*

Sofia: *I think our letters run into a lot of things before they get to Washington: red lights, big intersections with cars...*

Alioscia: *They run into the ocean, too... I think they go to America on a ship.*

Luca: *And what about if one gets lost? Then nobody would find it and it would never get there.*

Giacomo: *It can't get lost—it has the address on it, and anyway it's not the message that gets lost, it's the mailman who gets lost and he says, "Oh no, I forgot this letter, now I'll deliver it right away!" Then he takes the letter that gets there later—it's late.*

Teacher: Yes, you're all right, lots of things can happen to our letters... I wonder if there's a faster way to send the messages to our friends and get their answers.

Sofia: *Well, maybe so, but we don't know it!*

Lucia: *I can ask my dad—he knows lots of stuff!*

Roberta: *You need a FSSSSTTT that's fast as lightning!*

Matteo: *But lightning's no good—it would burn our message that's made of paper, and what then?*

Giacomo: *I think we need, um... I don't know what.*

Conversations with the children on engaging topics produce discussions, shared thoughts, and initial hypotheses for a strategic resolution of the problem under investigation.

216

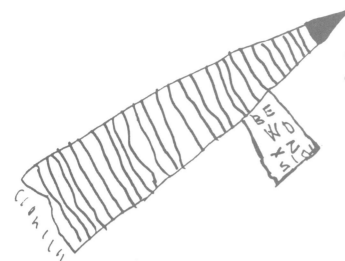

Initial theories on long-distance communication

Matteo:
If we want our message to our friends in Washington to get there fast, maybe we could send it with a rocket!

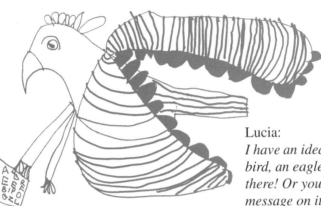

Lucia:
I have an idea. Let's call a bird, an eagle, who can take it there! Or you can attach the message on its foot, like the carrier pigeons, and it takes it where you want.

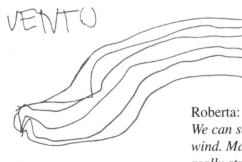

Roberta:
We can send it with the wind. Maybe we need a really strong wind that goes really fast to get it there in a hurry.

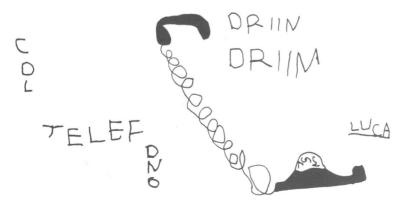

Luca:
Maybe we can put a message in the telephone. But how can we show them the drawings we made? I guess we have to send them by mail like the other times.

217

Lucia: *I know what we need! I saw it on TV, it's a kind of telephone. They took a letter, they put it inside a little slot, and they sent it to somebody. Inside the telephone there's a printer that maybe copied the letter, then the letter stayed there and the copied one went where there was a strong wind and it made it fly to the country where they wanted to send it.*

Giacomo: *I think it's called a "fax." It looks like a telephone but it's not a telephone, because the sheets of paper with the messages on them go inside it.*

Lucia: *Oh, now I remember! My dad has one in his office and he knows how to send a letter with the fax. When he comes to pick me up we can ask him about it.*

Teacher: That sounds like a good idea. What do you think?

Matteo: *We can ask him if he'll help us do the letter.*

Lucia's father is invited to school the following day to hear about the children's ideas.

Lucia's father: The fax is a kind of telephone that reads the messages that you want to send and then sends them to the fax number of your friend.

Lucia's father agrees to answer the children's questions about how the fax works. This will enable the children afterward to discuss in groups the ideas they've heard in more depth, and to develop possible questions and theories on fax operation.

Giacomo:
It's like a telephone with a box under it. Maybe it has some wires inside it and a kind of printer that copies the letter you want to send.

Luca: *So the fax is like a sheet of paper with a message written on it. It's like a thought... as fast as a thought.*

Lucia: *Maybe they gave it a short name so it gets there faster.*

Giacomo: *Listen to how it sounds: FAAXXX. It's like a missile.*

Sofia: *Lucia's dad said that you need the address, then the message, and then the signature of the person who's writing it—it's easy.*

Luca: *But you can't put things made of clay, because the fax would break and then everything gets broken—the message, too.*

Roberta: *We need to send a drawing of friendship, too, so that way they understand that it's us, their friends from the Villetta.*

It seems to us that the children are thinking about a fax message that's very simple. They seem to be more interested in how to use the fax than in the content of the message to be written.

Teacher: So should we try to write this fax and send it? How should we organize it?

Lucia: *There has to be a lot of us, because when you do something for the first time and you don't know how to do it very well, maybe somebody else knows how to do it.*

Alessandra: *I know! The ones who know how to write can do it.*

Luca: *We can have some kids who know how to do hard things and some kids who know how to do easy things... you have to have friends who know how to do different things.*

Giacomo: *We need Matteo who knows how to write numbers and Sofia who knows how to make nice drawings of friendship.*

Alessandra: *Well, if you say a word, and then somebody else says a word, and then somebody else says another one, then the idea comes out...*

Preparation

The group that works on writing the fax is formed in part based on individual skills identified by the children themselves and in part based on the desire to participate.

Matteo: *I know how to read and write good. My mom told me so!*
Giacomo: *I know how to count up to a hundred, and Matteo is my friend, too.*
Lucia: *I think we need a drawing, a nice drawing of friendship. We can use the one Lorenzo made with the two friends talking.*
Roberta: *I like sending a fax to our American friends!*

While preparing the fax, the children discuss what time to send it.
Alioscia: *We can ask them if when it's day here it's night there.*
Lucia: *We can wait a minute to see if they send us a message to say they got ours.*
Alessandra: *We hope they answer as fast as lightning.*
Matteo: *As fast as the wind!*

The fax is ready to be sent to Washington, and is shown to the other children in the class for their consent.

Among the many rules that the various groups of children establish for their group work, one is considered to be essential: everyone must be informed about what is happening in the groups. Before the fax is sent everyone has to see it, discuss it, and give their approval.

Matteo: *Here's the fax. We did it all together.*
Simone: *That's a fax?? That's a message, not a machine!*
Lucia: *Well, you say "fax." My dad said that the message is called a fax, too!*
Alessandra: *That's how you say it! It's like when you say "give me five," but you don't give them a five, but you use your hand that has five fingers. You say, okay guys!*
Simone: *But it's a pretty normal fax. It doesn't even have any colors.*
Giacomo: *But the fax doesn't see the colors. It's not like how we see them with our eyes. It traces them but it doesn't have the colors inside.*
Sofia: *We made it like this so that the fax doesn't make a mistake when it reads it.*
Matteo: *We made it like this because we have to see if it gets there fast, not because it has to be beautiful.*

Transmission

When working together, the children often give each other mutual support, as if they had to follow a recipe. The procedural rhythm, voice, and timing are underscored by multiple voices, as if it were a ritual in which you can find solidarity and a sense of belonging to the group, but also a way to consolidate those actions and gestures that are not always clear, that help to construct new knowledge.

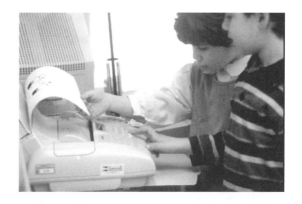

Sofia: *How do you put the sheet in?*
Giacomo: *Remember we have to put it in upside-down, so the fax can read it.*
Sofia: *You mean like with the photocopier?*
Giacomo: *Hey! Look what happens, it's eating the paper!*
Sofia: *It's a paper-eater... but... if it eats it, how can it send the sheet to America?*
Giacomo: *Maybe inside the fax there's a sort of brain that copies the message and then sends it off.*
Giacomo: *When the fax took the message in its mouth, it seemed like it was learning the words we wrote.*
Sofia: *Then maybe it made a fax for our friends.*
Roberta: *Or maybe it made a sheet that's really really light and then it flew to America...*

Sofia:
A fax is like a telephone-printer. You put the paper in the slot underneath. Inside the fax there are some special stamps, pencils, and pens that write and draw. There are some holes where the color comes out that makes the writing on the paper.

The children follow the fax's automatic procedures with curiosity and wonder.
What questions are crossing their minds?
Are they perhaps already developing their initial hypotheses about what is happening?
How can we support them in letting their thoughts emerge?

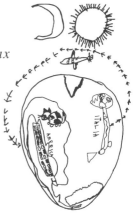

Sofia:
Maybe our fax paper took a plane and flew to our friends in Washington. It started in Italy and went all the way to America.

Individual theories

In the course of the project thus far, we have followed the children in their attempt to construct hypotheses, first on how to make the communication faster, then on the preparation and transmission of the fax, and now on how a fax reaches America.

One of our tasks as teachers is to be able to relaunch the ideas that emerge from the children's discussions.

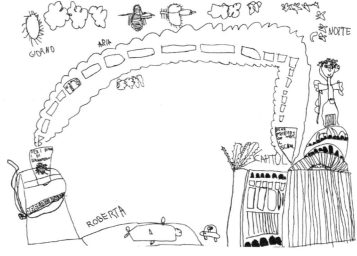

Roberta's theory:

I think the fax went a long, long way. It flew by itself. Now I'll explain it: here's the fax and here's Washington. In the middle, there's the ocean with sharks, and the paper goes inside the fax. Then a sheet of paper with the drawings stays here where we are, and another one with the writing in English goes in the sky and the air takes it to America. When it goes out, it gets really little, and then when it gets there it gets big again so that way the children can read it. The fax starts from here when it's daytime and gets there when it's night.

Alioscia's theory:

I think there's a big pipe inside the machine that goes all the way to America. Inside it there's a spring that launches the message really fast; a fake hand that's inside the fax machine pushes it.

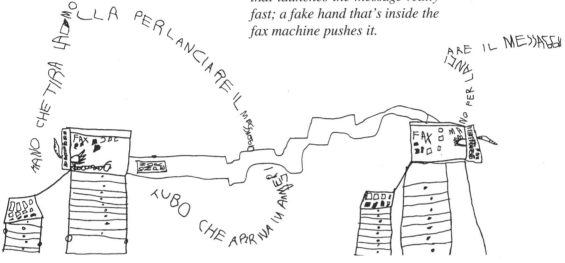

Lucia's theory:

Our message started from the Villetta and went into the sky. With the wind it went way up high and traveled in the middle of the clouds with the birds and airplanes. It went all the way around the world and then it stopped at the MELC school.

Toward a group graphic theory

The formation of a group is important for the learning dynamics that can take place inside it. The capacity for sharing thoughts, assessing and self-assessing, respecting the ideas of others, and the close link between the objectives of personal research and those of the group, can all be necessary conditions for the learning of each individual and of the group itself. Within this framework of movement between the micro and macro levels, the children compare their theories, developing a strong sense of respect for the thoughts of the others and also the idea that some parts can coexist and create together a more complex group theory.

From the group's revisiting of the individual theories emerges the final theory on the journey of a fax between Reggio Emilia and Washington, D.C.

Roberta: *See? In Alioscia's drawing you can see how a fax gets to America. It goes inside a pipe, so it doesn't get lost on the way.*
Alioscia: *It's a long pipe that goes around the things that it runs into on the trip.*
Matteo: *But you can't tell where it starts and where it goes to. You can't tell which way it goes.*
Alessandra: *You can tell in Roberta's drawing. You can see that the fax goes over the sea. America is on the other side of the world, on the other side of the ocean.*
Roberta: *In Lucia's drawing you can tell that America is on the other side of the world—it's real far away.*
Matteo: *Yes, but how does a fax fly around the world? We don't see papers flying around in the sky that go around and then go into people's houses.*
Giacomo: *I think there's a long, long pipe, like Alioscia said, but it goes a long way around and real far...*

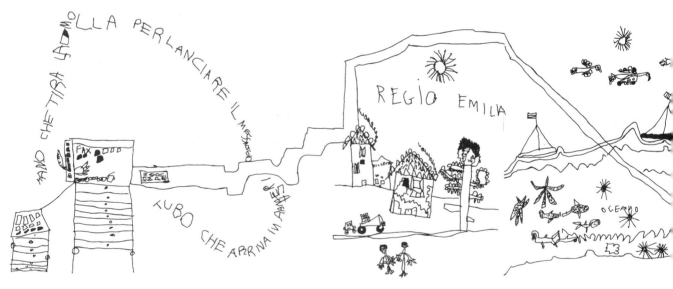

The pipe starts from Reggio.
There's a clear pipe that travels. The fax goes inside the pipe and when the pipe runs into trees, it goes up and then it comes back down, and when there are curves the pipe bends.

Then it goes under the ocean where there are fish, sea urchins, and octopuses, and it goes under the ground because it doesn't want to get all wet. Then it comes back up after the ocean is finished.

It seems that the idea gradually emerges that each individual theory is not sufficient to explain the journey of the fax. In their discussions, the children attempt to develop a provisional new theory that makes use of the contributions of the parts of the individual theories that they see as being significant.

Luca: *I think we can ask Alioscia to get a new piece of paper, a bigger one, and ask him if he can draw his fax, sort of the same, but longer, and then we can put in the other things, the houses like Lucia did, the ocean like Roberta's... Can I do the message?!*
Giacomo: *I'll draw Reggio, that's my town.*
Alioscia: *Yeah, I'll do Ireland, too, because it comes before America!*
Matteo: *Yeah, but we can't put in every single thing that it comes to before it gets there, because we'd have to have a really really long sheet of paper—as long as from here to Milan!*
Alessandra: *Hey, no, a lot, lot longer...*
Giacomo: *We have to draw it together, because just one person alone can't do the hard things.*
Lucia: *You can't understand everything that there is in the world—it's too big.*

By comparing their ideas, the children receive important information that enables them to assess their own theories and those of the others.

The fax crossing over the ocean in the sky

Lucia's buildings

Alioscia's pipe for carrying the fax

Then it gets to Ireland, which is a really different country. The cars jump, the houses are like huts, and there are mountains and lakes, and it rains all the time, even in the summer. In Ireland the boats are different, too—they have two sails. When the pipe goes to Ireland, it passes through the middle of the mountains.

Finally it gets to Washington where our friends and Amelia are. In America, the pipe passes over the skyscrapers, over the statues, and goes to the machine at the school. That way our friends can read the message and they'll think about how it managed to get there so fast, like we do.

Relaunching: a fax-modem for the children

Concluding notes and possible relaunches

The observations and interpretations that we documented during the project made it possible for us to see how the children are open to using technological instruments for communicating in real time. These instruments are used not only for their specific communicative potential but also as a sort of "training ground" for the children's thinking.

Other questions remain open:

How do we proceed now?

How can we maintain the plurality of forms and different systems of communication so that the children continue to use the methods that are most suitable and pertinent to their objectives?

How can we support the children in their communication by offering them other technologies that they can try out in order to advance their thinking?

For this purpose, together with the parents, we decided to give the children a fax-modem to connect to the school computers to broaden the communicative forms, but above all to broaden the contexts of discussion for the construction of new knowledge.

To provide a place where all the children and parents of the school can see our work and compare their thoughts and ideas, we (the teachers and the children of the group) displayed the documents produced during the experience, using documentation panels on the wall in the common area.

The City of Reggio Emilia

Giovanni Piazza
Angela Barozzi

Protagonists
Annarita, 5 yrs. 8 mos.
Cecilia, 5 yrs. 9 mos.
Francesca, 5 yrs. 7 mos.
Emiliano, 5 yrs. 6 mos.
Giacomo, 5 yrs. 8 mos.
Simone, 5 yrs. 9 mos.
Teachers
Angela Barozzi
Giovanni Piazza
Teresa Casarini
From a project by
Giovanni Piazza
Paola Cagliari
Photographs by
Giovanni Piazza

The focus of this fragment is the city: its forms, its relations, its transformations, and its identity, which progressively changes and is redefined in the eyes of the children. Here we offer some reflections of a group of five- and six-year-old children who had been exchanging ideas and thoughts about the theme of the city for a number of months.

As the investigation progressed, we saw different perceptions of the city on the part of girls and boys. This episode describes the thoughts and ideas represented graphically by a group of three girls and a group of three boys as each group designed and constructed collectively.

The girls' city

In the atelier three five-year-old girls, Francesca, Annarita, and Cecilia, are sitting with their teacher around a table on which drawing paper of various shapes and sizes and drawing tools have been placed. The girls have agreed with the teacher to make a collective graphic representation of a city.
Annarita, Cecilia, and Francesca had already made individual drawings of the city center.
Having the girls' previous work on hand will allow the teacher to revisit their thoughts and drawings with them as a premise for starting their work. This will enable each girl to compare her thoughts with those of the others so that they can start exchanging ideas, and will also stimulate their curiosity and foster the creation of a group "microclimate."

The girls choose together the type of paper they want to use. The size and shape of the paper itself seem to suggest the position of the town center. Annarita's finger points to and presses down on the middle of the sheet.

The topological identification of the center also determines their starting point, which will not be the town center but their school, which lies outside the center. They decide that they will draw the school as seen from above—a bird's-eye view.

Annarita, Francesca, and Cecilia all sit on the same side of the sheet of paper. It is Francesca, however, who takes the initiative.
The use of humor comes into the girls' relational strategies right from the start, immediately creating a group climate in which exchange comes easily.

Francesca: *We have to draw it like Simone did, where you can see all the roofs.*
Annarita: *Yeah, it was really nice, but we have to put the Amusement Park for Birds in it, too, so you can tell it's the Villetta.*
Cecilia: *And not Milan.*
Francesca: *Milan! That's silly, are we crazy? We have to do Reggio.*

The graphic representation of the school takes a good deal of time. While the girls are drawing, they hold a number of overlapping conversations. Many of these relate to friendships outside the school, and all three girls consistently use the language of prediction to communicate the things they intend to draw.

The fact that they started off by drawing a well-known place such as their school encourages and facilitates the establishment of the tasks that they assign to each person.

Cecilia

Francesca   Annarita

The task of representing the city from a bird's-eye view involves an exercise in comparing individual drawing skills, which is resolved quickly through the advice and help of friends. Having defined a topological point of orientation on the map, the girls get into a discussion of the location of each of their houses in relation to the school.

Francesca draws the road that leads to the park near her house.

The map of the city follows the girls' criteria of showing the houses. Children's styles, rhythms, and interests are different, and while Annarita and Francesca are exchanging invitations to each other's house, Cecilia continues to draw the school yard in minute detail.

At the same time, she keeps in touch with what is happening between her friends, to whom she pays close attention.

The girls' drawing evolves quickly, taking its points of reference from their real-life experiences.

The spoken language often precedes the action, as if this action needed to be supported by the opinion of the group.

Annarita: *If you make the road you're drawing a little bit longer, Francesca, you get to my house. But don't draw it, I'll do it myself later.*

Annarita: *My daddy works on the other side of town; now I'm going over there to do the place where he works.*

Cecilia: *Yes, go ahead, but make it small, otherwise we can't get the whole city to fit in.*

Francesca: *Reggio Emilia isn't Milan, you know!*

The children's viewpoints of the city are variable and their drawings represent these shifts: views from above, from the side, and in perspective get mixed together in a crescendo of ideas.

The girls are also more interested in a city built around the relationships it offers than in its function of spatial connection. To them, the relational function predominates: parks, streets, and squares are places of events and actions filled with real-life experiences, which are expressed in both their drawing and their spoken language.

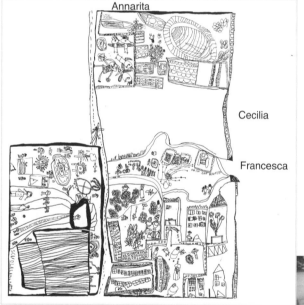

Francesca is particularly interested in the parks, and she begins to draw one that is in the town center.

Francesca: *It's the park where everybody goes to have fun. There are lots of people in the park in the afternoons. There are lots of parks in cities, where people can play and relax; if there weren't any, people wouldn't know where to go and relax.*

Streets become connecting links between related places, and it seems that there are two important ones: the Via Emilia, the main crosstown street that runs close to the school, and Via Città di Reggio, where Cecilia lives. It's Cecilia herself who makes a connecting link between what Francesca and Annarita are doing, by joining the two parts of the city, thus building a spatial boundary that allows a better estimation of what has to be done later.

Cecilia begins to draw her house and the other ones on her street.

It seems that the idea of the continuing city is very strong for this group of girls, where spaces are interwoven and run up against each other, and where streets are symbolic borders between microworlds.

After working individually, the girls change places again, and they are now coming together around a single objective: the city center and its buildings.

Cecilia: *Cities never end. They're all joined together like houses. I live on Via Città di Reggio and my house is joined to another one—it's a duplex.*

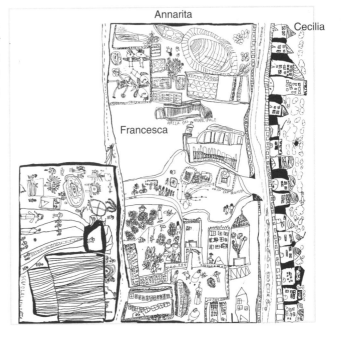

An animated discussion begins about familiar places that are going to be represented.

The girls agree that the mayor's house should be the first one to be drawn, followed by the theater and the cathedral with the tower in the main square.

The girls often stop to look at their work and assess it together, expressing a strong aesthetic pleasure in what they've done.

Once again the Via Emilia and the squares become the focal points of the city, as well as of the discussions they have about what to do.

Francesca: *There aren't just one or two squares in the city, there are lots of them—not two, like we did!*
Annarita: *I think there are a lot; there are a few on this side of the Via Emilia and a few on that side.*

In the end, they decide that each of them will draw one square, dividing the remaining territory into four sections.

At the end of their drawing, the three girls comment on their work.
Francesca: *See? When you walk in the town, you can see how the city is made. If you go up high on the top of a house, you can see the city all around and you can see the squares from up high.*
Cecilia: *Where the square stops, there's a sidewalk with all the houses attached.*
Annarita: *In the squares there's a lot of confusion, everybody's talking.*

The city represented by Cecilia, Francesca, and Annarita is a *city full of relationships and life.*

The parks, the squares, the houses, and the Villetta School, for example, are not only elements of a topological point of view, but they are also important elements for building relationships between the life of the people and their city.

The boys' city

In the atelier three five-year-old boys, Emiliano, Simone, and Giacomo, are sitting around a big table with various shapes and sizes of white paper and drawing materials. Their task is to work together to draw a city.

Before they begin, the teacher asks the children if they want to listen to their previous conversations and revisit the drawings they had made individually a few days before. The boys agree.

After a brief discussion, the three boys decide to choose the largest piece of paper on the table.

Emiliano: *To make a city that's really big you need a big piece of paper.*
Simone: *As big as the earth—as big as a city.*

235

Emiliano and Simone begin to draw, while Giacomo places himself at the side of the piece of paper.

Giacomo

Emiliano

Simone

Conversation among the boys is almost absent at the beginning; it seems that the initial agreement (about where to start in drawing their city) has been enough to enable them to proceed. While Emiliano and Simone sit close together and begin to draw the central square of the city, Giacomo, sitting beside the paper with his elbows on the table and his chin resting on his hands, seems for now to have decided just to observe what happens.

In this first phase, the verbal language that accompanies Emiliano and Simone's graphic representation focuses on the essential.

Emiliano: *All cities start from a square that's in the middle of the city.*
Simone: *Okay, we'll leave space at the bottom to make the street, that way people can leave and go out.*

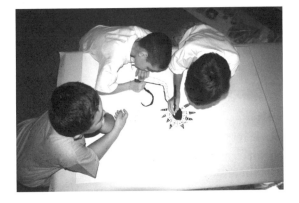

Giacomo still seems not to participate in the group. For the moment, the teacher decides not to urge him to take part; perhaps it is better to wait for him or for the situation to make the decision instead.

Emiliano and Simone, meanwhile, are drawing very close together—their hands overlap, they switch seats often—while the curves of the street they are drawing steadily approach Giacomo. Perhaps it is an initial invitation to their friend to take part in the project.

Simone: *The streets go to so many places, and there's one square after another in the city.*

Emiliano: *Yeah, otherwise you'd get lost. We'll make it with some curves that go that way. Toward where Giacomo is.*

After about twenty minutes, Simone explicitly invites Giacomo to participate.

Simone: *Giacomo, why aren't you doing anything?*

His friend's request makes Giacomo slightly uncomfortable, and after this call to participate he replies.

Giacomo: *Cities have to work, and I have to see if it works.*

Emiliano: *See, Giacomo, this is a different square, it's the one with the field where the children play, and all the houses are different.*

This explanation by Emiliano gives Giacomo the possibility of entering into a relationship with the other two children by way of an offer of competence.

Emiliano: *Giacomo, can you draw the roofs of the houses? Come on, try!*

Giacomo: *I know how to make houses with round roofs.*

Simone: *Will you help us then?*

Giacomo: *Okay!*

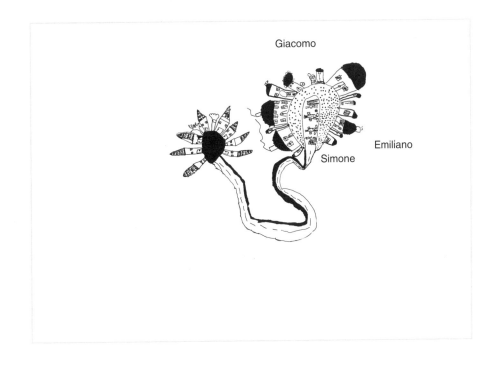

More than thirty minutes have passed since the work began, and in this phase the project becomes more clearly defined. The repetition of certain models (the square) facilitates the children's shared planning and executing. Now it is Giacomo who makes proposals.

Giacomo: *Let's make another square. I'm sure there are lots of squares in the city.*
Simone: *Should we make one with a soccer player who's practicing?*
Giacomo: *Yeah, good idea!*

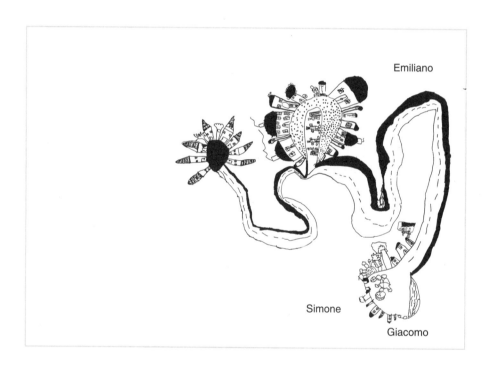

The three boys are now working side by side, with Simone occupying the central position in the group and engaging his companions in discussion. Just when the whole group has formed, however, it divides again. Emiliano, realizing that all three boys are working in a restricted space, decides to move to the other side of the paper to make the sidewalks.

Now Simone and Giacomo form a new pair. The square that is represented also becomes a resting point, a place of conversation, a stimulus for the boys' verbal and graphic development. It seems clear that the streets that are drawn become connections between one square and another, a kind of backbone that progressively traces the outlines of the city as it grows. The city that is developing seems to be defined by the functions carried out inside it.

Giacomo: *In the squares there are people talking.*
Simone: *There are pretty squares and ugly ones. Then there are also some squares for parked cars and for soccer players.*
Emiliano: *I think cities that don't have squares are kind of strange.*
Giacomo: *I think they don't work well because the people don't know where to be.*

Simone: *Cities are all connected by the streets and the railroads, right, Giacomo?*
Giacomo: *Well, yeah, the streets are important for keeping the city together and for making it work.*
Giacomo connects another street to Emiliano's street, while Simone adds the railroad and the playground.

The first elements of autobiographical narration emerge.
Simone: *In the afternoon I go to play at the playground where the train goes by, at Campo di Marte park.*

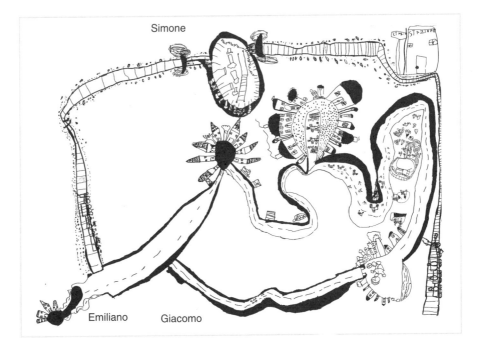

Simone

Emiliano   Giacomo

Each boy now focuses on his own ideas and the verbal interaction of the group is suspended. Simone's railroad, Giacomo's streets that lead to the center of town, and Emiliano's small squares that are being added to the map provide new connections and new complexities. As a group, the boys produce their own idea of a city and progressively define the objectives they want to reach together. The ultimate goal is to make an interconnected city: it must be possible to find a path through the whole city, and each boy steadfastly pursues this mission.

At this point, their city appears to be such a complex urban web that a pause is needed to check the new connections.

Emiliano

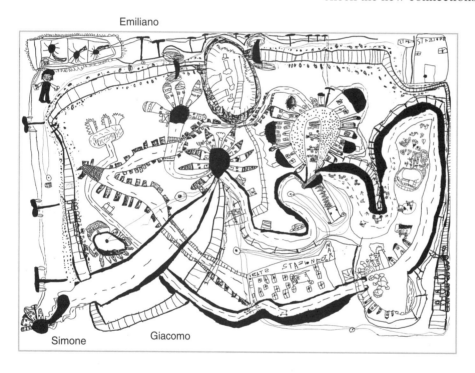

Simone   Giacomo

Emiliano: *We need to see if it's all connected.*
Simone: *Like in real cities.*
Giacomo: *We need to make sure that the whole city is connected and that nobody gets lost.*
The children think about how to verify this and finally agree to go over the streets with their fingers. The test will be carried out by each member of the group, a rule of fairness on which everyone agrees. Emiliano, after having traveled

through the city and its connections, gives a new impetus to the work by asking a question.
Emiliano: *Hey guys, but how can you live in this city at night? We don't have any light for the streets, we don't have electricity!*

This relaunching of the project generates new ideas and requires that new roles be taken on in the group.

240

When their work is finished and the children revisit the map with the teacher, they assess not only the aesthetic result of their representation, but also the consistency between the ideas expressed in the group as they worked and the final map of the city.

Giacomo: *We made a beautiful city even though it's a little bit messy.*
Emiliano: *All the streets take you somewhere. It's a city where you can't get lost, where you're not afraid.*
Simone: *It's a city that could be Reggio Emilia, because there's the Campo di Marte, but it isn't Reggio. Maybe it's called City of the World, because all the people in the world can live in this city.*

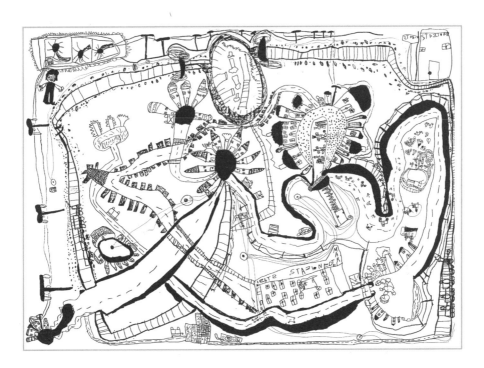

The city represented by Emiliano, Simone, and Giacomo is one full of functions and connections. The train station, the bus station, the aqueduct, the sewers, and the electrical system are not simply topological landmarks but are important elements for the real functioning of a city, essential to the life of the people.

The girls' city

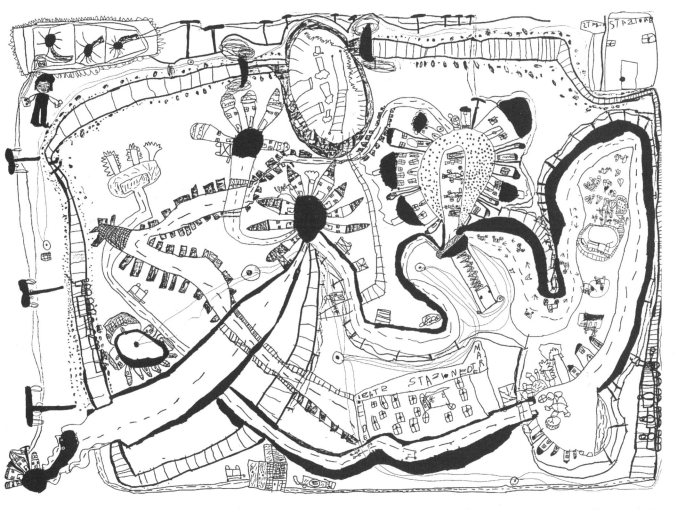

The boys' city

243

Points of view compared

The two maps highlight the different ideas of the city on which the representations are based.

The girls share the idea of a city made of recognizable places where they have actually lived, full of memories and relationships among the people who live there. The Villetta School, the girls' houses, their parents' workplaces, the market squares where their mothers go shopping, and the parks where they play daily with their friends are the coordinates of the memory of their city.

The boys seem more interested in describing, by means of an almost analytical drawing, a symbolic city, a generic city seen as an efficient urban network that fulfills the basic needs and necessities for living there: connectability and viability, high functionality and self-sufficiency.

The girls' project evolves and takes shape supported by wide-ranging verbal language, initially informative and negotiational, aimed at the construction of a dialoguing network that enables them to perceive the progressive development of the project. Each girl carries out her own role within the group, a role that is recognized by the others and supported by the fact that the girls have known each other for almost three years.

Cecilia seems to be the one who guides the relations, using highly articulate language, giving credit to her friends' competencies, making gestures of friendship and solidarity. Francesca uses language that reinforces the sense of group, but that also synthesizes their project design, referring to concrete experience and using her construction and design abilities. Annarita, whose language is warm and sustains the sense of friendship in the project design, has an important role in creating cohesion among the different identities. In addition, her sense of physical closeness leads the group to work very closely together, in contact, which increases the sense of group and of complicity.

Different relationships are constructed in the boys' group. The dialogue seems to be identified more in the silences, in the shared looks, and it is more reflective on the graphic accomplishments achieved in the evolution of their project. Emiliano and Simone immediately negotiate their ideas, and the language of reasoning and designing enables them initially to define the point of departure for the project. Giacomo needs more time to begin to feel part of the group, and half an hour of apparent extraneousness to the development of his friends' ideas passes before he is called to his duty on behalf of the group.

Time is another difference between the two groups. For the girls, the time of thinking together is important, enabling them to make progressive agreements on what to do and on the division of tasks. For the boys, it is a period of individual elaboration, with few exchanges, and the language used seems to pertain largely to the project they are developing.

These initial reflections, based on our discussions and interpretations of the different documentation materials, highlight the need to extend our listening capacity to the learning strategies of groups in order to gain a better understanding of the dynamics, the aspects of originality, and the contributions made by gender differences in the knowledge-building processes of girls and boys.

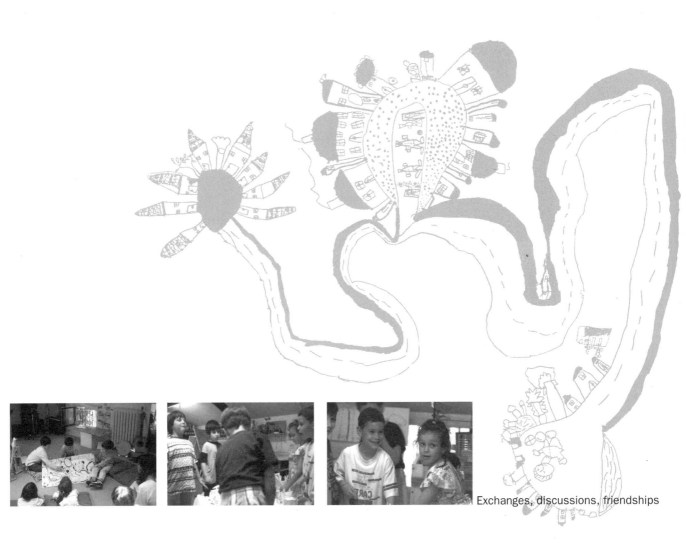

Exchanges, discussions, friendships

245

Form, Function, and Understanding in Learning Groups: Propositions from the Reggio Classrooms

Mara Krechevsky

Too many educational experiences live on only in the heads of the teachers who planned and participated in them. The visual and prose essays presented in the last chapters and the propositions elaborated here attempt to make some of these experiences visible in the hope that they can contribute to our understanding of how individual children and groups of children learn and how to support that learning in diverse settings. In this chapter we present a set of propositions about learning groups in early childhood that were identified by the Reggio educators. Many of them were described in the visual and prose essays of the last chapters; here we articulate them from the point of view of the Project Zero research team.

Seven Propositions

The propositions reported here are based on more than thirty years of observation, documentation, and interpretation of children's learning in the Reggio schools and classrooms. They are grounded in an educational and political context of collaboration among the teachers, children, parents, and wider community of Reggio Emilia. While some of the claims may be familiar to those versed in the early-childhood research literature, their innovativeness resides in part in the ways they were derived and their daily use by teachers to inform classroom practice.

We identify seven propositions (see figure 1). The first identifies six factors that influence the formation and functioning of learning groups; the next five describe different dimensions of the operation of learning groups; and the last identifies eight indicators that understanding is being supported and demonstrated by learning groups. While we enumerate seven distinct propositions, it is important to keep in mind that they are all interconnected. For example, becoming a group and forming a group identity are integrally tied to what individuals and the group as a whole come to know and understand. Thus, we consider "learning" to be both noun and verb: group formation and functioning are inextricably interwoven with what a group learns about content and concepts. Documentation is integral to this process.

The propositions are the result of a kind of dialogue between teachers and children that respects children's experience in the classroom. They reveal the enormous value of learning from the work and ideas of the children in front of us; we consider them every bit as important as what we read in textbooks and the developmental literature. The propositions should be considered flexible and modifiable: each one is reconsidered and re-elaborated in each classroom experience.

ring-around-the-rosy

246

figure 1

PROPOSITION I. Factors that influence the formation, functioning, and demonstration of understanding of learning groups in early childhood include the size of the group; the age, competencies, and interests of the children; gender; time spent together; friendships; and choice of materials.

PROPOSITION II. Individuals within a learning group have their own approaches to learning, which can nonetheless be influenced by the learning approaches of others. We refer to this phenomenon as the "modifiable fingerprint."

PROPOSITION III. When exploring ideas together, learning groups follow a set of rules—some tacit, some explicit.

PROPOSITION IV. Learning groups choose ideas according to an aesthetic of knowledge or "the pattern that connects."*

PROPOSITION V. Learning groups have different styles that are rhythmic in nature.

PROPOSITION VI. Learning groups can create and benefit from competent audiences.

PROPOSITION VII. Indicators that learning groups are supporting and demonstrating understanding include the following:

a) *Children and adults feel they are contributing to a larger, more meaningful whole.*

b) *The discoveries of individual children become part of the thinking of the learning group.*

c) *Children express a feeling of continuous growth and awareness that their theories are provisional, and they take pleasure in seeing them modified, developed, and advanced.***

d) *Over time the members of the learning group, alone or as a group, verify, consolidate, and apply concepts and competencies acquired in one context to other contexts and domains of knowledge.*

e) *Children and adults use a language of thinking and emotion.*

f) *The objective that the group sets for itself is reached by keeping together the procedural and content requirements of the work.*

g) *Assessment and self-assessment have a strong presence inside the learning group and serve to guide and orient the learning process.*

h) *Collaboration strategies are an integral part of the group learning process and can determine the quality of learning.*

* By *aesthetics*, the Reggio educators refer to the ability to judge and evaluate images or theories that work best for the particular project at hand. They also use the term to imply what is most pleasing, attractive, or satisfying to oneself or to others.

** We use the term *theory* to refer to a "system of concepts, strategies, and actions that provides a satisfactory explanation for the person who produces the theory."[1] (See also "Documentation and Assessment: What Is the Relationship?") Although theories are characterized by the coherence and interdependence of their concepts, they are not static but open to falsification by new evidence.[2]

In this chapter, we refer to the visual essays of the previous chapters and the ministories that appear throughout the book. To give additional dimension to the propositions, we draw also on the following sources: other literature produced by Reggio educators; studies of the Reggio experience by American and other educators; transcripts of roundtable discussions by the Reggio research team on documenting and assessing children's group learning; internal reports from the Reggio research team about children's work in groups; and eight trips by the Project Zero research team to Reggio Emilia between 1997 and 2000. During these trips, usually of a week's duration, Project Zero researchers observed in the classrooms and had in-depth discussions and interviews with teachers, atelieristi, and pedagogisti from the Diana and Villetta preschools.

One word of caution: While the propositions reflect how Reggio educators perceive learning groups in their schools and centers, our impression is that learning groups in the United States *can* function in these ways but do not always do so as successfully as they might. The establishment and nurturance of a culture of learning groups like the one in Reggio Emilia has considerable impact on the likelihood that children and adults will form effective learning groups and function well within them. Key components of this culture include the value placed on working in groups; attention to the range, quality, and choice of materials; the role of the adult as researcher and facilitator; a view of the environment as a powerful tool for learning; large blocks of uninterrupted, unscheduled time; and an image of the child as a powerful and competent researcher with a hypothesis. Readers will see reflections of this culture in the propositions, as well as in other parts of this book.

PROPOSITION I. Factors that influence the formation, functioning, and demonstration of understanding of learning groups in early childhood include the size of the group; the age, competencies, and interests of the children; gender; time spent together; friendships; and choice of materials.

a) Size

Children constructing rainbows (with a basin of water and a mirror turned toward the sun)

The number of children in a learning group significantly influences how and what the group learns. Groups of two, three, or four children are particularly effective in that they foster complex interactions, constructive conflicts, and self-monitoring.[3] Small groups allow for more frequent and dynamic communication than large groups; children can develop the capacity for listening, collaborating, and negotiating. Each child can be recognized by the others in the group as bringing a distinctive perspective and way of thinking. Teachers are also better able to listen to children because in the act of communicating, children make their thinking visible.

The right size for a learning group is frequently determined by the capacity of the group to maintain the rhythm of a conversation or work on a project and to negotiate conflicts. The group needs to be small enough for each person to keep track of everyone else's ideas and contributions. Of course, some children prefer to work alone, some in pairs, and some in groups of three. In unstructured situations, children tend to stay in groups of two, three (perhaps the most common), or at most four. Sometimes, when a third child is added to a group of two, he or she may break up a dialogue that was apparently easier in the pair of children.[4] But the conversation is sometimes enriched by the third person, who can revive the rhythm or mediate the discussion. A group of three children may have to focus more on organizing strategies for communicating with others. It may need to construct an equilibrium that is more readily achieved when children are in pairs. In "The Right Price," both Riccardo and Alessandro try to find ways to explain Riccardo's counting method to Silvia.

Sharing one's work with small and large groups is also different. Children's descriptions are likely to be more condensed when they are communicating with a large group. The conversation will tend not to go into depth because of the large size of the group. In "Landscapes of Light," an exploration of different instruments such as the overhead projector and slide projector that produce artificial light, children report to a large group the title of their composition of different objects on the overhead projector and they make a few other remarks. In small groups, the communication tends to be more precise and can yield sentences of considerable efficiency. Explaining their discoveries about the overhead in a small group, children made comments like: *Things change and become another kind of light. Light changes and then things become exchanged. When you took off one thing, another thing disappeared on the other side.*

Projections with the overhead projector

b) Age, Competencies, and Interests of the Children

For the most productive interactions in a learning group, Reggio educators have observed that the ages and developmental levels of the children should not be too separated.[5] Relative zones of proximal development—the distance between what children can accomplish independently and with the help of a more competent peer or adult[6]—are taken into account not only by the teacher, but also by the children. In addition, as we saw in the previous chapters, the types of competencies and interests of children in a learning group can be more or less complementary and suitable for the task at hand. A learning group of children who are all verbally expressive is likely to learn differently (and probably different things) than a group of children who are verbally, graphically, and musically expressive. In "Landscapes of Light" the teachers often form pairs with one child more oriented toward the verbal language and the other more oriented toward action. Interest is also a distinct factor. Small groups in Reggio are often formed by inviting the children with the greatest passion for a topic to become part of the group. The adults frequently make this determination after observing the larger group do some initial exploration of a topic.

Group discussing the choice of materials

Reggio educators try to bring together children with complementary communicative strategies and ways of working. In "The City of Reggio Emilia," after considering the graphic and verbal representations of several children, the teachers invite three boys and three girls to become part of two different learning groups. Of the boys, Simone likes to chat and is interested in the network of connections in towns; Giacomo is interested in how things work, but expresses his thoughts only when necessary; and Emiliano is interested in what happens in the centers of towns. In the girls' group, Cecilia is competent in verbal description, Francesca in drawing, and Annarita in three-dimensional construction. One motivation for bringing together these particular children is to see whether and how their different competencies (or intelligences) will influence and support one another as they carry out their work.

c) Gender

As is well documented in the literature, groups of young children learn and function differently, depending on whether they consist of all males, all females, or a mix.[7] Reggio educators purposefully set up single-sex and mixed groups in order to investigate further the approaches to learning exhibited by girls and boys. The research literature also shows that girls typically prefer smaller groups than boys.[8] As we saw earlier, girls seem to prefer learning groups of two or three, with a maximum of four children. Learning groups of boys are sometimes larger, but groups of more than six boys are rarely able to maintain the rhythm of a conversation. The flow of conversation typical of smaller groups is interrupted, and the group finds it difficult to maintain the focus that generated the research and discussion.

Boys and girls seem to determine and arrive at a common goal in different ways. For example, in one class of five-year-olds, the teacher invited a group of three boys and a group of three girls to work together to draw a single bicycle. Each of the three boys began by drawing his own bicycle—a kind of "proprietary production" of the object, which was then compared with the others.

Individual drawings of a bicycle by the boys' group

On the basis of this comparison, the boys chose the parts they considered most effective for composing the common bicycle. With the parts left over (that is, not used for the common bicycle) they set up a sort of garage for spare parts. (Children of both sexes seem to have a strong sense of parsimony, which leads them to try to preserve all that is produced in individual and group processes. This might also be interpreted as a sign of respect for the products and subjectivity of their companions.)*

The three girls, on the other hand, immediately adopted an organizational method in which they worked together on the same sheet of paper. They discussed the organization among themselves in an effort to negotiate and generate mutual satisfaction: *What would you like to do? If you do this part, then I will do that part. What do you think?* and so on. The distinctive ways of learning and collaborating are especially apparent when children encounter a problem for the first time. Yet, when the same problem is dealt with repeatedly, boys as well as girls tend to use the girls' strategy. The reasons for this are not clear. Perhaps when a problem is new, children choose a more immediate approach that tends to be characteristic of the boys' style. But when the problem is presented again, the approach is often more reflective and the school culture of negotiation and working together is more likely to emerge.

Boys and girls also seem to have different aesthetics or criteria for choosing "best" work. For example, in "The City of Reggio Emilia" the girls represent a city full of relationships and real-life experiences, whereas the boys create a city built around spatial and functional connections.[9] In "Landscapes of Light," when working with the overhead projector, the boys invent characters and create a verbal language narrative; the girls create a more visual narrative with a plot based on surprise and pleasure in the quality of materials.

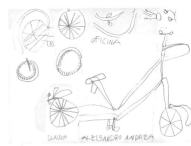

Drawing of a bicycle by the boys' group using parts of the individual bicycles

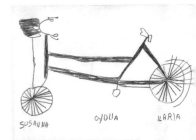

Collective drawing of a bicycle by three girls

d) Time Spent Together

The number of months or years that children spend together in a context influences the ways they come to know themselves and others. In "The City of Reggio Emilia" Simone and Emiliano have known each other for three years. They begin drawing the city together, sitting near each other, frequently overlapping hands and exchanging seats. On the other hand, in "The Beautiful Wall," a boy and girl who have not spent much time together previously seem to work together in a civilized way, but often move apart. Even when they work nearby, they appear to be working alone in tandem.

When children are given the opportunity to choose the members of a learning group, they may or may not follow criteria similar to those used by adults. Children who have been together for years often choose peers according to the competencies they can offer. But even in the infant-toddler centers, Reggio educators have noted that children will approach others because of their expertise. The more aware children are of the

---

* The term *subjectivity* is used by the Reggio educators to refer to the intellectual, psychological, and emotional composition that makes every person unique. It encompasses the meanings of the English words personality, identity, and individuality.

processes and competencies needed in a particular context, the more likely they are to choose group companions based on those qualities. Children who are not as familiar with the demands of the work tend to choose companions based on friendship (see below). Some children are chosen for both friendship and areas of competency.

e) Friendships

Children's friendship is often a criterion by which both adults and children determine a group. The girls in "The City of Reggio Emilia" are all friends, but they have different competencies and ways of working. We saw in the previous chapters that friendship can be a strong link between children, fostering curiosity and exchange. Cecilia, Annarita, and Francesca all start drawing on the same side of the paper, engage in a lot of conversation, and use humor and lighthearted teasing to solidify their identity as a group. Friends are also likely to motivate or prompt each other to try new things.

The early-childhood research literature shows that young children who are friends tend both to cooperate more with each other and to have more disagreements than children who are not friends. However, the disagreements are less likely to be overly confrontational or to disturb the friendship and are more likely to be resolved.[10] Children seem more able to test degrees of fairness in the safety of friendship.

For many children, friendship seems to be a guarantee of competency and security. Children may prefer to work with friends because they think, *They are friends of mine; therefore they are good.* Sometimes the opportunity to work together can consolidate a budding friendship. Friendship also provides confidence in the face of novelty. Even when children know they will need particular competencies to solve a problem, they often consider friendship a primary criterion in choosing their group companions. And friends provide an especially attentive audience when presenting work to others.

f) Choice of Materials

As we saw in "Daily Life at School" (page 58), the choice of materials and setup of the environment strongly influence how and what is learned by adults and children in learning groups.[11] Reggio educators define "intelligent materials" as those that invite questions, curiosity, and experimentation; intelligent materials involve a balance of simplicity and complexity. Whereas some materials guide children in specific directions, others are more evocative and facilitate discovery, exploration, and the creation of stories, metaphors, and games. These materials lead to a sense of wonder and excitement, so that children are motivated to come back to them. Tools like the overhead projector that modify one's perspective and support a combination of different languages are especially seductive.

In addition, the availability of a choice of materials for exploring a problem or expressing thoughts furthers the research of a learning group. If children have the opportunity to

Self-service material for the overhead projector

draw or represent their thinking   to
communicate with others in the   •   lia"
children choose the kind and siz   ... ɡ... ɪys

that cities never end and selects a big roll of paper. As we will see in "The Wheel and Movement," children find many different kinds of material to accomplish the task of making a robot that moves: paper of varying size, texture, and weight; corrugated cardboard; wood; wire; and tops.

In the "Dinosaur" project described by Baji Rankin, a small group of children tries to make a scale model of a life-size dinosaur on a piece of paper.[12] The atelierista offers the children a selection of lined, unlined, or blocked paper. This choice is crucial because it forces members of the group to make their hypotheses more concrete, accessible, and public.

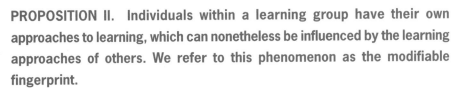

PROPOSITION II. Individuals within a learning group have their own approaches to learning, which can nonetheless be influenced by the learning approaches of others. We refer to this phenomenon as the modifiable fingerprint.

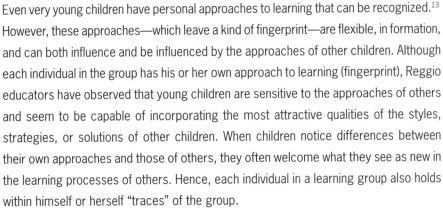

Large painting of a dinosaur mounted in a public park

Even very young children have personal approaches to learning that can be recognized.[13] However, these approaches—which leave a kind of fingerprint—are flexible, in formation, and can both influence and be influenced by the approaches of other children. Although each individual in the group has his or her own approach to learning (fingerprint), Reggio educators have observed that young children are sensitive to the approaches of others and seem to be capable of incorporating the most attractive qualities of the styles, strategies, or solutions of other children. When children notice differences between their own approaches and those of others, they often welcome what they see as new in the learning processes of others. Hence, each individual in a learning group also holds within himself or herself "traces" of the group.

In "The City of Reggio Emilia" the three girls each propose different graphic representations of the town. Cecilia draws a town with connections, houses, and streets; Annarita draws a long and narrow town; and Francesca focuses on the idea that the town is made of different squares. Each girl has a different point of view and way of representing the town, but they all adopt Francesca's idea of drawing the town from a bird's-eye view. Likewise, in "The Right Price" Silvia adopts Riccardo's counting strategies

when she needs to count up her own money. Usually we think of the identification process as Freudian, with children noticing and adopting traits from their parents. But in this context there seems to be a kind of intellectual identification with and adoption of traits from peers.[14] Children are not simply born with personal approaches to learning; rather, they construct their own approaches out of bits and fragments observed in the context of collaborations and interactions with other children at school, friends, siblings, parents, and grandparents.

PROPOSITION III. When exploring ideas together, learning groups follow a set of rules—some tacit, some explicit.

When young children in learning groups explore ideas together, they seem to operate according to two instinctive reference points: a strong sense of justice and the preservation of an atmosphere of pleasant cooperation. Reggio teachers note that at age three, children often seem to concentrate their efforts on learning the rules for discussing together—for example, learning to respect the turns and individual paces of other children in the group. Three-year-olds also recognize the pleasure of talking together. Often by age four, children develop a competency and respect for the pertinence of arguments or for staying "on track." (Of course, depending on the context, these attitudes and competencies can emerge earlier or later than the ages cited.)

A learning group may operate according to a shared understanding that everyone is allowed to express an opinion or elaborate a theory while discussing a particular topic. Children expect other members of the group to say what they think. If someone does not talk, the others encourage his or her contribution. In "The City of Reggio Emilia" Simone and Emiliano first draw a street toward Giacomo, perhaps to encourage his participation, and then Simone asks, *Giacomo, why aren't you doing anything?* This type of practice ensures democratic participation: children do not feel uneasy later because they did not take part in the conversation or development of the project.

In "The Beautiful Wall" three pairs of children work on a design for the wall. When the children need to choose which design will create the most beautiful wall, one subgroup proposes dividing the wall into three strips so that each pair can put its ideas in the layouts, and they can all have the ideas of everyone. However, the group ends up choosing Chiara's proposal of creating a new design *"all together,"* whereby each child contributes a piece with the agreement of the others. In this way the children in the group are *"all even in the end."*

The ultimate choice of a best theory is usually based on a complex network of cognitive, aesthetic, and social factors. The ideas that a group ends up preferring and using are usually those that enable the group to keep in mind both their search for a solution to the problem and their sense of justice and democracy. Children try to reach their objective by keeping their proposed aims and working methods in constant dialogue. These methods entail complete participation, which in fact seems to increase the effectiveness and quality of the result precisely because of the multiple contributions. The final result is certainly more appreciated by the children.

By means of this process the identity of each child is influenced, but not lost; rather, it is enriched. Each child recognizes the "stylistic traces" he or she has left as well as the traces of others. The group has a strong memory with respect to each member, but also a firm wish to declare the work the creation of all, perhaps to consolidate each individual identity with that of the others, or to affirm a shared sense of justice and democracy. The individual contributions are like multiple identities in a landscape that is constructed together and recognized both as a whole and in terms of its separate components.

Construction of a sculpture made of natural material

Other indicators that children are working in learning groups include:

• initially maintaining a certain physical distance from other group members, but as the work of the group progresses, increasing physical proximity;

• keeping the size of the group small;

• expressing verbal statements in the first person plural (*We can do this. Come on, let's do this.*);

• using different aspects of body language (gestures, facial expressions, tone of voice) to invite participation;

• dissolving a group when the negotiated goal is achieved or when interest in the topic or project fades.

PROPOSITION IV. Learning groups choose ideas according to an aesthetic of knowledge or "the pattern that connects."

Very early on, individuals and groups of children seem to develop a sensitivity to an aesthetic of knowledge. They exhibit the capacity to choose "what is best" among theories and to identify conceptual or formal solutions that advance the work of the group. They have a sense of excellence, both within a group and in their own work, though boys and girls seem to have different aesthetics. (For better or worse, powerful images from television and the other popular media contribute to creating these aesthetics of knowledge.) For example, in a clay project at the Diana School, each child is attempting to build a clay horse. The children look at each other's work and choose Elisa's horse as a kind of a model for the rest of the group. The model may have been chosen because it looks most like a horse, or because it is a structure the children can easily perceive and reproduce (a series of bridges that creates an elongated body). In either case, the choice is aesthetic; it enables them to carry out what they are motivated to do—make a horse.

Clay horse by Elisa, 3 years 6 months, which generates "contagions" and imitations in the class

Marco manages to reproduce the bridge structure but not the rest

Michele is attracted by the circular base and loses the structure

Federica finishes the reproduction

As we have seen, Reggio teachers often ask children to compare different pieces of work and to identify which works best for a particular task or project. (Neither teachers nor children shy away from comparing and choosing individual work in service of the group's attainment of a common goal.) In the "Crowd" project in which children explore the theme of crowds through different languages, after the teacher summarizes children's earlier comments about crowds she asks a small group to look at their drawings again.[15]

Group commenting on drawings of a crowd they had done previously

One of the crowd drawings analyzed by the group

The child who made the drawing explains the reasons for her graphic choices

These are the comments on Daria's drawing:
"Domenico: *Oh no!*
Daria (anticipating others' criticisms): *Mine's just a LITTLE crowd!*
Benedetta: *But you made the people all going the same way!*
Daria: *They are all friends, so they're all going in the same direction.*
Benedetta: *But in a crowd, the people aren't all friends or relatives, you know.*"

When children explore and develop their thinking in a group, their words and thoughts cross different domains of knowledge. The aesthetic dimension serves as a criterion for determining the quality of an idea or approach and motivates further learning. When we learn and build knowledge, we are putting into relation and evaluating what we are doing according to models that are attractive to us. We are engaged in a type of project in which a basic aesthetic or "pattern that connects"[16] leads us to evaluate and modify our interpretive constructs in order to "seduce" others toward our theories, ideas, and products. Children in learning groups are also engaged in this type of aesthetic project: they are attracted to the most pleasing or "nicest" models and make decisions  on this basis. In "The Right Price" Riccardo's counting strategy is adopted by other children in the class in part because of its musicality, the body movements, and the tapping sound it produces—all of which make it especially visible and attractive.

PROPOSITION V. Learning groups have different styles that are rhythmic in nature.

Just as individuals vary in their "fingerprints," so learning groups have different styles of learning that seem to produce a kind of rhythm or musicality inside the group. There is a kind of dance that balances the rhythms of individuals and the collective. Children continually modify their styles and strategies in relation to the others in the group. The rhythms change depending on the number of children in the group and the cognitive or other tensions that emerge at different points in the work (for example, if a particularly hard problem arises, or a topic that is familiar to one or more group members is chosen). Learning groups of children and adults can benefit greatly from cognitive tension (disagreements, conflicts, negotiations) inside the group if that tension is not too great. Two factors are key to letting this tension surface and flourish: (1) adults who listen to children, and (2) documents such as texts of conversation and photographs that can be referred to by the group. The teacher serves as a kind of memory for the group, either reminding children of what they or others have said or bringing previous drawings and work to the group. In "The City of Reggio Emilia" the teacher brings his notes and the children's earlier drawings to the table; children can revisit them as they go about their task.

Subgroups within the learning group also have their own rhythms and identities that serve different learning functions. In "The Beautiful Wall" the girls engage in more constant negotiation, questioning, and collaboration up front. *(If you do this, I could do that and she could do this.)* They stretch out the discussions, give more examples, tell more stories. The boys seem to have a more declarative style and produce more goal-directed repartee. *(You do this part and I'll do that part.)* The time frames for these different subgroups are frequently different. When groups are new, in order for learning to occur, certain roles seem to be fundamental, such as "the skeptic," "the negotiator," and "the coordinator." The presence of each of these individuals influences the rhythms of the learning group. As we saw in "The Curiosity to Understand," Ferruccio plays the role of coordinator when the boys construct tables in clay. In "The Right Price" Alessandro plays the role of negotiator, explaining Riccardo's method to himself and to Silvia. The repetition is useful for Alessandro's own understanding as well as for Silvia's.

A group listens to the initial proposal of a project with different attitudes: possiblist, enthusiast, skeptic

PROPOSITION VI. Learning groups can create and benefit from competent audiences.

Every day in the classroom, many different experiences take place simultaneously, with a continuous exchange of information, comments, and opinions. Often when children are involved in a long-term project, the small group of "protagonists" who are engaged in making discoveries receive numerous observations from the children around them. Some children merely stop near the group and watch what is happening; others are called over to admire what the group is doing. As the children working near the learning group become more competent from observing and tracking its work, they start to check in with the group more frequently—asking questions, making suggestions, evaluating what the group is doing.

Projections with the overhead projector

Light table

In "Landscapes of Light" three children working at a table next to the overhead projector make suggestions to the learning group regarding the optical aspects of the exploration. They point out that too many layers of material will make the projection too dark; they suggest that objects on the overhead surface will be more visible if they are moved toward the center. The learning group itself becomes more competent, thanks to the competent audience, because the children who are the protagonists must reflect on and find other ways to conceptualize what they have learned in order to respond to their peers.

Another variety of competent audience consists of children who already have experience with the task on which the group is working. These children generate and impart their own brand of wisdom. The learning group itself sometimes expands to include members of the competent audience.

Before moving on to Proposition VII, we need a few words about the difficulty of representing the complexities of any individual's understanding, let alone that of a group. As Nickerson puts it, "If we were able—and we are not—to represent the knowledge of a single individual in such a way as to do justice to its richness and breadth, its various degrees of specificity and certainty, its mix of explicitly and implicitly included facts and beliefs, its inconsistencies and contradictions, and its understanding, more or less, of countless concepts, principles, relationships, and processes, it would be a complex representation indeed."[17] In this spirit, we view the learning indicators in Proposition VII as reference points that can orient and guide teachers' observations, helping them become more aware of the learning of individuals and groups and suggesting new paths to explore. They are flexible and open traces of understanding that need to be adjusted to each classroom situation.

PROPOSITION VII. Indicators that learning groups are supporting and demonstrating understanding include the following:

a) Children and adults feel they are contributing to a larger, more meaningful whole. Children and adults in Reggio seem to be engaged in creating two kinds of larger communities: a community of knowledge and a community of democratic participation. Karl Popper's concept of "World 3" suggests a way of thinking about group learning in the context of a larger community.[18] Popper makes a distinction between the physical world (World 1), the world of knowledge as it exists in the minds of individuals (World 2), and the world of knowledge as an abstraction that exists beyond the individual level (World 3). Examples of World 3 knowledge are the sciences or other disciplines in which the long-term focus is not on individuals, but on building a collective body of knowledge.[19] Individuals are not just constructing individual understanding but, over time, a public and collective understanding that has meaning beyond what each person has understood. Schools and classrooms in Reggio Emilia often seem to operate—and value operating—in this dimension.

Wall documentation on a project on robots

Documenting children's learning is a key element in forming the identity of this type of knowledge community. Documentation offers a research orientation, creates cultural artifacts, and serves as a collective memory. It gives children, parents, teachers, and others a basis for discussion and reflection about children's ways of learning and living. At the Villetta School, teachers chose to leave on the walls a large part of the documentation panels from a previous five-year-old class's work on robots because the new class was going to be involved in the same project. Some of the children saw the panels as "users' instructions" left to them from last year's class; others saw them as examples of how other children think about robots; still others thought they were left to support their understanding, since robots are so hard to comprehend. The panels also served as a professional development tool for new teachers and contributed to parents' understanding of how children learn. At another school, a group of children decided to leave a three-dimensional world they had created, called "Crystal City," as a gift for the incoming class. The new group greatly admired the work and decided to leave the landscape intact. Realizing the city lacked people, they created figures to add to the world.

This kind of knowledge community is simultaneously generating two kinds of knowledge: knowledge about a particular topic (for example, robotics) and knowledge about how children learn. The people who make up the community are constantly adding to the knowledge community. Through such democratic participation, collective knowledge-building occurs in projects and products in the schools and in the town of Reggio Emilia itself. Children contribute not just to their own work, but also to the work of others. Reggio schools often engage in multischool, multiyear research. This work is seen as important and is frequently shared with the rest of the community. One study, on the religious and moral dimensions of school, involves a collaboration between several schools and the diocese of Reggio. Over time, parents shift from being interested only or primarily in their own child, to being concerned with other children and the whole group, to an interest in childhood in general (an example of World 3!). For instance, at the Villetta School parents are working with the teachers to understand children's engagement with new technologies such as robots. This type of community involvement serves in addition as a valuable form of professional development for the Reggio teachers.

b) The discoveries of individual children become part of the thinking of the learning group.

In the kind of knowledge community just described, group learning depends on various attributes such as the number of members and, above all, the types of contributions individuals make to the group. Individual processes and discoveries become part of the group's thinking when they influence participation and agreement. In order to constitute part of the group's thinking, children's individual discoveries need to be organized, expressed, and discussed. Individual moments in a learning group need to be guaranteed and respected, so that each child can express his or her own theories and ideas. (Reggio educators frequently ask individual children to represent graphically an emerging theory that is first expressed verbally in a group discussion. This practice enables teachers to follow better the modifications and advances of the ideas that emerge in the passage from verbal to graphic languages.) Putting these hypotheses and ideas immediately into circulation for discussion with others allows the ideas to evolve and the group to produce knowledge that belongs to the group itself, and in which the group recognizes itself.

In "The Fax" the group makes use of and modifies a number of children's theories about how faxes travel in order to come up with a final theory that belongs to everyone. In "The Wheel and Movement" the girls circulate many different theories about how to make the robot move, and they accept numerous variations and additions. The group splits up and comes together many times. After finding a top and observing it spin on its axis, Alice becomes interested in the center of the wheel, while Federica and Erica focus on the outside of the wheel, experimenting with different shapes and materials. When Erica and Federica see Alice's wheel spinning, the two groups combine their designs. Although the girls' ideas do not remain individual, there is no sense of loss. On the contrary, they gain a sense of being part of the group and of the thinking process of others in trying to reach a goal.

c) Children express a feeling of continuous growth and awareness that their theories are provisional, and they take pleasure in seeing them modified, developed, and advanced.

When children work alone, they do not generally negotiate or test their perspectives against the theories of others. Children in learning groups are more likely to perceive the temporariness of their theories because they experience knowledge as a constant process of negotiation and reflection. Adults who are comfortable with ambiguity and not exclusively focused on right answers provide a welcoming context for this process.[20] In the project "The Amusement Park for Birds," in which children and adults created an amusement park for birds with fountains, waterwheels, boat rides, and more, Filippo questions himself about whether or not his waterwheel works and tests his theory by putting the wheel in the water tank.[21] At another point in the project Andrea graphically represents his theory of the fountain, which is then discussed by his two companions, Filippo and Giorgia. When Andrea tries to explain his theory, Giorgia says, *I don't think the water turns exactly like that.* When he tries to explain his theory again, Filippo says, *But this here isn't right either.* Andrea then makes minor modifications to his theory and succeeds in convincing the others.

As children assess themselves, they are usually aware of the provisional nature of their ideas and theories. In the "Shadow Landscapes" project, five- and six-year-old children explore light and shadows in the construction area of their classroom.[22] When the teacher invites Riccardo and Veronica to try to produce a colored shadow, Riccardo is willing to try Veronica's suggestion of using something light like a feather, even though he says he is sure that his theory (putting a sheet of colored paper in front of the screen) is right and thinks the feather will yield only a gray color. *Okay, let's try; but then we also try my idea that I'm sure works because I always do experiments; I like experiments.*

What makes the reflection of the shadow colored?

A lightweight feather?

A piece of colored cardboard?

Tests, hypotheses, discussions

The children know that different ideas can coexist. After they try both suggestions, neither of which produces a colored shadow, they generate another theory that also fails. *Let's try to put the [red] sheet near the light. Poor me, it's all dark...maybe we have to wait a little for the sheet to become warm: if the sheet gets warm, maybe the color melts and produces a substance that evaporates and colors the shadow on the screen.* But the pair eventually come up with a theory that works and feel themselves to be creators of impressive magic. Playful teasing often characterizes children's remarks in these contexts perhaps as a way to ease the conflicts and tensions that can be produced by the act of assessment and the feeling of being assessed.

d) Over time the members of the learning group, alone or as a group, verify, consolidate, and apply concepts and competencies acquired in one context to

Transparency in
the dress-up corner

other contexts and domains of knowledge.

Children and adults exhibit and construct understanding in a "constellation" of opportunities that may or may not be related to the project at hand. In "The Wheel and Movement" the girls carry out their research not just when they are specifically working on their project, but also during other parts of the day in other spaces in the classroom—for example, constructing other kinds of wheels in the construction space. In "Landscapes of Light" children learn about the concept of transparency while using the overhead, but they also learn about transparency in the dress-up corner or when they play near the window.

As we saw in "Ring-around-the-Rosy," Reggio educators often explicitly set up situations with analogous problems to see whether individual children and those in groups can apply what they learned in one situation to another, or to see how concepts are represented and developed from one language to another, or to look at learning over time. In this case teachers posed the problem of representing a three-dimensional subject in a two-dimensional medium. After children drew the game, teachers asked them to represent other games using both two- and three-dimensional media. In many of these situations, children first act out the scenario, then observe it, describe it verbally, make predictions about how it can be represented graphically, draw individual representations, reflect as a group on the drawings, make another set of drawings, and reflect on both sets of drawings.

In another study, teachers decided to look at children's notation strategies to see whether the strategies used in one situation transferred to another. The three contexts were organizing different shades of the same hue on the light table, recording the price of things in Shop, and relating the organization of colors to sound. Investigations such as these can reveal the transfer not only of conceptual understandings, but of modes of collaboration like the ability to think through a theory together or an understanding of the pleasure of working in a group.

The research literature suggests that transfer of knowledge and skills rarely occurs without explicit scaffolding or support.[23] In order for children to transfer strategies and solutions from one situation to the next, they must first notice the similarities between tasks and then map the relations between them. When preschool children are presented with structurally and perceptually similar problems, they can identify the similarities and transfer solutions learned in one context to another.[24] However, children do not always perceive structural similarities spontaneously; they benefit from prompting, a key aspect of scaffolding. The situations that Reggio educators set up for children to encounter analogous problems are one way to promote the kind of transfer desired for children's learning.

e) Children and adults use a language of thinking and emotion.

Individuals in learning groups often use a language of thinking and emotion:

Children:

What do you think?

I have an idea.

In my opinion...

In your opinion...

Do you like it?

Do you agree?

Can I help you?

Do you like it this way?

I don't agree.

Teachers:

How many discoveries can you come up with?

Why don't you try to make discoveries together?

Rereading all the things that you said, one thing came to our minds that you could understand better...

We need to decide...how we can take these things to your friends. How can we let them understand what you have done here?

You have time for discoveries with joy.

Children learn to see themselves as thinkers with different points of view. Children in learning groups accept one another's opinions and feelings and offer their own opinions and feelings, whether they are in agreement with or differ from their peers. Children's and adults' comments often build on one another. In the "Crowd" project, when the learning group is stuck because the boys want to make a crowd out of clay and the girls prefer to draw one, Elena says: *I have an idea. If we help you make the crowd out of clay, we do you a favor; then you have to do us a favor and help us make the drawing one.* Adults in Reggio frequently use a language of thinking and emotion when they ask children to comment on other children's ideas or theories. As we have seen, comparisons are not viewed as negative. In "Ring-around-the-Rosy" Davide says, *This Ring-around-the-Rosy is nice because of Filippo's idea. He made it nice.*

Of course, meaningful communication happens not just when there is shared language, but when there is the *desire* to communicate and understand. In "Landscapes of Light," one of the pairs of girls, Federica and Giulia, share common aims, feelings, and physical movements, as well as verbal language. They pose interrogative sentences that require an answer and make exclamations of wonder that attract the other's attention and elicit support. They jump and laugh and share the pleasure of their aesthetic and optical discoveries.

Crowd in clay by five- and six-year-old children

Rolling in the light designs on the floor produced by the overhead projector

f) The objective that the group sets for itself is reached by keeping together the procedural and content requirements of the work.

Learning groups search for and choose conceptual and organizational procedures that will enable them to arrive at the solution to a problem while at the same time sustaining the participation of all group members and their cohesion as a learning group. In "The Wheel and Movement" the learning group repeatedly divides and re-forms, but each subgroup is always aware of what the other is doing and neither loses sight of the overall objective of creating a mobile robot. In "The Fax," while incorporating aspects of a number of individual theories, the group tries to create a satisfactory explanation of how the fax can travel across the ocean. The children want to find a theory that belongs to everyone, but they also keep in mind the need to choose one that can best explain how the fax crosses the ocean. They end up choosing Lorenzo's suggestion of electrical wires and electricity, supplemented by Alessandra's idea about the wind.

Lorenzo's theory on how the fax travels from Reggio Emilia to Washington, D.C.

Children comparing their individual theories that they have represented graphically	Alessandra's theory on how the wind carries the fax on its journey	The children decide to add the idea of the wind to Lorenzo's idea of the electrical wires and electricity	The children combine Alessandra's theory on the wind with Lorenzo's theory, advancing their ideas and thus creating a first group theory

In "The City of Reggio Emilia" the repetition of drawing squares allows all the boys to participate in planning and carrying out their task both verbally and graphically. The drawing of streets also serves to keep the group together and to further their creation of a city that is functionally connected. The group's goal becomes intertwined with the way it is achieved. Toward the end of the task, the group agrees that each member will test the connectedness of the streets to see if they have reached their goal of a unified city.

g) Assessment and self-assessment have a strong presence inside the learning group and serve to guide and orient the learning process.

In trying to make meaning of their own and others' thinking, children need to assess themselves and others. By *assess* Reggio educators refer to an informal and "in-process" act of reflection: children pause in their actions to take stock of where they are in relation to what they hope to achieve (as opposed to more structured and formal assessments like portfolios or performance assessments). These acts of assessment and self-assessment are an essential part of the learning process because they allow the individual and the group to orient, modify, and advance their thinking in relation to a cognitive goal. This kind of assessment does not occur after the fact, but in moments of learning; therefore it is not dispassionate and detached, but full of emotion and passion.

In some cases, the assessment is built into the learning process: Does the robot move or not? Does the waterwheel rotate or not? When a child's or a group's theory succeeds, self-esteem and social status increase. Sometimes the assessment may not be so straightforward: Does the crowd seem like a crowd? Does the picture express the mood we want? How does the "beautiful wall" look? In these situations children generate their own standards in relation to a sense of purpose, whether for themselves or an audience.

In "The City of Reggio Emilia" the girls stop frequently to assess their work, noticing, for instance, that they need more squares in the city. When they are finished with their drawing, one of their first acts is to share their work with friends in order to know if the town is "beautiful." The boys too pause to make sure that in fact they have met their goal of making an interconnected city, using their fingers to trace the streets. At the end of the session, the boys also assess their drawing with the teacher, but in accordance with their own sense of aesthetics and coherence of ideas. In "The Right Price" Silvia explains to the teacher what she has learned about numbers, what was hard for her, and what and who helped her learn.

Learning groups demonstrate understanding when individuals in the group can monitor their own thinking, take responsibility for their own learning, and are themselves aware when they have understood something or made a discovery. Debate and discussion with others facilitate the self-assessment process and help children to develop the capacity for meta-cognition. One strategy Reggio teachers use is asking children to discuss together their individual drawings. In the "Crowd" project, after just such a discussion, children realize that they need to learn how to draw figures in profile and from the back.[25]

"Teacher: If you were to draw another crowd, how would you make it?
Benedetta: *We need a big paper!*

Federico: *And then a thousand tiny people.*

Stefano: *We don't have to draw all the people going in the same direction, but also from the back and from the side [profile] as Martina and Filippo.*

Cosimo: *I don't know how to do them from the back.*

Alice: *Neither do I.*

Domenico: *We have to learn how to do it!*

Federico: *To do the back ones it's easy, one makes someone without eyes; to do the side ones, one makes someone with only one eye. I know how they are from the profile, I am not blind!*

Stefano: *I am not stupid either. I know how people look in profile, but I didn't draw them like that because I didn't think about it.*

Domenico: *Listen, you don't know how to do the profile because you need a lot of time to learn how to understand that it's a profile, otherwise they look like monsters!"*

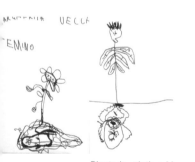

From the "Crowd" project: Soccer match – drawing by Giorgio, 5 years 9 months

After an intense discussion, with one group claiming that they already know how to draw people in profile and from the back, and the other saying they need to learn, Alice says, *I want to say an idea: you have to do the profile one time and then again and again until you learn how.* Domenico responds, *Yeah, or else somebody says, What kind of a crowd is "that"?* Through a democratic discussion process, the decision is reached to improve the group's abilities to carry out the task. We note again the use of teasing as a kind of social mediator to maintain a light and playful tone.

h) Collaboration strategies are an integral part of the group learning process and can determine the quality of learning.

By planning and working in a group from a very young age, children learn to make effective use of collaboration strategies that make thinking together productive: negotiating skills, flexible thinking, listening to the ideas of others, humor, and building on ideas that come from the group. Reggio teachers frequently ask children to create or draw things in relationship.[26]

Plants in relationship

"Teacher: Would you like to draw your plant in relation to something else: another plant, the plant of your friend, an insect, someone who is watering the plant…you decide.

Marco: *Let's make plants who love each other.*

Ale: *No, they're getting married.*

Teacher: You need to decide together what your two plants are doing…agree among yourselves. Remember the roots. Remember that last year you called them 'the little legs of life.'"

The children draw the plant either with or alongside another child. Through experiences like this, children spend a great deal of time exploring the relationships of things in relation to others. Relational modes on all levels are seen as critical to determining the quality of learning.

In "The City of Reggio Emilia" the girls begin by posing questions as a way to clarify the intentions of the group and some of the fundamental elements of representation. They use humor as a strategy to foster the exchange of ideas and increase the sense of belonging to the group. Sharing predictions about what they are going to draw also supports the group's completion of the map. In the boys' group, Simone and Emiliano draw the city streets so that they approach Giacomo, who has not yet participated. In "Landscapes of Light" Federica and Giulia use a number of collaborative and relational strategies. They speak in the first person plural and address each other with amused looks, gestures, and tones of voice. They jump, laugh, and exchange expressions of enthusiasm and interest in the overhead, its possibilities, and the opportunity to stay together. Giulia affectionately calls Federica "*Chica*," often searching for confirmation of her actions: *Chica, is this all right? Can we also put these?* The relationship is mainly sustained by Giulia, who shares with Federica pleasure in the aesthetic effects they are creating: *What a wonderful thing we are doing. Are we going to put the houses now? Shall we also put one like this? Look how nice. You can see the wonderful. How beautiful that is.*

Federica and Giulia playing with the overhead projector

Concluding Note

In her article "On Listening to What the Children Say," the preschool and kindergarten teacher Vivian Paley reflects on her discovery of the tape recorder:

"The tape recorder, with its unrelenting fidelity, captured the unheard or unfinished murmur, the misunderstood and mystifying context, the disembodied voices asking for clarification and comfort. It also captured the impatience in *my* voice as children struggled for attention, approval, and justice. The tape recordings created for me an overwhelming need to know more about the process of teaching and learning and about my own classroom as a unique society to be studied." [27]

Having put forth these propositions, we realize that they too will need to be studied further in the context of each unique classroom society. How do these propositions play out with learning groups of older students and even adults? What are the implications of these propositions for learning groups in other cultures and contexts? Which features are similar across cultures and which are different? Clearly, the Reggio schools foster a culture in which group learning is nurtured and enhanced. Which elements of this culture can be usefully built on in other contexts?

Moreover, while some propositions refer to the role of adults as members of the learning groups, we would like to look more closely at the learning of adults in relation to the propositions. For example, how are the adults' learning styles influenced by the individuals in the group, and how do they in turn influence the group? How do the adults participate in the process of deciding on a group goal for a particular project or product, or of generating an aesthetic of knowledge?

Paley talks about the key to her own teaching and research as curiosity—not just about children's learning and points of view, but about her own role in the teaching and learning process. We see these propositions as an example of what can emerge when teachers become, in Paley's words, their "own best witness." Through the process of documentation, teachers bring together theory and practice; they become researchers of the human experience of teaching and learning. The propositions illustrate the powerful role documentation can play in the learning of both teachers and children.

elephants kissing

RE
PZ

Protagonists
Aurelia, 5 yrs. 9 mos.
Ferruccio, 6 yrs.
Giacomo, 5 yrs. 7 mos.
Luca, 6 yrs. 2 mos.
Teacher
Laura Rubizzi
School
Diana
Photographs and text by
Vea Vecchi

For some time, we have planned and developed situations that support and encourage exchange and communication, even over distance, by setting up in each classroom an area with small personal drawers, one for each child, the teachers, the atelierista, the cook, and the helpers. Over the three years they attend the preschool, the children modify the quality and quantity of messages they send and they progressively, *naturally*, inevitably move from "offerings" of small objects and drawings to written messages (whose aesthetic quality continues to be important).

A Group Message

The teacher suggests to a group of children that they send a written message to anyone they want. The children have different writing competencies: Aurelia can read and write by herself; Luca can recognize and write all the letters and is starting to form words; Giacomo can recognize all the letters, but his understanding of how to put them together to form a word has yet to come. (Ferruccio will join the group later.)

The children want to write a message to the inhabitants of another planet. They set themselves a number of questions: in which language they should write, if they should send a message made up of only pictures, and how to send the message.

Luca: *Maybe they only communicate with sound waves or with magnetic waves.*

Aurelia: *They might be immortal, or like worms that turn into two worms when you cut them.*

The list of what they do not know but want to know is very long. They decide that the most authoritative intermediaries in answering their questions are astronauts, so the children's first message will be for them.

Luca: *The only ones to ask are scientists and astronauts!*

(From left to right: Luca, Giacomo, Aurelia)
The children set out the material that might be needed to write a beautiful message because, as they say: *It's nicer to read a beautiful letter and they'll be nicer to us when they write back.*
The children decide how to organize their work.
Luca: *Let's do eeny meeny miny moe to see who has to write.*
All three seem convinced that they know how to write.

They each simultaneously count off three times, cheating so that it turns out that each one is the one who should write.

Luca and Giacomo work out an agreement between them, while Aurelia waits calmly and stubbornly, certain that she is the only one who knows how to write.

The teacher, who is listening off at the side, intervenes delicately in order to help the discussion evolve and to lead it toward an at least partial definition of and agreement on the kind of information they want to ask the astronauts.

The teacher then distances herself and the children get three sheets of lightweight paper, each one a different color, and Luca beings to write.

Aurelia: *He can't write everything because then they're all his ideas.*

Luca: *Your ideas are here too. Let's each write one word. Or how about three words?*

Aurelia: *How about if each of us writes something and then we glue everything together on sticky paper?*

Problems arise immediately, however, because Luca's and Giacomo's competencies are still quite undeveloped. First Luca, then Giacomo, ask Aurelia to help read what they've written and to make some suggestions.

One of the problems the teacher highlights as she reads (or rather, interprets) the written sentences aloud in the right tone of voice concerns the point of view of the person who receives the message, when what is written is not questions but affirmations.

The children, not knowing the purpose of a question mark, discuss how to make the communication clear.

Luca: *Let's put "I ask you" to make questions.*

When the children have experimented and understood a bit more about communication differences between a spoken and a written phrase, the teachers will talk about some marks like the question mark that direct communication.

The children play and laugh about the mistakes they have made, which twist words or make them meaningless. Errors are accepted as a natural part of learning and at times these mistakes become the driving force behind new learning.

Ferruccio is attracted by the fun the others are having and because of it becomes involved in writing a message. He has replaced Luca who, having written his message, has become bored and gone off to the classroom to find something more interesting to do.

Of the group, Ferruccio is certainly the one who has the fewest autonomous writing skills. Even Giacomo, along with Aurelia, can become the "teacher."

The mistakes in this case reach the height of hilarity.

Verbal suggestions are not enough, and Aurelia is required to intervene with her expertise.

Ferruccio completes his sentence under the watchful eye of his two friends, who assist him until the end in various (and intelligently opportune) ways.

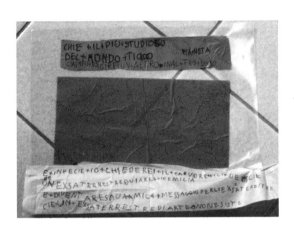

The message is finished.
The last discussion, which emerges after the teacher has intervened, concerns how to order the sentences in such a way that the communication is clear. The message is worked on in the following days and contains questions written by different children.

LETTER TO THE MOST EXPERT ASTRONAUT

HAVE YOU EVER HELPED AN EXTRATERRESTRIAL BE BORN?

*HOW DO EXTRATERRESTRIALS TALK?
I'M SURE THEY TALK; THEY AREN'T STUPID, BUT WE DON'T KNOW THEIR LANGUAGE.*

*ARE ALIENS AND EXTRATERRESTRIALS DIFFERENT KINDS OF PEOPLE?
ARE WE ANOTHER KIND OF PEOPLE?*

COULD THEY BE MADE OUT OF GREEN ROCK? OR SHOCKS? OR GAS? OR ARE THEY FULL OF OXYGEN AND CARBON DIOXIDE?

CAN EXTRATERRESTRIALS ALSO BE IMMORTAL?

CAN WE INVITE ALL THOSE GUYS FROM OTHER PLANETS TO COME TO EARTH?

DO YOU THINK THEY MIGHT BE BAD?

DO THEY HAVE CITIES OR ONLY GAS?

*IF THEY MEET US AND UNDERSTAND US WILL THEY FEEL BETTER?
IF WE SEND THEM SOME MAPS MAYBE THEY'LL BE MORE CONVINCED.*

Moving across the Atlantic

Ben Mardell

The Villetta School

Loom and overhead projector in the mini-atelier

In the winter of 1999, several members of the Project Zero research team visited the Villetta School in Reggio Emilia. After lunch we observed a meeting time in the five-year-olds' classroom. We sat just behind a circle of twenty children and their teachers who were discussing work that had taken place during the morning. A group of three children began to report on a project in which they were exploring the relationship between computer-generated and hand-created patterns and designs. In the current phase of their research, the children were decorating long strips of paper, which were then threaded into a large loom. Behind the loom an overhead projector illuminated a white bedsheet, simulating the glow of a computer screen. As the children explained how and why they had added several new strips to their pattern, the teacher involved in the project occasionally interjected comments; the other teacher and children asked clarifying questions. The report continued for fifteen minutes, taking up most of the meeting time.

The trio's report was, of course, in Italian. Part way through the explanation, one child became very concerned that we, the strangers sitting behind the group, were not understanding what had taken place. He stopped his presentation to the class, crossed the room, and addressed us directly, asking *Capite? Capite?* Through our translator, we communicated that yes, we had gotten the gist of the report. But the boy was not satisfied, and he was right to be concerned. We did not, despite the best efforts of our excellent translator, understand as he wanted us to. His standards for sharing were high, so he reexplained the situation to us, again in Italian, and again asked *Capite?*

It is now our turn to ask: *"Capite* (Do you understand)?" Like the boy from the Villetta School, we feel an urgency to convey our ideas. As even this brief story illustrates, groups can support a level of work and learning that is surprising and inspiring in its complexity. We believe that the ideas about learning in groups and the documentation presented here have tremendous potential to enrich American educational settings. Yet like the boy at Villetta, we suspect that despite the evocative prose and visual essays of the previous chapters, a full understanding may still be elusive.

Our suspicion is based on our own struggles with these complex ideas and our experiences describing them to other American educators. Our reports have been met with a mixture of excitement and skepticism. Although many have been intrigued by the possibilities of promoting group learning, a common reaction has been, "Isn't this just the same as cooperative learning?" In the face of a tendency to assimilate ideas into preexisting categories, differentiating our position from other perspectives and programs is a challenge.

The pedagogy of Reggio is especially difficult in this regard. The wide variety of responses that Reggio practices elicit bears witness to the confusion that they can cause among American educators. For example, many have been moved by the children's extraordinary drawings and sculptures, and by the teachers' beautiful and powerful documentation panels. At the same time, we have been told that it is impossible for young children to produce such outstanding work without undue adult interference, and that only by neglecting other more important responsibilities could teachers have the time to create such thoughtful pieces of documentation. While it is evident that there is much to be learned from this exemplary educational community, it is also clear that what happens in Reggio cannot simply be packaged and shipped across the Atlantic. The lessons we should derive from these schools are far from obvious.

In this section we continue to address the two main questions of this book: What is the nature of learning in groups? and How can documentation support this learning? We hope that the chapters in this section clarify our perspective on these questions. As we move into the American context, we add another question: Why are ideas about learning groups and documentation, especially as practiced in Reggio Emilia, challenging for Americans to understand? We feel that confronting this question directly affords the best opportunity to transcend these challenges and fully appreciate the significance of these ideas.

As the American half of the Making Learning Visible research team, we approach these questions informed by perspectives gleaned from work by our many colleagues at Project Zero. For more than thirty years Project Zero researchers have conducted studies with children, adults, and organizations aimed at understanding and enhancing thinking, learning, and creativity. Melding theory and practice, Project Zero's efforts often combine basic inquiry with work in schools toward the goal of fashioning more enlightened educational practices. (Background information about Project Zero is found in Appendix A.)

In this chapter we present several ways of thinking about issues that have been helpful in formulating our responses to the three questions above:

1) *Cultural knots*—assumptions, beliefs, and values that can block a full appreciation of situations;

2) *Reggio as a mirror*—using the schools in Reggio to help see our own practices in a clearer light;

3) *False dichotomies*—unnecessary simplifications of educational endeavors into either/ or terms.

Our intent is to provide a sense of how we formulated our American perspective as we, in this section, move across the Atlantic.

Cultural Knots

Be careful how you define the world; it is like that.
– Erich Heller, *The Disinherited Mind*

Educational decisions, from how to structure a meeting-time conversation, to when to intervene in a conflict between two children, to what to display on a bulletin board, are informed by assumptions, beliefs, and values about teaching and learning; in short, by educational worldviews. Take bulletin boards as a case in point. Display possibilities are endless. Options include commercially purchased artwork, posters with inspirational slogans ("We are all a team"), documentation of research by small groups of children (photographs, transcripts of conversations, products), and a piece of finished work by each child in the class. Though generally implicit, the decisions teachers make here are guided by their worldviews. For example, a decision to post work by each child is likely based on the assumption that fairness demands that all children be included in such displays, a belief in the importance of celebrating student achievements, and a belief that final products best represent these achievements. Other assumptions, beliefs, and values lead to other choices.

Educational worldviews—working theories of teaching and learning—are rooted in culture. They are indispensable in helping to make sense of classrooms and schools. Yet worldviews can limit as well as inform, at times preventing teachers, administrators, parents, and policymakers from fully appreciating situations and seeing possibilities. At this point, assumptions, beliefs, and values become what we call cultural knots.

Such a knot appears in the reaction of some to our story from the Villetta School. While most Americans see the value of children explaining their work to classmates, many American educators are surprised that the report of just three children would occupy the majority of such a sharing time. They see the apparent domination of a meeting by a few children as unfair. This reaction stems from assumptions, beliefs, and values about the relationship between individuals and groups. In general, Americans are wary of collectives, and assume that by joining groups, individuals risk forfeiting freedoms. We believe that individuals must be protected from groups. One popular protection is to establish mechanisms that ensure equity among group members. Thus, during meeting times in American early-childhood classrooms it is common for teachers to structure conversations to allow each child a brief opportunity to share thoughts on a given topic. Children often are not allowed to speak a second time until everyone has had a chance to speak once. Many teachers feel that there is no real alternative to such a structure. Yet fairness does not have to be equated with strict equity; important benefits can be sacrificed by such an interpretation of equal opportunity. Having come to see the importance of in-depth discussions and the power of children reporting about their work to others, we view the assumptions, beliefs, and values that constrain such conversations as a cultural knot.

Such knots are difficult to untie. We have deep, if largely unconscious, loyalties to familiar ways of thinking. We tend to assimilate reality into our existing worldviews rather than revise understandings based on experience.[1] Moreover,

crane
with passenger

280

because they are so deeply embedded in the social milieu, worldviews generally go unexamined.[2] The assumptions, beliefs, and values that form knots are part of our cultural legacy and are not easily transcended. However, encountering powerful ideas and educational practices with a spirit of self-reflection can help to identify and understand what lies behind our classroom practices.

Reggio as a Mirror

Cross-cultural comparisons, by throwing into sharp relief the assumptions, beliefs, and values that shape educational decisions, provide some of the most productive entry points into the examination of cultural knots.[3] Encounters with the pedagogical practice of other cultures make explicit our generally implicit educational worldviews, allowing an opportunity to reflect on the conceptual basis of our teaching. Contrasting practice can shake us into awareness by what T. S. Eliot, among others, called "making the familiar strange."[4]

Thus the cultural differences that make understanding the practices in Reggio difficult can also be a source of insight. Indeed, the pedagogy of the municipal preschools of Reggio Emilia provides a particularly rich opportunity for us to revisit our understandings of teaching and learning. Many similarities exist between progressive American education and the pedagogy of Reggio. On both sides of the Atlantic, there are attempts to engage students in long-term cooperative endeavors. Both cultures value education that nurtures the whole child, promotes individual children's potentials, and prepares children to be active members of their communities. The schools of Reggio draw us in because they represent an extraordinary realization of these goals. We view the exhibit "The Hundred Languages of Children," visit the Villetta School, or read about drawing "Ring-around-the-Rosy," and want to understand.

"Before we can understand the Reggio Emilia experience, we have to have an understanding of our own tradition and dominant discourses," writes Gunilla Dahlberg, a professor of education at the Institute of Education in Stockholm.[5] Dahlberg has been involved in more than twenty years of dialogue between Swedish and Reggio educators, the longest-standing international contact for Reggio schools. In order to engage fully with the ideas of Reggio, Swedish educators have had to wrestle with their own assumptions, beliefs, and values about pedagogical practice. For example, the Swedes had prided themselves on a "child-oriented" pedagogy. Encountering Reggio's image of the child forced them to examine the meaning of the term, determine whether they were living up to their own rhetoric, and explore how to achieve that goal. The results have been far-reaching, ultimately strengthening opportunities for children, parents, teachers, and even politicians (who have visited the schools of Reggio) to create and renew powerful educational settings. Swedish educators talk of Reggio serving "as a mirror in which we see ourselves and our traditions in a more conscious way."[6]

We believe Americans can approach Reggio in a similar spirit. By seeing what is and is not reflected in the mirror of Reggio, we can learn a great deal about American education. For example, in American schools we hear a lot about the importance of cooperation, teamwork, and children working together. Encountering the form and function of learning groups in Reggio forces us to examine the meaning of these terms, determine if we are living up to our rhetoric, and explore how to fully use the social nature of schooling to achieve our goals.

False Dichotomies

As we reflect on the pedagogy of Reggio, we note that many of the dichotomies that so many of us hold—teaching versus learning, theory versus practice, assessment versus curriculum, thinking versus feeling, adult versus child-directed curriculum, and individual versus group learning—are absent in Reggio schools. While it is convenient to think in either/or terms, many of these dichotomies strike us as false. In simplifying the complexity of the teaching and learning process, they do a disservice to our understanding of the classroom. Identifying and trying to resolve some of these dichotomies has proved useful in making sense of some very complex ideas about learning in groups and documentation.

If we think again about our visit to the Villetta School, we see that popular educational dichotomies have disappeared. Was the children's report to the class representative of individual or group learning? Was it part of an adult or child-directed curriculum? Were the children and teachers learning or teaching? Did the report involve teaching or the documentation of learning? The children's work comprised all of this and more. The children's explanation reflected their own individual learning as well as the learning of the group. Both children and adults played an active role in the report. As the children articulated their ideas and responded to questions from classmates and teachers, the entire class learned about the topic. At the same time, the trio's understanding of their research was deepened. Thus they were both teaching and learning. By providing insight into the thinking and competencies of the children, the report was also a kind of assessment.

The desire to simplify, to package reality into manageable categories, is a strong human impulse. Dichotomizing is a common strategy that flows from this impulse. While dichotomies provide an efficient way to categorize phenomena, they can be misleading in their oversimplification of the world's complexity. A passage from Italio Calvino's *Invisible Cities* is instructive here:[7]

"Marco Polo describes a bridge, stone by stone.

'But which is the stone that supports the bridge?' [asked the Khan]

'The bridge is not supported by one stone or another,' Marco answers, 'but by the line of the arch that they form.'

Kublai Khan remains silent, reflecting. Then he adds: 'Why do you speak to me of the stones? It is only the arch that matters to me.'
Polo answers: 'Without stones there is no arch.'"

As Calvino's Polo and the schools of Reggio exemplify, there are times when something is not one thing or the other, but both. This recognition can prove important when grappling with ideas about learning in groups and documentation.

Formulating an American Perspective

The previous sections of this book have focused on the theory and practice of learning groups and their documentation in the thirty-four municipal preschools and infant-toddler centers of Reggio Emilia. In this section we consider these issues in a more general way, and from an American perspective. Despite our move across the Atlantic, the fingerprints of our Italian colleagues are evident throughout this section. In fashioning responses to the three questions highlighted at the start of the chapter, we draw on and reflect on ideas and practices from Reggio, as well as from the United States.

In the four chapters that follow we employ several distinct styles of writing and draw on different disciplines, along with several Project Zero research initiatives, to afford further avenues to explore these topics. In our efforts to explain, we present a framework for understanding learning in groups, and use the theories and practices of Reggio as a mirror to reveal tensions in American education as well as to reflect promising practices in the United States. We also re-examine the relationship between teaching and research to suggest directions that can help us move forward in using these ideas.

Our exercise involves education writ large. While the Reggio schools focus on infants, toddlers, and preschoolers, we intentionally refer to and draw from learning contexts in elementary and secondary schools. Comparison of practices in American K-12 schools with those in the preschools in a relatively small Italian city may, at first glance, seem inappropriate, yet we believe the issues of learning in groups, and how documentation may be part of that learning, transcend age groups and subject matter.

Implicit in this book is the challenge of how to use these ideas to better support individual and group learning. This is not a simple challenge. Still, we believe that understanding the encounter of learning in groups and documentation is an important first step in forging new practices and in reclaiming valuable aspects of our own tradition.

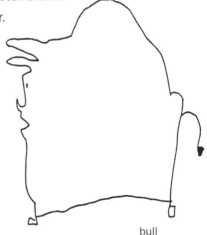

bull

Education will vary with the quality of life that prevails in a group.
– John Dewey, *Democracy and Education*

Four Features of Learning in Groups

Mara Krechevsky
and
Ben Mardell

Much, if not most, of the learning that goes on in and out of schools happens through the interactions of groups. Indeed, children are almost always in groups when they are in school. But are these learning groups? In most American schools, the focus of virtually all assessment and most aspects of instruction is on promoting individual work and learning. Yet the desire to learn from and with others is so powerful that even in institutions that tend to isolate children, students still learn from and with one another. How can teachers support and deepen the quality of learning that occurs whenever individuals are together in groups?

It is not always easy to distinguish between group and individual learning. At first glance, it seems that American practice is more focused on the individual and Reggio practice more on the group. Many American teachers are comfortable with a view of children as independent discoverers and constructors of their own meanings. They often take an inherently group setting—school—and try to individualize it; each child works on an individual product. Yet even with this emphasis on individual children and individual products, the types of activities, available materials, and time frame for working are often the same for all children in the class; the implicit message is one of conformity. Although there is no collective or group goal, all individuals in the group are working on the same individual things.

In this chapter we introduce a conceptualization of group learning that provides a framework for understanding and nurturing individual and group learning in the classroom. We offer a definition of learning groups and describe four features that distinguish our notions of group learning from other conceptualizations. The features suggest ways to reconcile some of the dichotomies so prevalent in education today, including the belief that teaching is for adults and learning is for children; that documentation and assessment are separate from the teaching and learning process; that learning and teaching are cognitive, rather than emotional and aesthetic, acts; and that learning groups are concerned with addressing individual, not group, knowledge. In putting forth this view, we draw on the experiences of the children, teachers, and parents in the Reggio Emilia preschools and infant-toddler centers as rich examples of learning in groups in early childhood.

tiger

One word about how this chapter relates to the propositions and visual essays in the previous section: While the propositions document individual and group learning strategies, the features offered here are an attempt to highlight the four aspects of group learning that have emerged most strongly for us in the course of our research collaboration with our Reggio colleagues. Although other features could be identified, we see these four as central to our view of group learning; without them, something important is lost. The features are one way to distinguish our conceptualization from other school-based notions of group learning, helping us determine the extent to which a group of individuals in school resembles a learning group. While the propositions can also be used in this way, they are the direct result of the pedagogical research of the Reggio educators. The propositions provide the visual and written documentation of how learning groups of young children and adults in Reggio classrooms form, function, and demonstrate understanding; the features are framed more generally with a view to understanding diverse learning contexts.

Our exploration of learning in groups is guided by two principles related to the nature of learning and the nature of groups. First, with regard to *learning*: Rather than reducing children's or adults' thinking and learning to discrete bits of information that can be produced via simple-answer questions, we are interested in the learning processes and outcomes involved in solving problems or creating products that are considered meaningful in a culture. This is in accord with Howard Gardner's definition of an intelligence as the ability to solve problems or fashion products that are valued in a culture or community.[1] We resist the tendency to simplify the complexity of either the individual's or the group's learning process or the content being learned. The type of learning in which we are interested engages students cognitively, emotionally, and aesthetically. It is situated in real-world problem solving that draws on critical and creative thinking as well as disciplinary knowledge and skills.

Second, by *group* we refer not only to what individuals learn by virtue of participating in a group, but also to a more distributed kind of learning that extends beyond the learning of any one person. Research suggests that we need to rethink our notions of human cognition as residing inside the heads of individuals and consider a view of knowledge as socially constructed and distributed among individuals, groups, and cultural tools and artifacts (such as books or computers).[2] We believe that participation in groups is key to the construction of individual learning. We also believe that group learning can lead to creating a community culture or collective knowledge that is larger than what any one individual knows.

We have defined a learning group as *a collection of persons who are emotionally, intellectually, and aesthetically engaged in solving problems, creating products, and making meaning—an assemblage in which each person learns autonomously and through the ways of learning of others*. Learning groups facilitate a kind of learning that is qualitatively different from that of individuals learning alone. Of course, even in groups individuals learn autonomously, constructing their personal understandings of the world. In this sense, all learning is individual. But when children and adults are in groups, they also learn from and with others. In groups we encounter new perspectives, strategies, and ways of thinking that enable us to learn from others. We also learn *with* others, modifying, extending, clarifying, and enriching our own ideas and those of others.

In putting forth this view of group learning, we draw on a long history of ideas about learning in groups ranging from studies on group processes in social psychology to current educational interest in cooperative and project-based learning. Although cognitive and developmental psychology have traditionally focused on the development and psychology of the individual, over the past few decades interest in the social and distributed nature of learning has increased dramatically. For example, according to Vygotsky's sociocultural perspective, development is inherently social.[3] Vygotsky maintained that all thought appears first on an interpersonal level, then on an intrapersonal level.[4] He believed that our ways of thinking are transformed internalizations of social interactions. The social nature of development reaches into all aspects of human experience. From birth most of us are guided into ways of thinking, feeling, and behaving by family, peers, and others. Even when ostensibly working alone, individuals rely on socially created tools and artifacts. In this way, all cognitive activity is bound to a social context.

Recent years have seen increasing interest of American educators in cooperative learning, which in the United States often takes the form of techniques used by teachers for organizing classroom activities.[5] It is primarily incorporated in elementary school classrooms above the first grade. Most of the research that looks at the effects of cooperative learning strategies focuses on the mastery of well-defined content or skills.[6] Typical cooperative learning techniques include using group rewards based on individual achievement, assigning particular roles or tasks to individual members of small groups of children, or peer tutoring. Teamwork skills such as building trust, managing conflict, and decision making are deemed crucial to the success of these efforts. While our conceptualization of group learning shares principles that underlie various forms of cooperative learning (for example, a commitment to providing experiences in which children can learn from and with one another), it differs from cooperative learning research and practice in a number of ways. Let us now describe the four features (see figure 2) that characterize our conceptualization of learning groups.

figure 2

The members of learning groups include adults as well as children.

Documenting children's learning processes helps to make learning visible and shapes the learning that takes place.

Members of learning groups are engaged in the emotional and aesthetic as well as the intellectual dimensions of learning.

The focus of learning in learning groups extends beyond the learning of individuals to create a collective body of knowledge.

1. The members of learning groups include adults as well as children.

One way in which our view of group learning in school departs from others is by the inclusion of adults (parents, teachers, other school staff, community members) as members of the learning group. In most American schools, even when we engage students in group learning, we maintain a view of children as learners and adults as teachers. In many cooperative learning approaches, the adult's role is seen as that of "implementer." In an article on peer education, William Damon suggests: "The role of the adult supervisor in a peer collaboration group should be first to keep the children focused on the task at hand and second to review with the children what they have learned after the task is completed. Adults should not interject their own knowledge or opinions about tasks during children's group discussions."[7]

While we would agree that adults and children play different roles in a learning group, we believe that every member of a learning group engages in inquiry. All individuals in a school contribute to a culture of teaching and learning. Teachers, of course, bring to this culture a different background and set of skills than children. The teachers' role includes listening to and observing children, providing occasions for discovery and joy, and intervening at critical moments. By systematically observing and documenting children's work, teachers develop new ideas about teaching and learning. Curriculum resembles a journey, and topics of study become research projects. Rather than being seen as the sole or primary sources of information, teachers help children enlist the cognitive and emotional support of their peers. Teachers also serve as the group's memory, reminding children of their earlier work and comments.

In American schools we are all familiar with learning goals for students. Less commonly considered are learning goals for teachers that identify what they would like to learn from classroom experiences. Reggio teachers generate learning goals for themselves such as: How can we expand and deepen our understanding of children's construction of their knowledge and skills? What are the connections between the mental images recalled from memory, the verbal language, and the visual language? What are the tools that can elicit the most cognitive and emotional processes for children? The focus is on the act of learning. Teachers try to make learning visible and collect data that will inform the design of other kinds of learning experiences for children. Through books, exhibits, and other products, teachers share what they learn with other teachers in the same school, teachers from other schools, and other audiences.

Parents too can actively participate in this culture by contributing their expertise and support and helping to document children's work in the learning groups. For example, teachers at the Villetta School noticed at the start of the year that children were spending a great deal of time experimenting and playing with water.[8] Observing the children more closely and recording their conversations, the teachers realized that the children were creating theories and hypotheses about the movement of the water. The teachers

A parents' meeting

shared their observations with parents, who decided to elect a committee of "experts" to work on the hypotheses generated by the children. The committee designed and built a system of pumps and pipes so that the children could continue experimenting with water.

In learning groups, parents become interested not just in their own child's learning, but in learning and child development in general. Parents bring to learning groups their knowledge of their children, their educational hopes and values, and their competencies and interests. Parents in Reggio often generate their own research questions to investigate (for example, How do children celebrate birthdays at home and at school? What is the role of action figures in children's play?) and then share their findings with others.

Community members and organizations extend the learning environment beyond the walls of the classroom and connect children to the life of the community. Rather than simply bringing in community members for isolated, one-time visits, teachers and children draw on the community as additional members of the learning group who contribute to the ongoing research. When children at the Diana School decided they needed another table for their classroom, they suggested calling in a carpenter.[9] When the carpenter arrived, he explained that he needed dimensions from the children. The challenge to provide measurements for the table became the focus of investigation for a small group of children, who kept the rest of the class informed about their progress. The teachers focused on understanding and supporting the children's learning processes as they went about creating a system of measurement.

The carpenter with the children

2. Documenting children's learning processes helps to make learning visible and shapes the learning that takes place.

At the heart of our conceptualization is the role of documentation and assessment in shaping the nature of individual and group learning and in making that learning visible. As education moves from a transmission model of knowledge to an inquiry orientation, documenting children's learning becomes a key tool for the learning of both teacher and children. Through documentation children and adults have the opportunity to revisit, individually and collectively, the work and activities they have planned and carried out. In many American classrooms engaged in cooperative learning, the separation between curriculum and assessment persists, and the assessment paradigm remains one of measurement and evaluation. Children are expected to master relatively well-defined skills or information, which can then be displayed and evaluated in measures that are designed to be quick, efficient, and "objective." The role of teachers as documenters of student thinking, activity, and learning is far too small a part of this model. Our conceptualization of group learning seeks to alter this situation fundamentally and promote assessment practices that involve teachers' observation and documentation skills.

Documentation makes children's ways of constructing knowledge—including the relational and emotional aspects—visible to both adults and children. Teachers share children's work and words with parents, they refer to children's conversations when they speak to them, and they put quotations from children's speech and samples of children's work on the walls. Teachers also generate and post their own reflections on a project or experience. Documenting children's learning is not about creating beautiful panels or displays, but about following and shaping the knowledge-building process. It allows teachers to deepen their understanding of children's strengths and interests, different languages or domains of knowledge, their own actions and pedagogical decisions, and the processes of learning.

Teachers discussing documentation

Documenting children's learning can help create a collective memory for the group, allowing children to return to their thoughts and ideas and pursue them either individually or in groups. When children work on projects and products that are stored in personal places without opportunity for exchange and comparison of ideas and activities, the group remains merely a collection of individuals. We will see in the next chapter that portfolios, for example, are often considered personal collections of work. Making visible in the classroom images of learning and being together in a group fosters a sense of group identity and generates other possibilities for extending and deepening learning. Looking at earlier drawings and comments allows children to build on and critique their previous thoughts and hear reactions from their peers. Theories can be developed and modified. Documenting children's work in this way enables everyone involved to learn about a particular project and about children's learning processes more generally. Such documentation helps children tell the story of their own learning and sustains the continuity of their experience.

Further, the act of documenting changes teachers' understanding of what goes on in the classroom. It slows them down, encouraging them to reflect on and understand the deeper meaning and value of a learning experience. It forces them to compare what they thought they would observe to what really went on, and informs their decisions about where to go next. Documenting children's learning entails making decisions about the moments and experiences that are most meaningful to record. Rather than trying to tell the whole story of an experience or putting up the work of every child, teachers become selective about what to document. Instead of simply describing the experience of a learning group, this view of documentation involves a deeper analysis of the purposes behind it and behind the related learning processes and products. Since it is often through discussion with others that we become clearer about our beliefs and values, collaboration with colleagues becomes a particularly significant part of the process. Both Reggio educators and American teachers who have learned from the Reggio experience attest to the importance of documenting, studying, and collectively analyzing children's individual and group work for sharpening and deepening the focus of learning.[10]

Documentation also contributes to children's own developing understanding of how they learn, and of how others learn. It offers them an opportunity for reflection, for evaluation of other children's theories and hypotheses, and for self-assessment. It provides a structured way for children to remember their own progress, knowledge, and doubts as well as those of others. As we have seen, Reggio educators frequently ask children to share with their friends or a teacher what they have learned in an activity or experience. A common question during work on a project is, "What can you do to remember what you did and communicate it to others?" Moreover, as children learn how to learn in groups, they come to rely as much on their peers and themselves as on the teacher for feedback and problem solving. Teachers are not seen as the only source of information. One by-product of this shift is that teachers can devote more time to documentation, or engage in extended interactions or conversations with one or more children, while the rest of the class continues to work on its own. Documenting children's work in this way sends a strong message that children's efforts and ideas are taken seriously.

3. Members of learning groups are engaged in the emotional and aesthetic as well as the intellectual dimensions of learning.

In our view, learning in groups—like all meaningful learning—should engage the emotions as well as the intellect. Many teachers, when choosing topics of study that meet the learning goals of their curriculum, try to take into account the interests of their students. Yet cognitive learning goals often remain unconnected to other forms of learning. Most approaches to cooperative learning involve learning basic skills, factual knowledge, and the application of basic algorithms.[11] In our view, children and adults in learning groups should be engaged in the emotional and aesthetic as well as the cognitive dimensions of learning.

Reggio educators consider the environment the "third educator." They often look to materials and the environment to see what processes they promote. They seek out materials or phenomena that will turn the ordinary into the extraordinary. For example, in the study of light in which children explored different objects projected on the overhead, teachers sought out materials that would charm, trick, and amuse the children. They decided to give them vellum, an architectural paper that looks transparent but casts an opaque shadow, and provide water in a bowl and in a plastic bottle to create unusual effects of fluidity and motion.

Often, before introducing a particular set of materials or tools into the classroom, Reggio educators investigate the objects themselves. They study the materials with an eye to the types of intellectual, emotional, and aesthetic processes potentially induced. For example, teachers might ask themselves, Do

cable lift

these materials promote a sense of wonder? Do they generate unexpected transformations or strong aesthetic effects? They believe that pleasure is aesthetic and can coordinate the actions of children. When children take pleasure in materials immersed in light, for example, the experience becomes precious to them. Reggio educators believe that scientific thought is advanced through this aesthetic dimension. As we saw in the last section, young children in Reggio seem to develop a sensitivity to an aesthetic of knowledge that enables them to choose among competing ideas and theories.

Teachers look for topics of study and projects that will be intellectually and emotionally stimulating for the adults as well. They nurture within themselves a sense of adventure and a willingness to take risks in following the varied paths of children's interests. Teachers experience the excitement of learning along with the children. Indeed, they may propose projects for which they themselves are not sure of the outcomes. In the "Dinosaur" project described by Rankin, the adults decided to challenge the children to draw a life-size dinosaur and find a way to hang it so that it would stand upright.[12] The teachers did not know if the children could succeed at this task; they based their proposal on the intensity of interest that children had exhibited—and the teachers had documented—in the size of dinosaurs.

Small groups are particularly effective for this kind of learning, typically involving no more than five or six children (see Proposition I). Most cooperative learning methods suggest four-person groups, though few studies have actually compared learning and interaction in small groups of different sizes.[13] Because of the small size, it is often possible to create groups of children who share high passion for a topic. Indeed, as we have noted, Reggio educators frequently set up initial explorations of a topic in which they can observe which children show the greatest interest and enthusiasm before forming a learning group.

When documenting children's activity, teachers maintain their multiple foci on the intellectual, emotional, and aesthetic aspects of learning. In studying and analyzing tape-recorded conversations, adults listen for the topics that stimulate the most interest and passion. In the "Landscapes of Light" project, teachers noticed that children used the overhead projector and materials in at least three ways. Some children told narratives with characters and plot based on surprise and aesthetic pleasure; others created performances of their own, using the beam of light as a stage; still others concentrated on making optical discoveries. This knowledge informed the opportunities teachers provided to extend and deepen children's learning and motivation. In this instance, they decided to welcome children and parents to school in the mornings by placing on the overhead a natural material such as a leaf, which generated a strong aesthetic effect. Over time, children began to bring in objects from home to place on the overhead. Teachers eventually projected a scenario of arranged objects on the overhead above

Images from a project on trees at the Diana School

the children's mattresses in the nap room.

Another way to think about this feature is that *what* a learning group learns is not separate from *how* the group learns (another false dichotomy). The way learning groups form and function is integrally related to what the group comes to understand. The process of working, feeling, and thinking together can be as important as the content of learning. Too often in the United States, even in classrooms where students engage in cooperative and project-based learning, the focus of the curriculum is on individual skill development. We do not believe that cognitive moments should be separated from other aspects of an experience. Carla Rinaldi refers to a research project motivated by the children's interest in a family of cats living on the school grounds as a process of research on "catness."[14] Rather than separating out bits of knowledge about "cats," the term "catness" suggests exploring the range of meanings we associate with cats, from cultural to emotional to scientific.

In a project on trees at the Diana School, children learned about trees in at least three ways: exploring them through the senses; close observation and representations of trees and parts of trees in different media; and conversations and drawings about various aspects of trees, including how they might feel and look in different situations.[15] To bring trees and children into even closer relationship, the adults proposed that the children adopt a tree. Significant attention was given to the scientific knowledge and aesthetic qualities of trees, as well as to children's feelings and attitudes about trees.

4. The focus of learning in learning groups extends beyond the learning of individuals to create a collective body of knowledge.

Learning groups, in our view, are much like scientific communities or scholarly disciplines in that they focus on building collective as well as individual knowledge. Most cooperative learning and other group learning techniques are seen primarily as instructional strategies that can help raise individual achievement. Even when collaborative learning refers to "give-and-take," it is usually give-and-take between children working on their own individual products and end results.[16] According to one well-known set of cooperative learning proponents, "the purpose of cooperative groups is to make each student a stronger individual...[S]tudents learn together how to perform even better individually."[17] Mixed-age grouping and peer consultation are other ways to allow teachers to give one-on-one attention to individual students.

While we acknowledge that learning is always individual, we think it is critical to consider the social construction and existence of knowledge as well. Learning in a group supports a quality of learning that is different from individual learning. A focus on collective understanding—requiring constant comparison, discussion, and modification of ideas—makes possible learning that is not accessible to individuals working alone. Individual ideas are immediately put in circulation for discussion with the group. Team sports provide an instructive example. When individuals learn how to play together on a team, they need to learn how to coordinate their actions. Although what the players learn resides in their individual minds, the knowledge is by and large useless to them as individuals; their skills emerge only when they are playing with others on the team. In school, as in sports, it is important not to artificially separate individual from group learning. Each must be considered in the context of the other.

As we noted earlier, interdisciplinary research on situated learning and cognition suggests that we will understand more about human learning and development if we recognize the distributed nature of knowledge among both individuals and the tools and artifacts of a culture.[18] For example, Ann Brown and her colleagues have designed classroom environments in which a distributed network of expertise is created among all the learners in the community.[19] Marlene Scardamalia, Carl Bereiter, and their colleagues have put forth a model of knowledge-building communities in which individuals are dedicated to sharing and advancing the knowledge of the group.[20] In these classrooms the focus of learning goes beyond individual learning to the goal of advancing the body of knowledge itself. Rather than simply completing a series of discrete activities and school tasks, children and adults feel they are contributing to a larger, more meaningful whole, one they can share in and communicate to others.

As part of this process of generating collective knowledge, members of learning groups sometimes try to create what Reggio educators call "work in agreement." Children and adults might agree on which elements a project or product needs to share—say, the size of the clay figures in the group representation of a crowd or the role of public spaces in the creation of a city map. This agreement results not from a sense of conformity, but from a sense of aesthetic integrity. The group performance or product builds on the work of each individual; it is not antagonistic to it. Teachers play a delicate and complex role here: they may help to facilitate discussion or frame goals, serve as resources, or intervene when children get bogged down.

Crowd made of paper

Many Americans view schools as a way to prepare children to be effective citizens by helping them acquire certain skills, key bodies of knowledge and ideas, and habits of mind. Preschools, in particular, do not receive much support or respect in our culture. They are regarded as serving a custodial function for socialization and play, or as places to develop pre-reading, pre-writing, and pre-arithmetic skills. In Reggio, schools—preprimary schools—are seen as places to document human learning, places where children's voices can be heard, respected, and shared with the wider community. Schools are based on a network of relationships. They do not simply prepare children for adult or later life; they are seen as essential to life. Schools in Reggio are considered privileged places where culture should be reproduced and developed. They are sites of educational research that are fundamental to our understanding of how knowledge is constructed. Teachers try to enact in daily life a permanent process of research that occurs whenever children and teachers work together in groups. Through systematic documentation of children's learning, teachers and children create the artifacts that become a school's culture. Schools do not merely reflect the surrounding culture, they re-elaborate and develop that culture. In this view, learning groups not only transmit culture and knowledge, they create them.

John Dewey claimed that education varies with the quality of life in a group. The work of the political scientist Robert Putnam suggests that the quality of our public—if not private—lives will vary with the groups of which we are members.[21] Putnam's work demonstrates the critical importance of social networks and civic engagement for the success of our social institutions and a democratic way of life. (In fact, Putnam points to northern Italy as an example of a community that works, having functioned successfully for seven centuries as a civil society.)[22] The experiences of the preschools and infant-toddler centers of Reggio Emilia challenge us to rethink our notions about the relationship between individual and group learning. As Carla Rinaldi says: "The intellectual and emotional learning which come about in and through the group create a quality of individual knowledge which is completely different. We not only learn how to be social, but we learn through this sociality, which leads us to become different individuals."[23] In the United States, the rhetoric and practice around groups is not aligned. Our future depends on our ability to provide children with opportunities to become "different individuals"—individuals who know how to listen, who acknowledge and respect diverse points of view, who work with others to solve problems, and who can interpret and understand the world in increasingly complex ways.

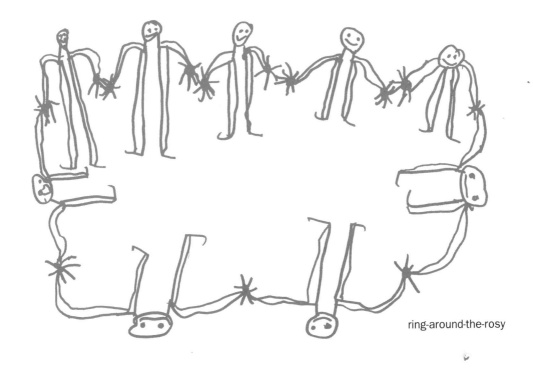

ring-around-the-rosy

Protagonists
Alice, 5 yrs. 8 mos.
Erika, 6 yrs.
Federica, 5 yrs. 7 mos.
Teachers
Simona Laiacona
Paola Barchi
Giovanni Piazza
School
Villetta
Photographs by
Giovanni Piazza
Text by
Giovanni Piazza

The Wheel and Movement

In the historical period we are living through, children and youths have more and more opportunities to play and experiment with intelligent and interactive machine models. In their homes, we find many different kinds of toys that use diverse technologies and mechanical systems, such as small humanoid and transformer robots.

The technological complexity of these objects, their functions, which are not always easy to infer, and the fascinating power of their movements and transformations, envelop them with an aura of mystery that immediately captures children's attention.

It also seems to us that the children can perceive these complex relationships which, as they often state in their discussions, make the robots behave as if they were alive, almost like living organisms, endowed not only with intelligence but also with human sensitivity, moods, expectations, and thoughts. At school as well, among the many materials available, the children can find toy robots or, if they wish, they can bring their own from home, as they do with many other kinds of toys.

While working within a broader project, a group of girls decides to build a robot.

At this initial stage, the girls choose to start the project using paper, because of its great pliability and their familiarity in working with it.

This material, however, despite being pertinent to the project in many respects, turns out to present a number of problems in relation to construction that the children could not have anticipated.

Federica: *Hey, you know what happened yesterday? The robot played a trick on us.*

Alice: *Yeah, a trick. It wouldn't stand up, it kept falling down because the wheels we built were wobbly and it was falling down.*

Federica: *I think it fell down because we put lots of wheels on, but we made a mistake when we put them on, so it got wobbly.*

Erika: *Look, mine fell off too! All of them!*

Alice: *We have to think about them more carefully! We need stronger wheels! I'm going to make them wider so they're sturdier.*

The group goes right back into action. Alice combs through the atelier looking for ideas. She moves from shelf to shelf but not in a superficial way; perhaps she already has an intuition but is not cognizant of its form, and perhaps she is not able to express it through verbal language.

Alice: *We need some round shapes.*

Erika joins Federica; together they think that it would be better to make some new and stronger wheels. They take the white cardboard again and start cutting.

Erika: *We have to make a little tube like the one we made to stand the robot up.*

Federica: *Nice and tough, strong like a pillar!*

Meanwhile, Alice has found a spinning top with the colors of the spectrum. The object immediately captures her attention.

Alice: *That's what I was looking for, a round wheel. Look how it turns... see how fast it goes... it's got strength inside it.*

The three girls, Alice on one side of the table and Federica and Erika on the other, are working out some new construction strategies. During this stage of the work, action prevails over the spoken language: the few comments they make act as reinforcement to the more operational aspect of the investigation.

Alice: *This is a fast wheel, see how well it turns? If you push it, it turns really fast.*

Alice has definitely speeded up the pace of her construction work.

She takes a piece of white cardboard, places the spinning top on it and traces the wheel twice, making sure that she traces the center very carefully. Then she looks for a punch and makes a hole in the center of the wheel. She then widens the hole with a pencil and checks to see if the wheel works.

Alice proceeds with her investigation and keeps making disks for her wheels. The rings of paper that Federica and Erika are constructing attract her attention. She seems to be interested in the development of their investigation.

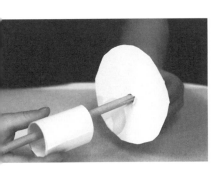 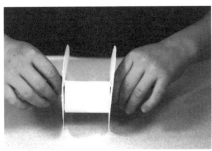 

After watching her friends, Alice borrows the idea of Erika's tube of paper and works out a new solution for the wheel that is a combination of the two thoughts that are being worked with in the group.

Alice is highly satisfied with the new wheel model she has made.
Alice: *Federica, do you like my wheel? Look how it turns!*
Federica: *Yeah, I've seen it, it's great. It's nearly a real wheel, and ours is great, too.*

Erika and Federica's idea is to work on the wheel's circumference. They are interested in making their wheels sturdier, and construct different wheel models that they try out on the robot as they go along.

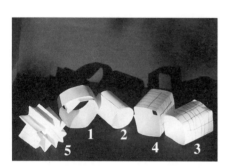

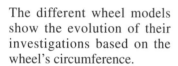

The different wheel models show the evolution of their investigations based on the wheel's circumference.

Despite the variations of shape from a cylinder to a square to a star, the wheel does not achieve the necessary degree of sturdiness to support the robot.

The attempt to strengthen the tube seems to have been successful. The girls feel the tube with their hands; they check to see how strong it is and declare it to be fit for its purpose.

Erika and Federica are satisfied. When submitted to the test, the tube supports the weight of the robot but does not turn.

Federica: *I think you need a stick inside it, in the middle, like Alice's, so it can turn.*

Erika: *Maybe that's what it needs.*

Alice's approach clearly shows a search for new possibilities of combination. From one initial model, she goes on to make structures with two, three, and four elements.

During this stage of the work there is little use of verbal language. Alice speaks only when testing her models. In the meantime, she checks to see what the others are doing, glancing across to the other side of the table.

Alice uses a piece of wire to hold the wooden rod.

Alice: *This wheel is just what we needed for the spiderstar robot. All you need is a piece of wire to hold the wheel. It sure doesn't have any bolts, it's made of paper!*

Federica: *I think you need the outside of the wheel, too, so it looks more like a wheel.*

Erika and Federica ask Alice to explain to them what they need to do. She feels very important in her role as an expert on wheels.

At this point, the construction models are all based on the same model and the individual and group strategies overlap. When combined in different structures, the models give rise to different forms, but they all work. Testing the models will provide a comparison of their different technical and mechanical characteristics.

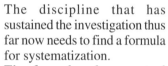

The discipline that has sustained the investigation thus far now needs to find a formula for systematization.

The formal and perceptual acceptance of a model is not sufficient: what is needed now is to find a kind of construction rule that belongs to the whole group.

Alice: *Erika, your wheel looks like the wheel of a truck. It rolls and it's real strong. See? You can put both your hands on it and it won't break.*

Federica: *Your wheel is a four-wheel one, Alice. There are four of them and it rolls well, but the circles outside are kind of thin. See how they bend if you press them down?*

The new wheel, which the girls construct together and represents an aggregate of the research of each child, seems to be more functional and more attractive. The girls adopt it as the model for making the other wheels that are still needed for the robot.

Federica: *But wait a minute! We've only made three wheels—we need lots more. I'm just going to count them.*

Erika: *More wheels, always wheels, what a drag! But we already know how to make them!*

Federica: *Well, but if you don't help us, how's the robot going to work?*

Erika: *It's like a train of wheels!*

Alice: *A train of all our wheels.*

302

In the course of their work, the girls used the stumbling blocks and construction "errors" they encountered as a reason for reworking the meaning of movement and relaunching it as a theme.

The process of individual learning within the group brought into focus the progressive construction of a body of knowledge that belongs to the group itself. During the final stage of the experience, the girls' sense of being a group engaged in research gradually became consolidated.

They also showed an increased awareness that they could, either individually or together, draw from the knowledge produced by the group, on the basis that this knowledge, in itself, is not tied to the uniqueness of any one person, but is available to everyone for building new knowledge.

Understanding Documentation Starts at Home

Steve Seidel

The actual practice of documentation and assessment in most American schools provides a stark contrast to the same type of work in the preschools of Reggio Emilia. The differences in these practices are multiple and deep. Certainly they grow from profound distinctions between the social, political, aesthetic, and historical environments of the preschools in Reggio Emilia and the environments of schools in the United States. Indeed, the words at the heart of this conversation—assessment, documentation, teaching, learning, group—are in some cases understood so differently that it is reasonable to wonder how to establish a basis for meaningful conversation.

Every aspect of our collaboration has provoked conversation, debate, and reflection on the meanings of words, how contexts inform meanings, and the understandings and values that inform practices. Our project was not, strictly speaking, a one-way study of practices in Reggio. It was, rather, a collaborative investigation of our separate and joint understandings of the nature of learning in groups and of ways in which documentation can play a critical role in nurturing that learning. Experiences and perspectives from both sides of the ocean have contributed. We grounded much of our investigation of learning groups in the Reggio experience, for it provided a mirror in which to reflect and reconsider American practices and perspectives. Yet the degree to which we developed our understanding of these aspects of learning and teaching is due in large measure to the identification of common values and meaning, while not denying significant areas of difference.

In this chapter we examine certain aspects of the American practice of documentation and assessment, explore Project Zero's work in these areas, and consider possible connections between documentation, assessment, and learning in groups—activities that many American educators tend to think of as separate endeavors. The chapter reflects our own vacillations between perspectives that generate feelings of hope and inspiration, and those that provoke frustration and inadequacy. We recognize many aspects of our experience as an internalization of extraordinary tensions within American education—in particular, differences in the perception of children and childhood, the teacher and teaching, and the school and its relation to its community.

Documentation as Assessment

In the preschools in Reggio Emilia, documentation is viewed as "assessment." As demonstrated in the visual essays that appear earlier in this book, in other books from Reggio, and in the many panels of documentation on the walls of Reggio preschools, documentation is both a product and a process that seeks to represent in words and images the working, playing, and learning of groups and individuals.

In the United States, the practice of assessment is most often thought of as synonymous with evaluation and, in an American context, evaluation is a process of

dragonfly

judgment, measuring or placing one work in relation to other works. Documentation is frequently seen as marks in a record book. When documentation is thought of in more elaborate terms, it becomes something for which there is no time. There has been considerable struggle and tension relative to this subject. Throughout the last century, though with notable exceptions, assessment in American schools has been dominated by the practice of giving tests to determine whether children have learned what they were supposed to learn. These tests have taken many forms—from pop quizzes to short essays to standardized tests administered to students across an entire district, state, or even the whole country. While there is little standardized testing in American preschools, anecdotal evidence from early-childhood educators notes that recent rounds of testing of second graders have had a significant effect on prekindergarten and kindergarten curriculum, pushing it toward more traditional "skill and drill."

What characterizes virtually all of these tests is a tendency toward short answers, choices between various options, and quick responses to decontextualized "factual" questions.[1] Few options are available for representing one's thoughts. A premium is placed on speed. These tests rarely, if ever, allow children to think and work together, let alone solve problems in an environment approximating "real-life" conditions. In short, our approach to assessment is individual, decontextualized, and focused on bits of knowledge or problem solving by use of the taught algorithm.

At Project Zero we have often found it useful to make a more marked distinction between assessment and evaluation. Rather than seeing them as identical processes, we have argued for a distinction that identifies assessment as processes for coming to understand many and varied aspects of ways of learning and teaching. It can be related directly to a particular child, to groups of children, to work in particular disciplines or across disciplines. The purpose of this conception is a deeper understanding of learning and the development of stimulating learning environments. At Project Zero, we thereby identify an affinity with Reggio's perspective on documentation and assessment, recognizing that our distinction between assessment and evaluation is not one commonly made in the United States.

Certainly the contrast between these practices and the forms of documentation presented by our Reggio colleagues is dramatic. It is hardly standard practice in American schools to consider "documentation as assessment" or to see documentation as an inextricable element in the effective functioning of a learning group.

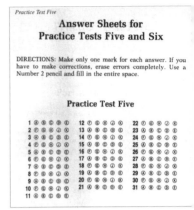

Standardized test score sheet

Affinities within Our Traditions

Our American schools and Reggio's preschools seem in many ways to be an ocean apart— literally and metaphorically. Yet many practices and, indeed, many pedagogical traditions exist in the United States that provide a rich set of connections with the ideas and pedagogy of the preschools in Reggio. The strength of these practices and traditions,

Children involved
in visual arts and music
(Project Spectrum)

if not their widespread acceptance, may help to explain the deep attraction many American educators feel to Reggio's pedagogy and unique approach to documentation. Considerable work at Project Zero also demonstrates an underlying deep affinity between our research and that of our Italian colleagues, despite some significant differences on the surface.

Notably, our "Spectrum" project, which developed approaches to assessment in early-childhood settings, shared with Reggio a mutual focus on children's capabilities and intellectual strengths, a respect for the integrity of materials, and a reliance on close observation and documentation of children's work. Further, they shared a deep concern for providing children with diverse materials and problems with which to work. The urgency of this need grows from the belief that children need multiple languages and intelligences in which to grow, develop, and learn.[2]

Beyond Project Zero, many elements of the progressive tradition in American education embrace visions of the child, the teacher, and the classroom that resonate with those held in Reggio. The nature study movement at the turn of the last century,[3] the "project method" promoted by William Heard Kirkpatrick in 1925,[4] and the child study movement[5] established both curricular and assessment practices that focused on the actions, language, ideas, and interactions of children at work in rich environments on complex problems. The proliferation of "lab schools" was a development drawing directly from the work of John Dewey and his colleagues in Chicago and then in New York City and elsewhere.[6] This tradition of schools that are also centers of research continues, though usually in more modest fashion, with a wide array of teacher research initiatives and study or inquiry groups. Some of these are directly connected to school improvement initiatives, and others have evolved from efforts such as the Philadelphia Learning Cooperative to make inquiry and research a significant element of teachers' professional practice.[7]

In recent decades, the distinctive work of Patricia Carini and her colleagues at the Prospect Archives and Center for Education and Research, and the Prospect School in North Bennington, Vermont, has demonstrated the possibility of creating school environments in which close observation of children is central to the work of teaching. Extensive documentation from the classroom provided the material for Carini's pioneering analytic processes for observations of children and examination of children's work.[8] The Prospect Center, with an archive of thousands of pieces of student work and countless observational records of children at work and play in school, is a resource and inspiration for teachers and others dedicated to the study of children and childhood. Many concerns and beliefs connect these various experiences and experiments with the work in Reggio: the image of the child as tremendously capable and ready to exercise intellectual, social, moral, and aesthetic potential in solving problems and exploring the world; the right of children to work with excellent materials; the social

306

nature of learning; and a sense of collaboration between children and adults in the learning enterprise.

Another affinity between our educational traditions is a concern for the epistemological questions at the center of the experience of teaching and learning.[9] How do we come to understand the world and our experience of it? How do we change our minds about how and why things are as they are, evolving and deepening our understanding? How can one person come to understand another's understanding? In what ways can the effort to understand another's understanding become the foundation of a serious pedagogy?

Through the clamor of recent educational debates in the United States over the purposes of schooling and the best ways to achieve those purposes, some voices maintain a focus on understanding as a primary goal of time spent in school. In Project Zero's work, "teaching for understanding" has emerged in the last decade as a central concern. This work addresses fundamental questions, such as What is understanding? How does it develop? How might we know it when we see it? What can we do to create learning environments that support and nurture the development of deep understandings?

These questions, and efforts to explore what answers might look like in the actual practice of teaching and learning in classrooms at various age levels, have led to the development of a framework that builds "ongoing assessment" into the fabric of the learning experience, involves students as well as teachers, and provides ample opportunity for self-assessment and reflection on one's work and thinking. Although the focus is on products and "performances of understanding," the concern remains centered on how one has come to understand ideas and phenomena, and how one demonstrates that understanding—all in a context that recognizes understanding as fluid and evolving.[10]

In this epistemological context, documentation in the classroom takes on a particular hue. It becomes focused on the "stuff" of understanding—ideas, theories, hypotheses, feelings, experiments, deductions, notions of cause and effect, imagination, intuitions, "performances," and the relationship of experience, skill, knowledge, and insight— cognitive processes involved in coming to know something. Reggio's documentation is full of such stuff. In documentation, we see that recording and presenting children's actions and interactions can reveal the genesis of ideas and then, in being shared with the group, can lead to new thoughts, questions, and discoveries.

In the visual essay "Ring-around-the-Rosy," for example, we can see the thinking of individual children as they struggle with the problems inherent in making two-dimensional representations of three-dimensional life. Following those children through the essay, we come to see not only the thinking of the individuals, but the ways in which the children encounter each other's thinking, how they work to make their ideas and ways of thinking clear to each other, and in the end how some appropriate the ways of thinking of others. In this close study of a slice of life in one room of the Diana School, we see the actual birth of ideas in the exchanges between Giulia, Leonardo, and Giovanni. For many reasons, not the least being a limited tradition of philosophy in our culture, and more specifically in our training of our teachers, these elements are far less likely to take center stage in American forms of documentation. Our efforts at documentation are typified in most schools by the mere display of artifacts with little serious attention to the aesthetic elements of their presentation or to the possibilities for interpretation and study implicit in the activity of producing these displays. Of course, far more rigorous attempts at analysis exist, but many of them maintain a measurement focus as they attempt to document the growth and development of individual students. Rarely is the action of teaching and learning—the complex interaction of students, teachers, materials, subject matter, and parents as played out in our schools—the central concern of our documentation. Yet it is that action that is at the heart of the life of a classroom. In our American context, we are far more driven by a desire to report on outcomes, achievement, or change in a child over a specific period.

Promise and Problems in Portfolio Assessment

Documentation in America is most often in the form of snapshots taken at the beginning and end of a process, and at isolated moments along the way. Various forms of alternative assessment popularized in America in the late 1980s and early 1990s, including exhibitions of student work and performance assessments, exemplified this snapshot approach. They sought to contextualize assessment in authentic projects or tasks and, in so doing, represented a significant alternative to traditional tests and quizzes. At their best, these forms of assessment are tremendously useful to teachers, parents, and students.

In exploring the relationship between documentation and assessment, we find that portfolios, another alternative assessment, are an especially revealing practice. Grounded as they are in student work, portfolios provide a set of very concrete reference points for reflection on a child's journey through school. In many American schools, portfolios have become the focus of conversations between students, their teachers, and their parents, providing (in some cases for the first time) a central role for the student in discussing his or her learning.

Indeed, portfolios have provided the mechanism for some highly significant, even profound, shifts in educational practice in the United States. They make possible a nearly complete reorientation of our attitude toward what children are asked to do and make in school. Traditionally, we treat student work as essentially disposable. Over the years children are in K-12 classrooms, they are asked to create literally hundreds, if not thousands, of works—papers, drawings, diagrams, maps, problem sheets in math and science, labs, project exhibits, and so on. Overwhelmingly, these products are created, handed in, given some response (often cursory), returned, and then they go where? (One imagines a great black hole in the sky filled with the things children make in school, which then disappear—almost entirely forgotten in no time at all.)

The implications for students of this widespread treatment of student work are all too obvious in most of our schools, especially beyond the early years: little investment put into one's work, cynicism about the real significance of what one does in school, a focus on external rather than internal values—the grade rather than what one might learn from the experience of sharing one's work with a teacher or other students.

Compares maps drawn by two students

The collection of at least some of these products in portfolios restores a dignity to the whole enterprise in which children are asked to engage. Their work is collected and kept as both record and, more significantly, as opportunity for reflection—an occasion to look back, take stock, celebrate, contemplate, reconsider, and think ahead toward future projects, goals, and directions. In this way, portfolios help shift our collective perception of student work from that of disposable object to indispensable artifact.[11] While many states (Massachusetts, for one) have dropped portfolio assessment from their statewide comprehensive assessment systems, many teachers still use them in their classrooms.

Displays three pieces of work from an eighth grader's portfolio

My portfolio, your portfolio

The significance of the shifts made possible by collections of student work should not be underestimated. But, rich and useful as portfolios have proved to be in many classrooms and schools, they are almost always developed as records of the journey of an individual. My portfolio is "a picture of me," not of "us." I take mine home; you take yours. Indeed, one of the conundrums encountered by many American teachers using portfolios in their classrooms emerged in relation to project-based curriculum. Many projects in school are designed to engage students in collaboration. Ultimately, one student's contribution may be indistinguishable from any other's. In many respects this is the ideal. Yet in relation to each student's portfolio, it creates obvious problems. On a very practical level, who from the group gets to put the project in his or her portfolio, and what do the others get to keep as their record of the work? More profoundly, perhaps our ultimate concern with the individual in virtually every aspect of our assessments renders us helpless in relation to the assessment of group work. We often sense the development of a body of knowledge in a group of children working together over time. We know that, together, they develop capabilities beyond those of any one child in the group and we appreciate and honor this achievement. But in American assessment practices, we have few ways of representing this particular constitution of knowledge.

Displays five pieces of work from a first grader's portfolio

Contrasts end-of-year reflections from two students

A close reading of "The City of Reggio Emilia" demonstrates how collective knowledge develops. The essay focuses on two groups of children who are working together on drawings of their city. The contributions of each child are visible, but only in the larger context of the product and process of their collaboration. The drawings become a central part of the documentation produced by the teachers and the atelierista; all are made public through displays in the school and, in some cases, reproduction in book or pamphlet form.

Assessment as a Collaborative Effort at Understanding Learning and Teaching

From 1985 to 1990 Project Zero, along with the Pittsburgh public schools and the Educational Testing Service, was centrally involved in Arts PROPEL, a collaboration designed to explore the use of portfolios as a form of assessment in music, visual arts, and imaginative writing at the middle and high school levels.[12] The portfolio in this context was conceived as simultaneously serving multiple purposes: it was to be a tool for student learning, with reflection on one's work inextricably woven into the fabric of the curriculum; it would be a foundation of information for the district on student performance and, by extension, on the success of the schools; and it would serve as a source of information and insight for teachers about student learning and the work of teaching.

One of the unanticipated outcomes of Arts PROPEL was the development of protocols to structure teacher conversations about student work. This practice grew out of a deep concern that teacher conversations about student work, focused on specific pieces, were a highly unusual event in most schools and that it was not immediately obvious how to make those conversations productive. It was clear to all involved that the collection of student work in portfolios yielded a rich opportunity for conversations about educational practice. During the work on Arts PROPEL, teachers and researchers began structuring their collaborative examinations of student work with a protocol designed to elicit new insights, ideas, and questions about teaching and learning.

In the course of these and subsequent conversations among teachers about pieces of student work, one of the most significant discoveries was that those pieces of work, traditionally evaluated as though they were only a reflection of the intellect and effort of a single child, were, instead, reflections of both the child and the learning environment. A student essay, for example, on the death penalty would certainly contain the author's original thoughts on this topic. It would also have references (available newspapers, Web sources, books, articles), language, perspectives, and opinions the student had encountered in the learning environment. The essay would reflect not only ideas about the topic drawn from the environment, but ideas about what an essay is, how to make an argument, what constitutes acceptable grammar, and so on. Of course, this environment encompassed, in a sense, all of the worlds in which this young person moved. But this work would be especially reflective of classroom and school, teacher and fellow students. In short, student work was not just the work of one child or even a group of children. It was the result of a confluence of sources, resources, influences, values, materials, and—most important—minds at work and in interaction.

Of course, there are points at which a child is alone and fashions the work in particular ways. But even those unique contributions are never conceived in any absolute isolation. Every work is the product of the group, broadly construed, no matter how specific the stamp of the individual. In part, our embrace of the group as a unit of study, documentation, and assessment is recognition that an obsessive focus on the individual denies what we have found about the ecology of student work—that even at its most particular, it is always a product of an entire system.

Two differences

We have noted two profound differences in orientation between our American schools and those of our Reggio colleagues: first, our orientation to notice, document, and report only on the work of the individual, as opposed to Reggio's focus on the group and the ways in which individuals move, interact, contribute, and learn from "the ways of learning of others"; and second, our focus on outcomes, achievement, and measurement of improvement over time, as opposed to Reggio's focus on the actions of teaching, learning, playing, thinking, and other epistemological considerations.

It is important to notice that these are differences not only from the mainstream of American practice, but from some of the most progressive approaches to assessment in our schools. Our purpose here is not to argue every aspect of the relative values of these orientations, but rather to note them in an effort to identify the critical aspects of the "ocean" between us. It may well be that the significance of these differences is at the core of what is especially challenging about Reggio's practice to so many American educators. At the same time, it is probably the depth of the affinities in our values and perspectives on children, teaching, and learning that explain how attractive Reggio's practice is to those same American educators. Both forces matter—for without the attraction, there would be no desire to meet the challenge.

mare

311

To Be Part of Something Bigger than Oneself

Steve Seidel

Many young people wonder why they are in school. To learn, of course, they are told. But why and to what end, they rightfully ask. To become productive members of society; education is your portal and path to opportunity, they are reminded. But that is in the future, they protest. What does school have to do with now, today, this moment of life? For many young people the experience of school is an exercise in waiting for the present to matter. The justifications for their schoolwork seem related only to some invisible future. The present has little more than operational value; deeper meanings, understandings, contributions, and satisfactions are not the goal here. Childhood is little more than a holding pattern, a phase to pass through on the way to maturity. And children are not seen as capable of doing anything particularly useful, except "getting ready" to do something useful. This disregard for the capacities of children and this dismissal of any unique value in the period of life we call childhood are all too common in our educational system. No wonder young people question why they are in school.

The Group Holds the Individual in Its Arms

Being part of something bigger than oneself—whether a group, a community, or an enterprise that may have benefit for others—gives experience in the present meaning and satisfaction. This impulse to higher purpose is often at work when individuals come together to accomplish a complex task in any field. The recognition of one's limits in relation to one's ambitions brings these groups together. Even a group small in number is an entity larger than the individual. A small group with a big purpose—in terms of learning and in terms of producing—enlarges the significance of the group but, paradoxically, does not reduce the significance of the individual. On the contrary, the members of a group with large purposes, high standards, and rigorous demands become, potentially, major figures in their community, whether a classroom, school, neighborhood, disciplinary field, or some other grouping.

In the American cultural context, however, the experience, rights, and freedoms of the individual are a glory of our national heritage. From the protections provided individuals in the Constitution and the Bill of Rights to the debates at every level of society over affirmative action and gun control, our protection of the individual often trumps our consideration of the collective. These debates literally rage and consume our national conversation. (Even the right of individuals to accrue material possessions in staggering excess of others, and at the expense of others, seems to be held sacred and above moral question.)

The contradictions between our individualism and our impulses toward community confuse us personally and divide us collectively. We carry this focus on the individual into our schools and classrooms. Even when the desks are no longer in rows, each separated from the next, our curriculum and instruction remain constructed around the individual as a solo learning unit. Even when we design group activities, the default

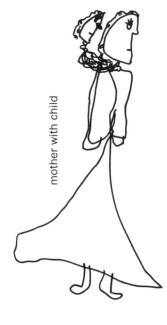

mother with child

312

setting on our assessments is the individual. (Assessment is so individual that rarely is a connection made even between the success and failure of the learning and that of the teaching. We act as though there are no problems with the teaching; it is just that the kids are not learning.)

Despite what significant research reminds us about the social nature of learning, most classrooms contain not so much a group as a collection of individuals. Indeed, virtually all learning in school is seen as an individual act, quite independent of other people. The group, in school settings, is often seen as the enemy of the individual. We fear we will lose our identity in the group, that our needs will not be met.

The experiences of our colleagues and their students in Reggio suggest that our focus on the individual need not completely dominate our educational philosophy, values, and practice. Indeed, their work and the research they contribute to this book reminds us that the rights, contributions, and learning of the individual do not necessarily contradict those of the group. In fact, it may well be that the opposite is the case—the individual may be best served by frequent opportunities to be part of intentional, purposeful learning groups. It is possible to see the group as holding the individual in its arms with care, respect, and love, rather than as some large and cold container in which the individual's rights, needs, and identity are inevitably lost and which crushes the spirit of the individual. Our sense is that the learning group as we discuss it in this book is an ideal setting for individuals to develop, to recognize their own ideas and potentials, their own minds, as they offer their perceptions, thoughts, and insights to the group and in turn consider those of others. The group that embraces the contributions of each member, however diverse or contradictory, may well provide exactly the right context for the emergence of strong individual identities. Through the debate, experimentation, and negotiation that characterize the work of these learning groups, each member comes to see, and in time to value, the particular, even idiosyncratic, qualities of the others. The valuing of each member's contributions means that each person not only develops respect for the others, but also has the experience of being valued for what he or she brings to the problem at hand.

But, once again, epistemological concerns emerge as critical to the formation and nurturance of high-functioning learning groups. If the goal of the group does not embrace each member's understanding the understanding of others, the focus of the group may shift subtly but quickly to other goals—being the best, winning, finishing first, getting the highest grade, and so on. A focus on understanding and on the attempt to follow each other's particular contributions and ideas may well distinguish a learning group from other kinds of group efforts. Indeed, we believe this focus is implicit in our definition of a learning group as individuals "engaged in solving problems, creating products, and making meaning… in which each person learns autonomously and through the ways of learning of others."

Learning With and From

Still marked by the tradition of desks in rows, with their suggestion of individuals as small self-contained islands, American classrooms remain environments in which attention is to be focused on the teacher, even though one's peers are often far more interesting. (The surreptitious passing of notes emerges as a symbol of the desire for social interaction despite the possible penalties that may reward this "inappropriate behavior.") Actual collaboration in learning can feel like a remote possibility in this environment.

Contrast now the "early hours of the day," as described by Paola Strozzi in the chapter "Daily Life at School." Reggio's preschools are marked by a flow of interactions and activities in an environment designed and equipped with the spaces and materials for children to engage in research into a wide range of phenomena and problems. In the doorway of the Diana School, among the panels that welcome students, parents, and staff every day is a reminder from Loris Malaguzzi, founder of these schools: "Nothing without joy."

In schools, we all—students, teachers, parents, and staff—are in groups and our success or failure to learn is inextricably bound to our success or failure to decipher how to learn with and from others. In the United States, we most often define teaching and learning as a one-way relationship in which the teacher does the teaching and each student, pretty much on his or her own, does (or does not do) the learning. Of course, this is hardly the only way to conceptualize the relationships of teachers and learners in schools or the processes of teaching and learning. It simply remains the dominant model in our American educational tradition, despite decades of research identifying the limits of that model and countless efforts to reform those practices.

Many American classrooms exist with little or no sense of the participants as members of a learning community or group. Most graduates of American schools know too well the possibility of loneliness and isolation in the classroom. The fact of being in the same room or building does not in itself make the group a learning group. There is often an arbitrary quality to these groups: assignment has brought them together, most often by virtue of age, but so also have other considerations—racial balance of the school or classroom, first language, or academic skills, for example.

At the core of this collaborative study is a view of learning as occurring within and between all members of the group. To be sure, not everyone in a classroom has exactly the same roles or responsibilities. On the contrary, within the learning group of the classroom everyone has, or will develop, particular roles, areas of expertise, and possibilities for learning and teaching. All of this, our Reggio colleagues remind us, is possible and can be accompanied by an atmosphere of joy.

The Role of Intention

In this collaborative research, our notion of a learning group focuses first on groups smaller than a whole classroom, often groups of three to five. As we noted in the four features of learning groups, adults as well as children are active agents of both teaching and learning. Who is in the group is determined by consideration of who might work together in productive and dynamic fashion, providing support and challenge to one another and bringing diverse ways of thinking to the effort. Proposition I posits that gender, interests, age and experience, and friendship are among the elements that inform the creation of these groups. Indeed, composing these groups requires thoughtful consideration by the teachers.

Why the group has come together—in relation to what purpose, project, problem, or study of a particular phenomenon—is an integral part of the identity of the group. The investigation of profound questions, the possibility of making wonderful objects, and the use of distinct symbol systems and diverse materials bring groups together. From the beginning, these newly evolving groups must find their points of mutual interest and engagement. This mutuality need not imply that all group members have exactly the same interests; rather, it can allow considerable diversity within the context of an identifiable focus.

In "The Beautiful Wall," decorating the courtyard of their school became a common concern for all members of the group; yet each child brought different interests and lenses to the problem of what should be represented, and the adult brought still other questions and motivations. In the making of a mural in an elementary school, whether in Italy or the United States, all members of the group may share a vision for the wall, but each person will bring a different set of concerns to the effort. One may be particularly conscious of the colors used and how they work in relation to each other and the colors surrounding the wall. Another may be concerned with accurate portrayal of the people in the mural, so that they can be recognized. And another may bring special attention to the challenges of representing depth in two dimensions. The artist-teacher may be balancing concerns about the final product and a desire to document the learning experiences of the group.

This diversity of concerns and interests is likely to affect not only the quality of the mural, but the quality of the learning experience for each individual in the group. (In producing the mural, the group learns many lessons and as the group learns, so do the individuals—though it would be wrong to assume that everything the group learns is learned by the individuals.) One of the distinctions between any random group of students in a classroom working together, often just side by side, and a learning group might be the degree of intentionality and design in the creation of the group.

Lessons for Learning Groups from the Ensemble Arts

An examination of work in the arts that requires collaboration and group effort—dance, theater, or music, for example—provides many images and points of reference relevant

The Beautiful Wall at the Diana School

Details from a mural on an outside wall of the Fletcher School in Cambridge, Massachusetts

315

to the work of groups in classrooms. In dance troupes, orchestras, and theater companies, as well as many other ensemble artistic groups, it is always a challenge to keep everybody learning as well as merely working effectively enough to get the job done. In many of these ensembles, in both professional and educational settings, the normal pressures of life (not enough time or money, for example) force many directors, conductors, or choreographers to simply "get the work up." The opportunity inherent in the rehearsal hall for achieving new insights and deeper understandings in any systematic fashion is often lost.

This loss probably derives not only from external pressures or inadequate resources. It may also be the result of dichotomies and beliefs that place insight, thinking, and understanding outside the work of making ensemble art. However, when learning and understanding are inextricably linked to the process of making the performance, the potential for the ensemble to become a learning group may well be realized. Dichotomies between process and product, learning and making, individual and group, begin to dissolve as each of these elements is recognized as impossible without the other. Once again, it is the attention of each person in the group to the understandings, ideas, and questions of the others that may well characterize the learning ensemble.

In the realm of professional artistic endeavors, it is the artistic directors and each member of the company who determine the degree to which understanding is or should be at the core of the artistic practices. In an educational environment, however, the responsibility to make artistic work a learning experience is undeniable. The way to achieve this goal is open to debate and interpretation, of course, but our study of learning groups in Italian preschools offers some insights. Similarly, the examination of performance ensembles in American schools has value for our understanding of the nature of learning groups. One study conducted by Project Zero has striking resonance with the findings of this collaborative research. We therefore shift focus from documentation of learning groups in preschools in Reggio Emilia to high school gymnasiums and auditoriums in the hills and mountains of Berkshire County, at the western edge of Massachusetts.

Checking-in session from Shakespeare & Company

Since 1995 researchers at Project Zero have been studying the educational programs of a professional theater group, Shakespeare & Company. This company is devoted to producing and teaching the works of William Shakespeare and has, for more than two decades, conducted educational programs in the schools of Berkshire County as well as in many other communities of the region. Project Zero's study focused on a program for high school students, the Fall Festival of Shakespeare, and a summer institute for high school teachers. Of the major findings, one set is particularly relevant to our understanding of the ways individuals learn in groups, and provides a view of learning by students considerably older than Reggio's preschool children, as well as by artists and teachers.

Learning to work and working to learn

Through some two hundred interviews and extensive observations, the research team came to recognize that the high school students in Shakespeare & Company's programs had become deeply engaged by the challenges implicit in studying and performing Shakespeare. Two aspects of the theater ensembles formed by the company further augment our understanding of the learning group. First, understanding is both the primary means and the goal of the company's educational programs and it is achieved through diverse activities. The primary materials of this work are the mind/body, including the voice; interaction with other performers, directors, and designers; and, of course, Shakespeare's text. The directors constantly ask the students/actors, individually and as a group, what sense they are making of the text—scene by scene, speech by speech, line by line, even word by word.

Second, the young actors are considered worthy interpreters of these classic texts. The directors often acknowledge that their own understanding of a line or a character or a scene is pushed to new levels by the particular group with which they are working. Confusion is embraced. Ideas are shared, but not just with verbal explanations. They are acted. Understanding is communicated in movement, tone of voice, intensity of feeling. In fact, feeling is considered the opening through which the deepest understandings of these texts may well emerge. In this way, the company's work resonates with the third feature of learning groups regarding the emotional and aesthetic dimensions of learning.

In the Shakespeare & Company rehearsals, understandings are treated as provisional: this is how we understand the scene today; tomorrow may well bring new insights, new possibilities of meaning. Instead of expressing frustration with this constantly evolving sense of the text, the high school students became even more fascinated with the multiple interpretations the texts allow. The discovery of a new way of understanding and playing the text provided delight and a feeling of accomplishment. This articulation by these teenage actors supports the proposition put forth in "Form, Function, and Understanding in Learning Groups" that "children express a feeling of continuous growth and awareness that their theories are provisional, and they take pleasure in seeing them modified, developed, and advanced."

Rehearsals are characterized by a feeling that time has been suspended. There is rarely a sense of haste. Time is taken to explore, to go over and over, to try out any new idea that arises. Observations and perspectives are solicited. Everyone's feelings are considered. Kevin Coleman, director of the company's educational programs, says, "Everyone counts." Students described this experience as almost the exact opposite of studying Shakespeare in the academic classroom.

The other relevant aspect of students' reports on their experience in these learning groups was the identification of "learning in four realms at once" as they studied with the company.[1] Two of the realms concerned the arts themselves: learning about Shakespeare and his language, and ways of reading the texts of his plays; and learning about acting and making theater. The other two realms related to the act of learning: learning about oneself, linking self-knowledge to social and intellectual development; and learning about working in creative communities. In particular, students identified learning that "a strong sense of community can be developed with people who share a common interest in Shakespeare by struggling together to make sense of his plays." These students made a connection between the formation of a strong community and the effort to understand something of shared significance.

The research revealed other aspects of learning to work in groups, as participants from across the ten schools articulated the benefits of participating in these plays. Some noted learning that every person had an important contribution to make to the work of the group. In other words, they identified inclusion as a powerful and positive principle, especially as it provides a setting for developing one's own identity. Others spoke about how in these challenging collective projects, each individual was pushed beyond his or her sense of personal limits. They became aware that each person needed support and attention from the group, and the ultimate success of the group's effort was dependent on providing that support and attention. Many spoke about coming to understand that high standards and discipline are important elements in the work of a creative community.

In discussing what they discovered about themselves as learners, students identified and agreed in significant numbers on numerous points. Two of these are particularly striking in relation to the ways in which a group can be instrumental to individuals' learning about self. Several of the students linked their personal growth or intellectual development to trusting their ideas and feelings, and to keeping their mind open to contradictory ideas. Others noted that treating oneself well, and being treated well by others—with kindness and generosity—increased the likelihood that they would be willing to take risks.[2]

These Shakespeare programs exist in the margins of the school. Rehearsals are held after school and students take over the school theater or gym, spilling into the hallways and any other spare space. Nonetheless, the experiences become central for most of the students who participate. They find in these rehearsals and performances a way to connect with peers and adults in a cognitively and physically demanding, intellectually stimulating, and emotionally provocative fashion. (There are no dichotomies between cognition and emotion, or between mind and body in the company's work.) The students connect intimately with some of the most beautiful poetry and drama ever written. They report feeling noticed, appreciated, and part of something bigger than themselves. They report feeling smarter—in part, ironically, because these ensembles become an environment in which they can acknowledge the

mother with baby carriage

318

uncertainty of their understandings. They describe falling in love with the work, with the group, even with Shakespeare.

Building Communities of Learners

In classrooms and schools, the learning group is hardly restricted to children. One of the features of a learning group is that in classrooms adults work and learn alongside children. At any one moment, the classroom is likely to contain multiple learning groups working on various projects. Groups last as long as the projects in which they are engaged. The rhythm of the classroom develops from the nature of the projects and the research these groups have undertaken. Any individual may be part of more than one group at a time and simultaneously serve as a member of a "competent audience" for other groups. (In this way, the classroom is like our own research organization. Individuals at Project Zero often work on multiple projects, moving from one to another, joining new teams, negotiating shifts in role and identity from one project to the next. We frequently take time to listen and respond to the work of other groups, providing a respectful and rigorous audience for ideas and products.)

The adults in Reggio and many American schools also form groups for pursuit of questions and projects. The processes of these groups—documentation, data collection, analysis, theorizing, design, reflection, and so on—mirror those of the learning groups of children in classrooms. The school, like the classroom or the research organization, becomes a learning environment in which many groups are simultaneously engaged in productive, purposeful projects. Through participation in these groups, the adults, like the children in Reggio and the high school students in western Massachusetts, continue to develop their sense of themselves as contributors, thinkers, and problem solvers with specific perspectives, inclinations, limitations, and possibilities. Teachers not only mirror, but also model, these processes for students. The significance of the project, the commitment of the individuals to the purposes of the group, and the degree to which all group members accept their dependence on the others, contribute to the ultimate quality of the experience and the product of the group's efforts.

Ann Brown's work provides another example of an American effort to build a community of learners in the classroom by drawing explicitly on the model of a professional research group. Citing influences primarily from psychological learning theory and cognitive research of the past forty years, Brown, the late professor of education at the University of California at Berkeley, sought to create a classroom pedagogy in which the goal was "to lure the students into enacting roles typical of a research community."[3] Numerous features of her communities resonate with the features of learning groups as described in this book.

In Brown's community of learners, students learn from each other and play multiple roles within the community, including the roles of "actor and audience." In this way, Brown connects with Reggio's concept of the "competent audience."

"Everyone in the community is a teacher as well as a learner; everyone is at some stage an actor and an audience. The sense of audience is an important aspect of the community. Audiences, be they adults or children, demand coherence; they push for higher levels of understanding; they require satisfactory explanations; they request clarification of obscure points. Students do not have to deal with a single audience, the teacher, as they usually do in school; the sense of audience is not imaginary, but palpable and real. Students are forced to teach what they know, and this is often the impetus for learners to recognize gaps in their knowledge that need attention before they take center stage again."[4]

Brown's vision of these communities of learners focuses on the "seeding, migration, and appropriation of ideas." Again, echoing perspectives explored in this book, she recognizes the enormous possibilities in children and adults "learning from and with others." She and Joseph Campione suggest that "learners of all ages and levels of expertise and interests seed the environment with ideas and knowledge that are appropriated by different learners at different rates, according to their needs and to the current state of the zones of proximal development in which they are engaged."[5]

More important, we believe, than any differences between communities of learners and the learning groups we explore here are the common and shared concerns for a radical reconceptualization of roles, responsibilities, patterns of interaction, and sense of purpose in the social environment of the classroom. Brown wonders why classroom structures and pedagogies that encourage student and teacher isolation, and focus on bits of knowledge, continue to dominate educational practice when developments in cognitive theory have long since discredited those approaches: "Why? I argue that this is because what the new theories ask is *so hard.* It is easier to organize drill and practice in decontextualized skills to mastery, or to manage 164 behavioral objectives, than it is to create and sustain environments that foster thought, thought about powerful ideas. We are asking a great deal from everyone in the learning community."[6]

In admiring the classroom and the school as human communities with the potential for remarkable achievements in both individuals' learning and the contributions of a group to the learning of others, we remind ourselves to pay close attention to the workings of these communities on every level. This is a potential, as Brown notes, profoundly difficult to realize.

Admiring the Workshop, Classroom, and School

Sometimes it becomes easier to realize new possibilities when we look at an analogous situation in a very different arena. In art history, some scholars are seeking ways to alter the usual discussions around the glorious achievements of the individual, and instead draw our attention to the group. Ivan Gaskell, in a study of "sketches in clay" that were models for finished sculptures produced in the seventeenth-century workshop of Gian Lorenzo Bernini, reassesses the significance of the workshop:

"We now have the opportunity to approach these sculptural models in a more complex manner—one that, while respecting individual achievement, does not value it as necessarily superior to group achievement; one in which individual achievement is not seen as necessarily the property of one imperatively identifiable and unconditionally admirable artist; one in which group achievements are held in as high esteem as those of any given individual within the group... At this juncture it seems far more urgent to realize that, *in addition to admiring things produced—the clay models that puzzle, bewilder, and inevitably get the better of us—we can admire the workshop itself as a social entity, for in its various manifestations it was no less an achievement historically than are the finished sculptural projects or their preparatory models* [italics added]."[7]

Gaskell's assertion that there is much to learn from considering the workshop itself is certainly provocative. It seems equally true when we consider classrooms from preschool through twelfth grade. The creation of a productive, innovative environment—whether sculptor's studio, rehearsal hall, fourth-grade classroom, or preschool—is no small achievement. It requires an extraordinary union of efforts and qualities combining vision, craftsmanship, political savvy, logistical wizardry, passion, patience, humility, arrogance, aesthetic sense, a community that values one's efforts, and enough time and money to experiment.

Whenever we come close to creating these kinds of learning groups and communities, even for a short period, our ability to recognize them as an accomplishment of great significance is preliminary to our analysis of what we have done to make them possible. Recognizing, admiring, documenting, and coming to understand such an accomplishment has been the goal of this study. Just as the scholars studying the "sketches in clay" for angels and other statues examine the fingerprints three centuries later to understand better the hands and minds at work, we can easily see the possibilities of an equally intense scrutiny of the hands and minds at work in our classrooms and staff rooms.

card game

321

Protagonists
Five- and
six-year-old
children
Schools
Villetta and Diana
Teachers
Angela Barozzi
Giovanni Piazza
Laura Rubizzi
Photographs by
Vea Vecchi

Children's Comments on Learning Groups and Group Learning

On one occasion, teachers at the Villetta and Diana schools suggested to the children, conscious protagonists of all the paths and processes illustrated here, that they discuss and reflect on the very same topics and questions that the adults themselves were discussing; that is, individual and group learning and learning in groups.

The objective was to increase our own—as well as the children's—awareness of these topics.

Teacher: Olimpia and I often suggest that you work and play in groups, or form groups with different children. What do you think about that?

Angela V.: *I like working in groups, because it's faster. When you work alone it takes longer... We can decide on things together. In a group you can do things together, so it's more fun for us and for everyone else.*

Teacher: How do you decide on things?

Anna C.: *You've got to agree first, and to do that you have to talk and talk until finally you decide.*

Athina: *When you agree on something, you can do something that's even nicer.*

Anna C.: *Because your brain works better. Because your ideas, when you say them out loud, they keep coming together, and when all the ideas come together you get a gigantic idea! You can think better in a group.*

Teacher: In your opinion, do you always think better in a group?

Anna: *Sometimes no. Sometimes it's better to do things by yourself. For example, I'm learning how to jump rope. When I practice I have to think really carefully about the jump and the rope. No one can be around or else I get confused and I do it wrong.*

Anna C.: *I like to work alone when I'm writing a special message to my friend, because it's a secret and I'm the only one who's supposed to know about it!*

Teacher: Do you like working with boys better, or with girls?

Athina: *Girls know how to do things that are nicer than boys.*

Anna C.: *But boys are smarter, because their heads are bigger and full of ideas.*

Anna: *Like Luca—his head's as big as his brain!*

Anna C.: *I like working with girls better, because boys are too much trouble. They tease you or play tricks on you.*

Anna: *So it's easier to learn together when you choose your friends. You choose them because of what they know how to do, too. We teach each other and we learn from each other.*

Anna C.: *I think it's better to choose the one who's the smartest. That way she can help you do things even more.*

Athina: *But sometimes even if someone's smart but she always complains, like Ramona, it's better not to choose her!*

Anna: *I like to choose Giulia, because she's always nice and generous and she always follows directions!*

Angela V.: *It's better when there are friends in the group who know how to do different things, because otherwise you'd always learn the same things!*

Athina: *I think girls learn more in a group than boys.*

Angela V.: *You have to see if someone is smarter, because you never know.*

Anna C.: *I like building stuff with Jacopo because he always says funny things that make me laugh even if he makes them up!*

Anna C.: *Like Lorenzo. He's always making things up, even stuff he hasn't even learned yet.*

Teacher: When you choose groups, do you always choose the same children or do you change?

Athina: *You have to change the groups sometimes, because otherwise you start to get sick of the same kids!*

Anna: *Lots of kids can be in a group—even everybody in our whole school!*

Angela: *Maybe for some things it's better for there to be only seven or eight, or even three.*

Athina: *I think you learn a lot in a small group.*

Anna: *You learn different things. For example, in a big group there are a lot more ideas.*

Angela V.: *Sometimes when two or three kids start something, if it gets really big you need other kids to help you, because otherwise you can't finish. Sometimes the teachers decide who can come and help and what to do, but sometimes we decide or just one of us does.*

Athina: *When one person decides, everyone else has to listen to him.*

Angela V.: *Oh, come on! You have to agree first, and if someone doesn't agree, that kid can do something else.*

Anna C.: *Sometimes, though, we all have to agree. If not, we can't do anything. Like last year when we did that big mural. If we hadn't all agreed what to do, we never would have finished it! We'd still be there painting it!*

Teacher: We often ask you if you want to work in a group. Sometimes we form the groups but sometimes we ask you to choose the children you want to be with in a group to work on a project. What do you think about that?

Andrea: *We're in a group now—a small group. See? There are five of us [including the teacher].*

Francesco: *You work better in a group.*

Nicola: *You think better.*

Francesco: *You can help each other better. For example, if you have to make a plane and you don't know where a piece goes, your friend can help you figure out where it goes, and so you learn better.*

Teacher: So you think that you work better and learn more in a group?

Andrea: *Yes, because you become even more of an expert.*

Nicola: *But I'm not an expert! My dad is, because when he was a kid his father—that's my grandfather—explained everything to him and so he became an expert.*

Luca: *We're learning how to do a lot of things and when you learn a lot, you become an expert too, and even more... a super expert! If you build stuff a lot, you turn into an expert builder because you've learned a lot of times how to do it. You can even do it with your eyes closed. I know how to do some things, but not everything. I'm sort of a robot expert.*

Francesco: *When you work together, you learn things from your friends. When you choose a group, you have to choose friends who know how to do things but not the same things as you, because then you'd all know how to do the same things.*

Teacher: So what you're telling me is that you learn more in a group? That maybe you have to choose your friends, too?

Nicola: *You have to know how to do different things, because if everyone knows how to do different things the whole group knows how to do everything. Even the best things.*

Luca: *But you don't need fifty people in the group—a little bit less. You don't need very many...*

Francesco: *In a class you don't need just one group of kids but a lot who do different things.*

Luca: *Sure, but if there are a lot of you, you can do things faster.*

Andrea: *But if you don't agree first, you end up fighting.*

Nicola: *You argue, and then you don't know what's going on. You don't know what you're supposed to do and then you get tired of it and go and do something else.*

Francesco: *If there are a lot of you, you don't know what's going on, but if there are only five of you, like us* [including the teacher], *you can really think. If I don't have any more ideas about something, someone else does...*

Andrea: *And that way the one who doesn't have any more ideas gets another one that goes on top...*

Luca: *And another one on that one, and another one on that one...*

Andrea: *And then all the ideas go together.*

Teacher: Ideas go together?

Luca: *They go together like when you're building. You hear them come out of our mouths and they go here* [in the middle of the table] *and they hook up to Francesco's and Nicola's...*

Nicola: *But ideas don't have any glue.*

Andrea: *It's like... something you have inside of you.*

Francesco: *For example, when you're with a group you feel like you don't know some things, because you're not an expert, and someone else helps you and that way you learn stuff, like building walls, and the thing you learned sticks inside and it never comes off because it sticks to the other ideas you've already got.*

Teacher: So where are all of these ideas?

Andrea: *They're in your head.*

Francesco: *For example, our ideas are in our head. Now we know more than before—all of the ideas are stuck to each other and we all know them. We're friends who know different things.*

Nicola: *Sometimes you do some things alone.*

Teacher: What kinds of things do you do alone?

Francesco: *When you have to do something with your memories that only you know, or when there are things you have to think about by yourself.*

Teacher: Can you give me an example?

Francesco: *When you have your own thought in your head, that only you think, that the grown-ups can't know about.*

Luca: *When you have to do an experiment that no one else wants to do.*

Andrea: *Okay, but you can't always do things by yourself, because the world would be stupider and no one would know anything.*

Luca: *If you do things together, you feel how nice those things are. You feel a feeling that you like and you say, look at this nice thing we did. Do you want to do something else?*

Teacher: When we ask you to form groups, how do you do it? Do you have any strategies for forming groups?

Nicola: *Sometimes we just look at each other to see if someone feels like doing something or not.*

Luca: *You have to say what you want to do, and then you go look for someone who wants to do the same thing and who can help you.*

Nicola: *I go to Luca and ask him if he wants to do something with me and if he says yes, we do it.*

Andrea: *Boys know different things from girls.*

Luca: *We like working with groups of boys.*

Andrea: *With girls too. Their ideas are different.*

Luca: *Girls are better at dancing and the ideas they have inside are more beautiful.*

Francesco: *When you make a group with girls you have to think about the things they like, too, because otherwise you don't know what to do.*

Nicola: *And then you don't know what to say.*

Luca: *Well, you have to say, "Do you want to make a train?"*

Teacher: Why a train?

Luca: *Girls like trains, too. You have to like the things that everyone else likes.*

Nicola: *But if we have robots that are so ugly they almost look like monsters, well, they* [the girls] *don't like them.*

Luca: *We're the only ones who like them!*

Nicola: *We love them. We think they're great!*

Francesco: *Well, let's just say that when we work in a group with girls, there's a rule: Everyone has to like whatever we build!*

Teacher: Are there rules when you work in a group?

Luca: *Sure! One rule is that you can't interrupt when someone's talking.*

Francesco: *You can't say anything that doesn't have to do with anything.*

Luca: *You have to have a lot of ideas in your head about what you want to do and then everyone decides together.*

Michele: *Let me ask a question: It's not fun to be alone when you're playing, but what about when you're writing something that's hard? If I have to write, "I love you, my dearest, more than me," well, if I write it when there's other people, it's kind of hard for me.*

Luca: *It's easy! You concentrate more.*

Armando: *If there are smart kids I can concentrate, but not if there are kids who aren't so smart.*

Teacher: Are there any children who aren't intelligent?

Armando: *There's some.*

Teacher: I don't think there are any children who aren't intelligent. Children are different. Some can concentrate more easily, while others, a little less so. When you work in a group, do you all learn the same things?

Luca: *No, different!*

Ferruccio: *I think so, too.*

Luca: *Okay, for example, I say a rule: "Don't be mean." Maybe someone doesn't learn it. I learn what other people say, and other people can learn the things I say.*

Teacher: What should a group do to get down to work?

Luca: *First you have to decide what to do—for example, "a table." You have to figure out how big it is, how heavy it is, wide, square, long… It's like with games. One person asks someone else.*

Teacher: Working in a group isn't easy. What should you do to work well?

Benedetta: *You have to agree.*

Aurelia: *You say something, if you want one thing and the other person wants it, you agree. The group has to listen and obey. I even use blackmail.*

Caterina: *It's easier to share ideas with your friends, and you get new ideas. If someone doesn't understand something, the other person helps her. It's better when the ideas are all different; a group is for learning other things, not the things you already know. Friends can have different ideas. Being friends means always being happy about the ideas we said. When there are kids in a group who don't know each other, the hardest thing is to explain so that they understand.*

"The Question Cannot Be Satisfied with Waiting": Perspectives on Research in Education

Steve Seidel

Those who ask, however, must become or already be committed to the process of an answer, as much as they expect those they ask the question of to be. In other words, the question cannot be satisfied with waiting. Of course, whoever asks a question expects an answer, but those who inquire critically are willing to deal with the answer obtained and also to attempt their own answer.

– Paulo Freire, *Letters to Cristina*

Being with children offers countless moments and situations that test our understanding of their complex world, of ourselves, and of a broad range of issues related to learning and teaching. These include moments when a child is struggling to grasp a concept and we are not able to understand the real nature of her or his difficulty. Or moments when one child experiences frustrations with another and we are unsure of our role in working out the conflict. A child may ask us questions in areas where our knowledge is scant, and we become confused by our own uncertainty, in relation to both the topic and how to handle our confusion in front of the child.

As adults, our responses to these moments, especially those that press the limits of our own understandings, reveal the stance we take in the world as learners and as teachers. Clearly, our students are watching. They want to see what we do when we do not know the answer. They watch to see how we gather resources—personal, material, and social—to pursue answers or insights into what we do not understand. They want to know if we have the interest and the will to gain the knowledge we lack.

"Every Question Reveals a Dissatisfaction..."

It cannot be said of any question that it is the first. Every question reveals a dissatisfaction with previous answers to previous questions. To inquire is to take on the curiosity of those who search.

– Paulo Freire, *Letters to Cristina*

When is a piece of student work finished? After an hourlong examination of a piece of historical fiction, a group of thirty educators, members of a monthly conversation/study group held at Project Zero and the Harvard Graduate School of Education, came to this question. The session had begun with a quiet reading of the story by a fifth-grade student in California about the experiences of a young girl in China during the Tang dynasty. As the discussion opened, everyone in the circle described particular aspects of the story that they had noticed. A very complex work emerged from the descriptions. Dozens of questions also emerged. Finally the child's teacher spoke at length about her own understanding of the work, answering many of the questions that had been raised, but certainly not all of them.

As the group reflected further, a series of questions seemed to capture the collective curiosity.

Did this young writer believe the story was finished?

If she thought it was finished, did that mean she didn't think it could be improved in any way, that it was as good as it could be?

Is a piece of writing finished just because the writer is finished with it?

Even if the child thought the story was finished, should the teacher point out ways in which it might be improved?

Who decides anyway when to consider a work complete?

And on it went. These were questions everyone present had confronted in one way or another and believed to be significant in the realm of teaching and learning.

A group of teachers looking over a student's work

Genuine questions—questions that, as Freire suggests, "cannot be satisfied with waiting"—and the curiosity that sparks their articulation mark the turning point when the act of teaching may become, simultaneously, an act of research. The questions may be specific to one child, asking, for example, how she came to her conclusions. They may be about a particular group, how the ideas of one child influenced others and whether any child has been unable to follow the newer ideas. They can be specific to a discipline, how students justify their interpretations of primary source materials from the American Civil War when they have already encountered contradictory interpretations by professional historians. Materials may spark inquiries, such as how explicit training in techniques for working with clay may influence a child's capacity to express thoughts in that form.

Questions may be broader and focus on elements of teaching: Am I talking too much in class? Have I been clear in making assignments? How can I learn from students what standards they hold for their own work? Or they may deal with aspects of school structure, such as how best to use substantially longer class periods, or the potential advantages of multiage classrooms. Or they could be questions with an epistemological focus, such as how these children have come to their understanding of a phenomenon, and what experience convinced them to let go of their previous understanding.

Discussion groups

It is obvious that questions about how learning groups form and function have been central to Project Zero's collaboration with Reggio Emilia. For example, we asked how effective learning groups come together and how children come to acknowledge, appreciate, and utilize the particular insights and contributions of others. Considering the role of the teacher, we have wondered when it is especially useful for a teacher to introduce a new question, idea, or material into the group's work. The possibilities may not be endless, but they are not easily exhausted.

Indeed, these questions and the very real situations and decisions that give them urgency confront most educators in some way at some time, and many educators confront them daily. Answers are not obvious. Thinking hard about these questions, refining them, determining how to think more deeply about them alone and with others, gathering documentation that might provide insight into the situations to which they relate, arguing interpretations of the documentation, and sharing perspectives—in short, working on these questions in serious, intellectually rigorous ways—seems a starting point for a confrontation with one's "dissatisfaction with previous answers to previous questions." In the arena of the improvement of public education, it is hard to imagine significant progress without engagement of the full intellectual curiosity and investigative powers of the adults.

Committed to the Process of an Answer

Research is a behavior for living.

– Carla Rinaldi

Whether it is a group in Cambridge on a Saturday morning, the second-grade team in an elementary school in rural Massachusetts, a research team from a university, the staff of the Diana School in Reggio Emilia, or a single teacher in a classroom, everyone struggles with how to investigate questions about learning. This problem of method is even more complicated, as its resolution is linked to who is framing the question and who will do the investigating.

The examples of pedagogical research practiced by our Reggio colleagues and shared in this book (and other Reggio publications) are both reminders and models. They remind us of the power of the investigative vantage point of those who work most closely with children on a daily basis. The processes of learning and teaching are entwined on a daily basis in intimate and subtle ways such that a teacher's-eye view is needed to capture the minute details that are the essential data of the investigation. The intimacy of daily contact and deep immersion in the life, rhythm, energy, and ecology of the classroom and school provide teachers and other adults in the school building an extraordinary opportunity to follow "the minute particulars" of learning.[1]

There are, of course, ways to study learning in the classroom and school. Different purposes, questions, and circumstances suggest different methodologies. Many methods evolve from philosophical perspectives on best ways to come to understand a phenomenon, problem, or question. At the same time, methods evolve in direct relation to what is possible for the researcher to accomplish. Funding, access, contact, and time frame drive methodological choices significantly, often far more than researchers would like. Still, limitations and constraints often unwittingly serve as provocation to creative solutions and methodological breakthroughs.

Reggio's ongoing projects in pedagogical research—over decades, on a daily basis, and in collaborative teams (including pedagogistas, atelieristas, parents, and other colleagues)—are much more intimately tuned to the rhythms of life and learning in classrooms than most research projects conducted by "outside" researchers.

Researchers who would be teachers, teachers who would be researchers

In Reggio, documentation of children at work and play is understood both as assessment and as research methodology. These actions, instead of being considered exclusive of each other, are considered inextricable. They are one and the same. At Project Zero, assessment has long been understood as containing within it the possibility of its being "an episode of learning."[2] The dichotomy between curriculum and assessment is, in this view, inappropriate and unnecessary. The actions of instruction, assessment, documentation, and research come to contain each other. They cannot be pulled apart in any practical sense; they are of a piece. No dichotomy between teaching and research remains. Neither is fully possible in the absence of the other. The rejection of either responsibility is to limit the effectiveness of the other. In this way, documentation and research are not something added on to teaching. They are part and parcel of the action of teaching.

Many have envisioned a reconceptualization of the profession of the classroom teacher to embrace teaching as an act of research, investigation, and learning. Our Reggio colleagues are hardly alone in seeing this possibility, or even in sharing a deep urgency in calling for a profound transformation of the teaching profession. However, few programs have existed for so long, on such a scale, or with such a large body of documentation as the preschools and infant-toddler centers in Reggio Emilia. And few have achieved such a level of accomplishment in their pursuit of this vision of the role of the educator.

Though it is difficult for some to imagine this transformation of teaching in the American context, Eleanor Duckworth refines the vision for us:

"I am not proposing that schoolteachers single-handedly become published researchers in the development of human learning. Rather, I am proposing that teaching, understood as engaging learners in phenomena and working to understand the sense they are making, might be the sine qua non of such research.

This kind of researcher would be a teacher in the sense of caring about some part of the world and how it works enough to want to make it accessible to others; he or she would be fascinated by the questions of how to engage people in it and how people make sense of it; would have time and resources to pursue these questions to the depth of his or her interest, to write what he or she learned, and to contribute to the theoretical and pedagogical discussions on the nature and development of human learning."[3]

From the perspective of Project Zero's three decades of research into human learning and the working of the mind at its best, understanding another's understanding of something is especially compelling as it calls for both self and other to be thinking hard and well. Starting from the platform of a research institute and not from within a school (though we are located at the Harvard Graduate School of Education), we have increasingly recognized the potential of close collaboration with schoolteachers in conducting research. To this end, at the beginning of this new decade we continue to extend our collaborations with teachers and administrators in schools. We follow and join with others in the United States who have made major assaults on the traditions that divide research, teaching, and the people who engage in these activities. Carini and the Brookline teachers group are among the distinctive, though still far too few, adventurers into the zone where these fields are redefined and interconnected.[4]

At Project Zero, these collaborations take various forms. In one case, for example, our research staff are in the classroom working with children alongside teachers, collectively investigating students' understandings of the various types of causal relationships implicit in complex concepts of physics and biology. The staff is attempting to deepen students' scientific understandings by exploring with them the different ways causality behaves.[5]

In another project, teachers identify questions about the effectiveness of their own instructional practices and children's ways of learning. With their colleagues and researchers from Project Zero, they meet regularly to explore these questions, gathering various forms of data from their classrooms and engaging in collaborative analysis of the artifacts, such as pieces of student work, that they bring to the group.[6]

Cognizant of the American construct of the relationship of teaching and research, we recognize that bringing the two fields together is unlikely. Indeed, the great divide between educational research and what actually goes on in our classrooms raises questions about the efficacy of our current policies, assumptions, and structures for both fields. Yet we are inspired by the pedagogical research of our Reggio colleagues and yearn for policies and structures that support reconsideration of how best to investigate what works in teaching and learning.

Therefore, we must ask how best to continue our American experiments in pedagogical research, building on our own traditions as well as those developed in Reggio. Whether or not we can accelerate our movement toward this vision of teaching and research, certainly this is one of the questions that, as Freire observed, "cannot be satisfied with waiting."[7]

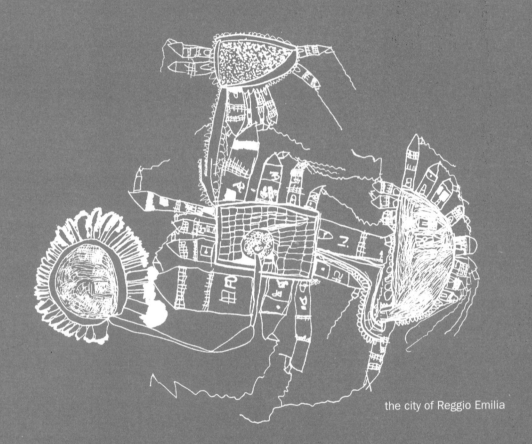

the city of Reggio Emilia

Final Reflections

Making Our Learning Visible

Literary critics say that poetry is the most difficult genre to translate. As a social scientist, I have to demur. I would argue that disciplinary concepts—ideas drawn from physics or history or psychology or education—are even more difficult to translate. In poetry, we deal with common human experiences. Even if the languages parse the world of experience somewhat differently, there is an opportunity to recreate the basic ideas and images in a second natural language. In contrast, in much of disciplinary work, we deal with *new concepts*, new paradigms. Ideas like gravity or relativity, evolution or "jumping genes," democracy or e-commerce, are not just difficult to describe. They represent new inventions, for which no earlier experience or metaphor proves truly adequate. Just as scientists must unlearn much of what they believe if they wish to master a new paradigm,[1] so, too, ordinary readers have to be able to expunge misleading conceptions and construct new knowledge, if they are to be able to appreciate a hitherto unfamiliar concept.

Howard Gardner

Our experiences with our friends and colleagues at Reggio Emilia have constituted an extended lesson in the challenges of conceptual translation. Whether the terms are seemingly new—like *pedagogista*—or all too familiar to readers of Romance languages —like *apprendimento* or *insegnamento* or *valutazione*—or deceptively cognate, like *documentazione*—we have had to avert simple lapsing into one of our already understood concepts and try to construct the concept afresh. I am sure that our colleagues have experienced analogous difficulty with terms bandied about Project Zero—like intelligences, or processfolios, or performances of understanding—but fortunately that is *their* problem, not ours!

Concepts are not the only entities that are difficult to translate, comprehend, construct. At least as difficult are those long-standing practices, disciplines, and habits that are taken wholly for granted by practitioners but are either invisible to outsiders or erroneously assimilated into prior categorical schemes. To use a term made familiar by the French sociologist Pierre Bourdieu, we can speak of the customary *habitus* of any well-worked-out environment. Over a decades-long period, our colleagues at Reggio Emilia have worked out countless routines that are well known and understood by participants and to which novices are gradually introduced in their native Italian. To swoop in on occasion and attempt to master these practices, what they mean, and how to implement them properly, is a daunting task to say the least.

And so our goals in this volume can be simply stated: 1. to reflect on our own learning of concepts, our own incipient mastery of the Reggio habitus; and 2. to make this

337

learning as visible as possible to ourselves and to others. The Project Zero pages represent, in effect, one extensive linguistic "performance of understanding."

Let me be frank—perhaps uncharacteristically frank for a volume of this sort— and mention three obstacles to understanding the Reggio experience, at least on my part and perhaps on the part of other Americans.

First of all, as a scientifically trained psychologist and scholar, my inclination is to begin with theories and definitions and then to test them against practices. Often, particular recommendations grow out of conceptual analysis or theoretical claims. In contrast, much of what is special about Reggio has grown out of promising practices that have been worked out over the years. To be sure, there is a definite theoretical superstructure for the Reggio enterprise, and the architects rightly insist on the need to master it. But in a sense that is simply not true of Project Zero, the heart of the Reggio enterprise lies in daily practices in the thirty-four schools and infant-toddler centers in the municipality.

Second, my own favored ways of representing information are linguistic and musical— and both of these modes happen to favor the auditory modality. In contrast, there is little question that the intellectual heartland of the Reggio team lies in visual and graphic means of representation—definitely external and probably "in the head as well." As such, Reggio probably represents the majority of the population that is visually oriented. However, it makes understanding points and documentations and projects that much more difficult for those of us who do not think primarily in visual-imagistic terms.

Finally, there is a question of how one goes about conceptualizing a complex terrain. Like many scholars, and particularly American ones, I am more comfortable as a "splitter"—one who makes distinctions, and then even finer distinctions, and tries to learn from those distinctions. Thus, as just one example, I would take a concept like "documentation" and right away ask what it means, whether it can be done equivalently in different symbol systems, how much it can be condensed or elaborated, how much of it is interpretive, what its various purposes are, how they can best be evaluated, and so on.

But there is an equally respectable and venerable tradition in scholarship that goes by the inelegant name "lumper," but might as well be termed "holistic thinking." I believe that the Reggio educators are more comfortable approaching their own creation in a holistic spirit. They stress the interconnection—indeed the inseparability—of teaching, learning, documentation, assessment, individual and group learning, and many other terms and practices, and they are equivalently suspicious of efforts to distinguish sharply (they would probably say, *too* sharply) among these various elements.

As a result of these and probably other differences, I have found it challenging to make sense of the Reggio experience, one that I thought I understood moderately well when we began this collaboration but one where I now have as many doubts as certitudes. Like many other smoothly operative but deeply introspective entities, Reggio is well guarded and not readily accessible to outsiders. It has a "feel" to it—like Greenwich Village in the 1920s, or Hollywood in the 1940s, or Silicon Valley in the 1990s—that is self-evident to residents but not easily caught by others. Such communities are best captured by art and metaphor, and perhaps that is why the hundred languages, and the stories of the poppies, the city in the rain, and the amusement park for birds are such popular introductions to Reggio.

This conundrum suggests, to an old student of the brain, that perhaps the best alternative is to take advantage of the bilateral nature of the human nervous system: to have both a "left hemisphere" (linguistic and analytic) approach and a "right hemisphere" (imagistic, visual, holistic) approach to this educational enterprise. Happily, the diligent reader will have the opportunity to adopt both lenses and, if equipped with a serviceable corpus callosum, to effect the necessary connections and integration.

Still, this work does have a focus and the reader does well to keep it in mind. The spotlight falls on documentation and reflection, two processes that are integral to the operation of both the American and the Italian team, and two processes that we value in young children as much as we value them in our relatively ancient selves. We have sought to convey our ideas about these processes in a multitude of ways—though they fall somewhat shy of one hundred. Our effort has a certain postmodern touch to it; and though I do not think that either group is deeply wedded to postmodern methods or madness, we cannot escape being imbued with a smattering of postmodern values and sensibilities.

We travel to learn about other places, other people, other ways of doing things. But of course in the end, the ultimate reason—and the ultimate reward—for travel is to learn more about oneself. Reggio challenges individuals from all over the world to reverse some common figure/ground relations: the relation between description and evaluation; the relative importance of the individual versus the group; the tensions between intuition and theory, intuition and reflection; the connections between knowledge and meta-knowledge in youngsters and oldsters; the advantages of democratic as opposed to socialistic regimes, to mention just a few.

Travel often begins with initial disorientation. We confess to having been disoriented—physically and imaginatively—more than a few times in our three-year adventure in the hills and valleys, the communities and countryside of Emilia-Romagna. We hope—we believe—that this disorientation has subsided and that the resulting amalgam is greater than the sum of its parts. We hope that, whether you have approached it as a researcher or an educator, a lumper or a splitter, a visualizer or a linguistic creature, this volume has given you a sense of both the intriguing parts and the stunning whole.

mountain climbing

Dialogues

As I was reading the various chapters of this book prior to writing this conclusion, a number of aspects appeared to me to stand out so clearly that I was persuaded to share them with the reader.

The first concerns the learning processes of children and adults. For a long time now, Piagetian epistemological genetics has demonstrated that, from a very specific and abstract point of view, the logical structures of an adult are quite different from those of a child. According to this view, when an adult and a child are faced with the same problem, they will react and behave in very different ways. However, if we place adults and children in concrete situations that are different and yet require them both to make a cognitive effort that is commensurate with their respective potentials, it would seem as if the processes enacted do not differ so significantly.

Carla Rinaldi

In my view, this can be seen from much that has been written in this book. We notice, in fact, how, when faced with the need to reflect and to reformulate their existing knowledge, as happens when documentation is used, adults and children develop strategies that are often comparable. Essentially, these strategies involve a search for a theoretical, moral, and sometimes even physical "stance" that allows the subjects to exercise greater control over the changes that are taking place: changes that refer to and sometimes undermine both the conceptual and the value systems that they have previously formulated. The nature of the relationship between the problem that arises and the person who has to resolve it is essentially analogous, just as the nature of the strategies that children and adults use for exploring, defining, and hypothesizing, and the emotional involvement, passion, sense of irony, and fun they experience can be similar. A learning experience is therefore an "educational endeavor," whether it involves adults, children, or both.

The second aspect that I think can be gleaned from this book concerns the work of the teachers. Thanks to our colleagues from Project Zero, their questions and the relentless way in which they delved into the everyday activities of our schools, it has become even more apparent to us that the teacher's "practical" work is an "interpretive theory" that integrates stories and micro-stories of research with real-life contexts. This ennobling of the teachers' practical work, which we have always believed in, has now acquired even greater value in being shared by our Project Zero colleagues.

This research project and this book demonstrate that, however one might look at it, the work of the teachers—provided they are not left on their own, without rules or collegial support—not only produces daily experience and action, but can also become the object of critical reappraisal and theory building. In this way, practice is not only a field of action necessary for the success of the theory, but is an active part of the theory itself: it contains it, generates it, and is generated by it.

A further aspect that deserves careful consideration is the way our dialogue with our Project Zero partners evolved. It was a complex process, at times made more difficult by linguistic and cultural differences. Yet language, which started off as a barrier, turned out to be a sort of "forum" that provided an opportunity to submit our own understandings to further scrutiny and clarification. A number of terms, in fact, seemed impossible to translate because the concepts they expressed were not easily transferable across the two experiences.

In Reggio, we use a language that originates from a microworld which, despite its openness to dialogue and exchange, has had to and has sought to construct a language that is both generated by experience and generates experience. The fact that this language is highly visual and metaphorical has often made it extremely attractive to our Project Zero colleagues, but has also been the source of a few understandable suspicions.

First among these is the idea that we might be trying to skirt the issue, refusing, even if only momentarily, to decontextualize it. Perhaps our colleagues were right. At times we were a little too vague, letting ourselves be perceived as enveloped in a kind of haziness that had much in common with vagueness. Occasionally however, we perceived their persistent and punctilious questions as a sort of deviation, which we felt could generate some possible philological and conceptual misrepresentations.

We undoubtedly have a great love of metaphor; and this is primarily because children love and often make use of it. We see metaphor not as a rhetorical or stylistic device but as a genuine tool of cognition. As many other studies and investigations confirm, we have noticed that metaphors are particularly useful when new ideas are emerging from within groups of people (and therefore also groups of children), and the use of previous concepts and expressions is avoided on the grounds that they might be misleading. In this case, metaphorical language, precisely because it is more undefined, allusive, and sometimes ambiguous, but at the same time open to new concepts, becomes the only tool available to the new understanding that is seeking to emerge and find an audience.

Perhaps it was due to the fact that we were trying to find new understandings in this research, and we ourselves were trying to understand, that metaphor (and, with it, examples) appeared to provide a supportive strategy. It seems to me that we were able to structure—though the reader will be a better judge of this—what Kenneth J. Gergen calls a "transformational dialogue": a dialogue that is able to transform our relationship and therefore, in a certain way, our professional and group identities. Instead of adopting a "top-down" approach, with a prior definition of identical rules, ethics, and practices for everyone involved, we managed to move into a sphere of action in which children and adults alike struggled successfully, it seems, with the problems of learning in multiple and conflictual contexts. We thus compiled a sort of "dictionary of experiences," which helped us to reflect, infer, hypothesize, and understand.

For all this, I would like to thank Mara, Steve, and Ben; for their heuristic skill, their ability to participate and enable us to participate in their philosophical thinking, knowledge, and experience. I particularly thank Howard Gardner, because during the joint meetings of the Project Zero and Reggio research teams he was frequently able to confound our accumulated knowledge with a single question, forcing us to engage in healthy rethinking processes. Finally, I am grateful to our readers for their faith in us; by reading this book, they enable our research to live on.

Appendixes

History and Description of **Project Zero**

Project Zero, a research group at the Harvard Graduate School of Education, has investigated the development of learning processes in children, adults, and organizations for over three decades. Today Project Zero is building on this research to help create communities of reflective, independent learners; to enhance deep understanding within disciplines; and to promote critical and creative thinking. Project Zero's mission is to understand and enhance learning, thinking, and creativity in the arts and other disciplines, both at the individual and the institutional levels.

Project Zero was founded in 1967 by the philosopher Nelson Goodman to study and improve education in the arts. Goodman believed that arts learning should be studied as a serious cognitive activity, but that "zero" had been firmly established about the field; hence, the project was given its name.

David Perkins and Howard Gardner became the codirectors of Project Zero in 1972. In July 2000 Steve Seidel assumed the directorship. Over the years, Project Zero has maintained a strong research commitment in the arts while gradually expanding its concerns to include education across all disciplines, and including not just the individual, but whole classrooms and schools as well. Much of this work takes place in American public schools, particularly those that serve disadvantaged populations. An increasing amount is taking place in other educational and cultural organizations, the business world, and overseas.

Project Zero's research projects are based on detailed understandings of human cognitive development and of the process of learning in the arts and other disciplines. Project Zero researchers place the learner at the center of the educational process, respecting the different ways in which an individual learns at various stages of life, as well as differences among individuals in the ways they perceive the world and express their ideas. Research spans a wide variety of ages, academic disciplines, and sites, but shares a common goal: the development of new approaches to help individuals, groups, and institutions learn to the best of their capacities. Current investigations include, but are not limited to:
• exploring how to teach for understanding—in other words, to help students learn to use knowledge to solve unexpected problems, rather than simply recite back facts;
• designing strategies for creating a "culture of thinking" in the classroom that encourages students to think critically and creatively;
• making assessment an ongoing and integral part of the curriculum, so that it reinforces instruction and guides students in reflecting upon their work;
• relating classroom instruction to the tasks and experiences students will encounter outside of school and particularly in the world of work; and
• marshaling the power of new technologies, especially computers, to advance learning and provide access to new realms of knowledge.

Project Zero's work is documented extensively in a variety of publications and materials by Principal Investigators and other Project Zero researchers. In addition, Project Zero offers symposia and workshops, most notably an annual summer institute.

PZ

The Municipal Infant-toddler Centers and Preschools of **Reggio Emilia**

The Municipal Infant-toddler Centers and Preschools of Reggio Emilia have their origins in popular initiatives carried out just after the end of World War II, when a number of community-run schools were built literally "brick by brick." The municipal early-childhood institutions were therefore generated by an act of social solidarity and democratic coparticipation that involved parents and citizens in the building and management of the schools.

The present network of early-childhood educational services operated by the municipality of Reggio Emilia is made up of twenty-one preschools and thirteen infant-toddler centers. Currently, 1,508 children between the ages of three and six attend the municipal preschools, and 835 children from three months to three years old attend the infant-toddler centers.

The city also has five infant-toddler centers and one early-childhood center for children aged one to six that are run by cooperatives which have a special agreement with the local administration, and one infant-toddler center that is managed by a parents' association which has a similar agreement with the municipality. These facilities serve a total of 351 children between the ages of three months and three years, and twenty-seven children between the ages of three and six.

The presence of a substantial number of other early-childhood services in the local territory (state-run preschools as well as private preschools, most of which are run by religious orders) means that 94.6% of all children between the ages of three and six and 38% of children from three months to three years old residing in the city are served.*

* Excerpt from *The Municipal Infant-toddler Centers and Preschools of Reggio Emilia: historical notes and general information*, Reggio Emilia, Italy: Comune di Reggio Emilia, 2000.

The Community-Early Childhood Council

Participation is a distinguishing feature of the Municipal Infant-toddler Centers and Preschools of Reggio Emilia. Effected through actions relating to the organization and the physical environment, it becomes concrete in the daily practice of relationships and communication based on dialogue, exchange, and reciprocity. Participation is constructed and consolidated on a daily basis but is also embodied in a number of organizations such as the Community-Early Childhood Council (formerly called Advisory Council).

The Community-Early Childhood Council is an elected body in each infant-toddler center and preschool, which is composed of all of the staff, who take turns participating, and of parents and other community members in unrestricted numbers. The Council is a democratic body whose task is to promote participation and social management as well as the coresponsibility of the families served and the citizens for educational issues. The Council therefore has both organizational and cultural responsibilities.

In order to carry out its tasks more effectively, the Council may organize itself as it deems most appropriate and most functional, based on the number of members, its objectives, its time frames, and so on. Study groups and work committees are often set up within the Council, a choice that has shown positive results. "In order to optimize management time, to ensure more time-effective discussions, and to enable a form of participation which corresponds more closely to the interests and abilities of each member, the Council may organize specific Work Committees."*

The committees have different functions. They may:

• have pedagogical-didactic objectives;

• promote cultural initiatives;

• assess and reflect on the special characteristics and designation of the indoor and outdoor spaces of an infant-toddler center or preschool;

• design and add to furnishings and materials;

• take part in the organization of school or city events;

• ensure that close relations with local agencies and organizations are maintained (with the objective of defining policy concerning early childhood and the family);

• develop proposals connected to the municipal administration's policies concerning early childhood; and

• promote encounters between educational and scholastic institutions of different levels in order to ensure better mutual understanding and educational continuity.

The committees do not work independently of each other; joint meetings are organized to exchange and develop ideas, providing opportunities for exchanging feedback on the work being carried out not only for the Council itself but also for all the families of the school. These meetings are arranged and coordinated by a Secretariat made up of staff members of the infant-toddler center or preschool and parent members of the Council. The Secretariat identifies the issues and operational priorities the Council needs to deal with, and is responsible for the organizational aspects of the Council (calling meetings, making announcements, writing minutes and reports, setting agendas, and so on). Meetings of all of the Councils system-wide and the Director of the Infant-toddler Centers and Preschools and the Superintendent of Education are also held.

The Councils publish a periodic newsletter called "La Mongolfiera" (The Hot Air Balloon), which is distributed free in the infant-toddler centers and preschools and around the city.

The Councils are elected every three years, although parents can also become participating members each new school year by expressing their interest and availability during a class meeting.

One of the characteristics of the Council elections is that they represent an act of solidarity. The elections take place not to select or support one party against the others, but to express support for the willingness and generosity of those parents who volunteer to assume the role of parent-citizen on behalf of all. In this role, the parents take into consideration not just their own children, but also the whole class, the school, and the city.

The election process is made up of a number of events and special initiatives. "Thinking about the elections as a path means acting in a true democratic spirit which involves the protagonists in the building of that path (listening, receptiveness, development, and so on), and also allows each person—through

* Excerpt from *Partecipazione e gestione sociale. Significati e finalità*, Reggio Emilia, Italy: Municipality of Reggio Emilia, 1984.

assimilating information and building shared sense, meaning, and values—to be aware of the meaning of casting his or her vote. It is therefore a path of information-gathering and personal growth for the candidates, as well as one of personal growth and professional development for staff members, alternating events, meetings, and occasions within each school with events, meetings, and occasions more generally related to the city at large."*

The Council elections are an important moment not only for the municipal infant-toddler centers and preschools but for many citizens and the city as well. This is why the elections are made visible through posters displayed publicly throughout the city.

In the 1999-2000 school year elections 584 parents and 107 citizens were elected.

* Paola Cagliari, presentation at the Inter-Council Meeting, Reggio Emilia, Italy: October 27, 1999 (unpublished).

Appendix D
Organizational Aspects of the Infant-toddler Centers and Preschools

In the educational project of the Municipal Infant-toddler Centers and Preschools of Reggio Emilia, organization is a cornerstone. It is a choice of content within the theoretical and scientific framework as well as within the educational aims and purposes. The Reggio Emilia approach to education is characterized by this attempt to combine the organizational bases of the work with the bases of educational research and project-based thinking.
The organization of the infant-toddler centers and preschools is based on collegial work, which means affirming and applying the value of coresponsibility among all those who work in the centers and schools. Thus, the work schedule must provide time for professional development for the teaching staff as well as for the kitchen and cleaning personnel, with their different professional roles.
The infant-toddler centers and preschools are coordinated by a *pedagogical coordinating team* composed of nine pedagogistas and one psychologist. Each pedagogista, who is required to have a university degree with specialization in pedagogy or psychology, coordinates a number of infant-toddler centers and preschools.
This coordination of services for children from birth to six is crucial in order not to create and legitimate separation between the early childhood ages (the 0-3 range and the 3-6 range), differentiations between the various types of institutions, or differentiated economic and administrative treatment of the teachers in the infant-toddler centers and preschools. Attention to these matters fosters a sense of belonging to a system, a project of continuity among the early-childhood services.

Hours of the Infant-toddler Centers and Preschools
Monday through Friday from 8:00 a.m. to 4:00 p.m., with the possibility of early entry at 7:30 a.m. and extended day to 6:20 p.m. for families who make a specific request for work reasons.

Annual calendar for the children

September 1 - June 30

A number of infant-toddler centers and preschools, depending on the demand, stay open for the month of July for families who make a specific request for work reasons.

Annual calendar for staff

August 24 - July 13

From August 24 to August 30 and July 1 to July 13 all personnel (teachers, cook, helpers) are in service to organize the environment and meet with the families of the children who will be attending the center or school for the first time.

Infant-toddler Center Organization

Children (4 groups)			
Total children	Group	No. of children	Age
70	Infants	27	from 3 to 9 months
	Toddlers 1		from 10 to 18 months
	Toddlers 2	43	from 19 to 24 months
	Toddlers 3		over 24 months
Staff			
Teachers		11	
Cook		1	
Full-time helpers (cleaning staff who participate actively in the overall life of the center)		3	
Part-time helpers		3	

Teaching staff work schedule		
Total hours per week	With the children	Other activities*
36	31	5

* Professional development, planning, preparation of materials, community management, meetings with families, other meetings, etc.

Staff work shifts		
Role	Schedule	
Four teachers*	8:00 a.m.	2:00 p.m.
Four teachers*	8:33 a.m.	4:00 p.m.
Two teachers*	9:03 a.m.	4:00 p.m.
One teacher*	9:09 a.m.	4:00 p.m.
Cook	8:00 a.m.	3:21 p.m.
Full-time helper*	8:00 a.m.	3:21 p.m.
Full-time helper*	8:30 a.m.	3:51 p.m.
Full-time helper*	9:39 a.m.	5:00 p.m.
Part-time helper	4:00 p.m.	7:00 p.m.

*   weekly rotation

Preschool Organization

Children			
	2 classes[1]	3 classes[2]	4 classes[3]
Children	52	78	104
Staff			
Teachers	4	6	8
Extended-day teacher (part-time)	1*	1*	1*
Atelierista	1	1	1
Cook	1	1	1
Full-time helpers	2	2	3
Part-time helpers	1	3	3

* A second teacher may be added depending on the number of children attending.

[1] Classes composed of children of two age groups that may vary from year to year: three- and four-year-olds, three- and five-year-olds, four- and five-year-olds.

[2] Classes composed of children of the same age: three, four, and five years old.

[3] Three classes composed of children of the same age: three, four, and five years old. The fourth class is composed of children of two age groups that may vary from year to year: three- and four-year-olds, three- and five-year-olds, four- and five-year-olds.

Teaching staff work schedule		
Total hours per week	With the children	Other activities*
36	30	6

* Professional development, planning, preparation of materials, community management, meetings with families, other meetings, etc.

An example of staff work shifts in a three-classroom school		
Role	Schedule	
Classroom teacher*	8:00 a.m.	1:48 p.m.
Classroom teacher*	8:27 a.m.	4:00 p.m.
Atelierista	8:30 a.m.	3:33 p.m.
Cook	8:00 a.m.	3:21 p.m.
Full-time helper*	8:00 a.m.	3:21 p.m.
Full-time helper*	9:00 a.m.	4:21 p.m.
Part-time helper	12:36 p.m.	4:30 p.m.
Part-time helper	4:00 p.m.	7:00 p.m.

* weekly rotation

Reggio Children

Reggio Children, International Center for the Defense and Promotion of the Rights and Potential of All Children, was established on March 11, 1994, with the Municipality of Reggio Emilia as the majority shareholder. It was based on an idea suggested by Loris Malaguzzi and promoted by a community-based group, and public and private institutions as well.

Reggio Children's mission is to protect and disseminate the wealth of knowledge and experience accumulated over many years of work in the field of early-childhood education by the Infant-toddler Centers and Preschools run by the Municipality of Reggio Emilia.

In the context of a widespread crisis in education, cultural impoverishment of educational systems, and neglect of the rights of children, the Reggio Children project was designed to create opportunities for exchange of ideas, discussion, and research on a topic that will be decisive for our future: a new culture of childhood that places real value on the potential and creativity of children.

In promoting what has come to be known as the "Reggio Approach" to early-childhood education, Reggio Children oversees an extensive network of national and international cultural exchanges, with specific activities that include:
• organizing initiatives for disseminating information on the pedagogical experience of Reggio Emilia (study tours, seminars, conferences)
• professional development initiatives
• on-site consultancy
• publishing and sale of books and audiovisual materials
• promotion of educational research in collaboration with universities, foundations, and government ministries
• management of the exhibit "The Hundred Languages of Children," which has been touring Europe and North America for more than twenty years, hosted by government organizations, museums, universities, and art centers.

The company profits are reinvested for the further development of schools and educational research.

Bibliography and Notes

Arnheim, R., *Art and Visual Perception: A Psychology of the Creative Eye* (Berkeley-Los Angeles: University of California Press, 1954).

Arnheim, R., *To the Rescue of Art. Twenty-Six Essays* (Berkeley-Los Angeles: University of California Press, 1992).

Balducci, E., *L'uomo planetario* (Firenze: Cultura della Pace, 1990).

Bateson, G., *Steps to an Ecology of Mind* (San Francisco: Chandler Publishing, 1972).

Bateson, G., *Mind and Nature. A Necessary Unit* (New York: E. P. Dutton, 1979).

Bateson, G. and Bateson, M. C., *Angels Fear: Towards an Epistemology of the Sacred* (New York: MacMillan, 1987).

Becchi, E., *I bambini nella storia*, (Bari, Italy: Edizioni Laterza, 1994).

Berandi, F., *Mutazione e cyberpunk. Immaginario e tecnologia negli scenari di fine millennio* (Genova, Italy: Edizione Costa e Nolan, 1994).

Bocchi, G., Ceruti, M., Fabbri, D., and Munari, A., *Epistemologia genetica e teorie dell'evoluzione* (Bari, Italy: Dedalo, 1983).

Bocchi, G. et al., *L'altro Piaget. Strategie delle genesi* (Milano: Emme Edizione, 1983).

Bocchi, G. and Ceruti, M. (eds.), *La sfida della complessità* (Milano: Feltrinelli, 1985).

Bondioli, A., *Gioco e educazione* (Milano: Franco Angeli, 1996).

Borges, J. L., *Ficciones* (Buenos Aires: Emece Editores, 1956).

Branzi, A., *La crisi della qualità* (Milano: ArtBook, 1996).

Bronfenbrenner, U., *Ecology of Human Development* (Cambridge, MA: Harvard University Press, 1981).

Bruner, J. S., *On Knowing: Essays for the Left Hand* (Cambridge, MA: Harvard University Press, 1964).

Bruner, J. S., *The Relevance of Education* (New York: Norton, 1971).

Bruner, J. S., *Toward a Theory of Instruction* (Cambridge, MA: Harvard University Press, 1974).

Bruner, J. S., *The Process of Education* (Cambridge, MA: Harvard University Press, 1977).

Bruner, J. S., *Savoire faire, savoire dire. Le développement de l'enfant* (Paris: Presses Universitaires de France, 1983).

Bruner, J. S., *In Search of Mind: Essays in Autobiography* (New York, Harper & Row, 1983).

Bruner, J. S., *Actual Minds, Possible Worlds* (Cambridge, MA: Harvard University Press, 1986).

Bruner, J. S., *Acts of Meaning* (Cambridge, MA: Harvard University Press, 1990).

Bruner, J. S., *The Culture of Education* (Cambridge, MA: Harvard University Press, 1996).

Cagliari, P., *La partecipazione: valori, significati, problemi e strumenti* (Reggio Emilia, Italy: Comune di Reggio Emilia, 1994).

Calvino, I., *Le città invisibili* (Torino, Italy: Einaudi, 1972).

Calvino, I., *Lezioni Americane* (Torino, Italy: Einaudi, 1988).

Camaioni, L., *La prima infanzia* (Bologna, Italy: Il Mulino, 1980).

Camaioni, L. (ed.), *Manuale di psicologia dello sviluppo* (Bologna, Italy: Il Mulino, 1993).

Ceccato, S., *La fabbrica del bello* (Milano: Rizzoli, 1987).

Ceppi, G. and Zini, M. (eds.), *Children, spaces, relations – Metaproject for an Environment for Young Children* (Reggio Emilia, Italy: Reggio Children, 1998).

Ceruti, M., *La danza che crea* (Milano: Feltrinelli, 1989).

Ceruti, M., *Evoluzione senza fondamenta* (Bari, Italy: Laterza, 1995).

Chomsky, N., *Syntactic Structures* (Paris-The Hague, France: Mauton, 1957).

Chomsky, N., *Language and Mind* (New York: Harcourt, Brace and World, 1968).

Chomsky, N., *Rules and Representations* (New York: Columbia University Press, 1980).

Cornoldi, C., *Metacognizione e memoria* (Bologna, Italy: Il Mulino, 1995).

Dal Lago, A. and Rovatti, P. A., *Per gioco. Piccolo manuale dell'esperienza ludica* (Milano: Raffaello Cortina Editore, 1993).

Dewey, J., *Democracy and Education* (New York: MacMillan, 1916).

Dewey, J., *Education Today* (New York: Putnam, 1940).

Dewey, J., *Experience and Education* (New York: MacMillan, 1959).

Edelman, G. M., *The Remembered Present* (New York: Basic Books, 1989).

Edelman, G. M., *Bright Air, Brilliant Fire: On the Matter of the Mind* (New York: Basic Books - Harper Collins, 1992).

Edwards, C., Gandini, L., and Forman, G. (eds.), *The Hundred Languages of Children* (Norwood, NJ: Ablex, 1993).

Fabbri, D., *La memoria della regina* (Milano: Guerini e Associati, 1990).

Fabbri, D. and Munari, A., *Strategie del sapere. Verso una psicologia culturale* (Bari, Italy: Dedalo, 1984).

Fodor, J. A., *The Modularity of Mind: An Essay on Faculty Psychology* (Cambridge, MA: MIT Press, 1983).

Fodor, J. A., *Psychosemantics: The Problem of Meaning in the Philosophy of Mind* (Cambridge, MA: MIT Press, 1987).

Freinet, C., *Education through Work: A Model for Child Centered Learning* (Lewiston, NY: Edwin Mellen Press, 1960).

Galimberti, U., *Il corpo* (Milano: Feltrinelli, 1997).

Galimberti, U., *Psiche e techne. L'uomo nell'età della tecnica* (Milano: Feltrinelli, 1999).

Gardner, H., *Frames of Mind: The Theory of Multiple Intelligences* (New York: Basic Books, 1983).

Gardner, H., *The Mind's New Science* (New York: Basic Books, 1985).

Gardner, H., *To Open Minds* (New York: Basic Books, 1989).

Gardner, H., *The Disciplined Mind* (New York: Simon and Schuster, 1999).

Gergen, K. J., *Reality and Relationships: Soundings in Social Construction* (Cambridge, MA: Harvard University Press, 1994).

Gergen, K. J., "Verso un vocabolario del dialogo trasformativo," *Pluriverso*, 5(2) (aprile-giugno 2000): 100-113.

Goleman, D., *Emotional Intelligence* (New York: Bantam Books, 1995).

Gombrich, E. H., *The Story of Art* (London: Phaidon Press, 1966).

Harris, J., *The Nurture Assumption* (New York: Free Press, 1998).

Johnson, G., *In the Palaces of Memory* (New York: Alfred A. Knopf, 1991).

Katz, L. and Chard, S., *Engaging Children's Minds: The Project Approach* (Norwood, NJ: Ablex, 1989).

Katz, L. and Cesarone, B. (eds.), *Reflections on the Reggio Emilia Approach* (Urbana, IL: ERIC/EECE, 1994).

Kellog, R., *Analyzing Children's Art* (Mountain View, CA: Mayfield Publishing, 1969).

Lanzi, D. and Soncini, I., *I significati dell'educare oggi*, Lecture presented at the International Symposium "Learning About Learning," Reggio Emilia, June 16-18, 1999.

Levy, P., *L'intelligence collective. Pour une anthropologie du cyberspace* (Paris: Découverte, 1994).

Luria, A. R., *Cognitive Development: Its Cultural and Social Foundations* (Cambridge, MA: Harvard University Press, 1976).

Lussu, G., *La lettera uccide* (Roma: Stampa Alternativa e Graffiti, 1999).

Malaguzzi, L., "Il ruolo dell'ambiente nel processo educativo," *Arredo Scuola 75 - per la scuola che cambia* (Como, Italy: Luigi Massoni Editore, 1975).

Malaguzzi, L., "For an Education Based on Relationships," *Young Children* (1993, November): 9-13.

Malaguzzi, L., *Una carta per tre diritti* (Reggio Emilia, Italy: Comune di Reggio Emilia, 1995).

Malaguzzi, L., *The Hundred Languages of Children*, Catalogue of the Exhibition (Reggio Emilia, Italy: Reggio Children, 1996).

Manghi, S. (ed.), *Attraverso Bateson. Ecologia della mente e relazioni sociali* (Milano: Raffaello Cortina Editore, 1998).

Mantovani, S., *Asili Nido: psicologia e pedagogia* (Milano: Franco Angeli, 1975).

Mantovani, S., *La ricerca in Asilo Nido* (Bergamo, Italy: Juvenilia, 1983).

Mantovani, S. (ed.), *Nostalgia del futuro* (Bergamo, Italy: Junior, 1997).

Maturana, H. R. and Varela, F. J., *Autopoiesis and Cognition. The Realization of the Living* (Dordrecht, Holland: D. Reidel Publishing Company, 1980).

Maturana, H. R. and Varela, F. J., *El Árbol del Conocimiento–Las Bases Biologicas para el Entendimiento Humano* (Santiago, Chile: Editorial Universitaria, 1990).

Morin, E., *La méthode. La nature de la nature* (Paris: Editions du Seuil, 1977).

Morin, E., *Science avec conscience* (Paris: Editions du Seuil, 1982).

Morin, E., *La tête bien faite* (Paris: Editions du Seuil, 1999).

Munari, A., *Il sapere ritrovato. Conoscenza, apprendimento, formazione* (Milano: Edizioni Guerini e Associati, 1993).

Munari, B., *Fantasia* (Bari, Italy: Laterza, 1977).

Munari, B., *Da cosa nasce cosa* (Roma: Laterza, 1981).

Neisser, U., *Cognitive Psychology* (Englewood Cliffs, NJ: Prentice Hall, 1967).

Piaget, J., *Six études de Psychologie* (Paris: Editions Gouthier, 1964).

Piaget, J., *La situation des sciences de l'homme dans le système des sciences-Psychologie-problèmes généreaux de la recherche entredisciplinaire et mécanism communs* (Paris-The Hague: Mauton, 1970).

Piaget, J., *Psychologie et epistemologie* (Paris: Denoël, 1970).

Piaget, J., *L'équilibration des structures cognitives* (Paris: Ed. Presses Universitaires de France, 1975).

Pierantoni, R., *Verità a bassissima definizione. Critica e percezione del quotidiano* (Torino, Italy: Einaudi, 1998).

Pontecorvo, C. (ed.), *La condivisione della conoscenza* (Firenze, Italy: La Nuova Italia, 1993).

Popper, K. R., *Conjectures and Refutations* (London: Routledge, 1969).

Popper, K. R., *Objective Knowledge: An Evolutionary Approach*, (Oxford, U.K.: Clarendon Press, 1972).

Popper, K. R., *Alles Leben ist Problemlösen. Über Erkenntnis, Geschichte und Politik* (Munchen: R. Piper, 1994).

Popper, K. R., *Knowledge and the Body-Mind Problem: In Defence of Interaction*, (London: Routledge, 1994).

Rabitti, G., *Alla scoperta della dimensione perduta* (Bologna: CLUEB, 1994).

Read, H., *Education through Art* (London: Faber and Faber, 1943).

Rinaldi, C., *I pensieri che sostengono l'azione educativa* (Reggio Emilia, Italy: Comune di Reggio Emilia, 1994).

Rinaldi, C., *L'ascolto visibile* (Reggio Emilia, Italy: Comune di Reggio Emilia, 1999).

Rinaldi, C., *I processi di conoscenza dei bambini tra soggettività ed intersoggettività* (Reggio Emilia, Italy: Comune di Reggio Emilia, 1999).

Rinaldi, C., *Le domande dell'educare oggi* (Reggio Emilia, Italy: Comune di Reggio Emilia, 1999).

Rinaldi, C., "Organization as a Value," *Innovations* (Fall 2000): 2-7.

Rinaldi, C. and Cagliari, P., *Educazione e creatività* (Reggio Emilia, Italy: Comune di Reggio Emilia, 1994).

Rodari, G., *Grammatica della fantasia* (Torino: Einaudi, 1973).

Rogers, C. R., *Person to Person: The Problem of Being Human* (Lafayette, CA: Real People Press, 1969).

Schneider, M., "Die historischen Grundlagen der musikalischen Symbolik," *Musikforschung*, IV, 1951, 113-128.

Stein, E., *Zum Problem der Einfühlung* (2nd ed.) (Munich: Kaffke, 1980).

Süskind, P., *Das Parfum* (Zurich: Diogenes, 1994).

Tanizaki, J., *In Praise of Shadows* (New Haven, CT: Leete's Island Books, 1998).

Vattimo, G. and Rovatti, A. (eds.), *Il pensiero debole* (Milano: Feltrinelli, 1983).

Vecchi, V., "The Role of Atelierista" in *The Hundred Languages of Children*, ed. C. Edwards, L. Gandini, and G. Forman (Norwood, NJ: Ablex, 1993).

Vygotskij, L. S., *Istorijarazvitija vyssih psihiceskih funktcij* (Mosca, 1960).

Vygotskij, L. S., *Razvitie vysich psichiceskick funkcij* (Mosca, 1960).

Vygotskij, L. S., *Izbrannja psichologicakia issledovaya* (Mosca, 1970).

Vygotskij, L. S., *Mind in Society* (Cambridge, MA: Harvard University Press, 1978).

Vygotskij, L. S., *Thought and Language* (Cambridge, MA: MIT, 1986).

Weick, K., *The Social Psychology of Organizing* (2nd ed.) (Reading, MA: Addison-Wesley, 1969).

Zolla, E., *Lo stupore infantile* (Milano: Adelphi, 1994).

Introduction (page 25 - page 27)

1. **R. Putnam**, *Making Democracy Work: Civic Traditions in Modern Italy* (Princeton, NJ: Princeton University Press, 1993).

2. **H. Gardner**, *Frames of Mind* (New York: Basic Books, 1983/93).

3. **H. Gardner**, *The Unschooled Mind* (New York: Basic Books, 1991); **H. Gardner**, *Multiple Intelligences* (New York: Basic Books, 1993); **H. Gardner**, *The Disciplined Mind* (New York: Simon and Schuster, 1999).

Form, Function, and Understanding in Learning Groups: Propositions from the Reggio Classrooms (page 246 - page 268)

1. **C. Rinaldi**, *L'ascolto visibile* (Reggio Emilia, Italy: Comune di Reggio Emilia, 1999).

2. See also **J. Astington**, *The Child's Discovery of the Mind* (Cambridge, MA: Harvard University Press, 1993).

3. **L. Malaguzzi**, "For an Education Based on Relationships," *Young Children* (1993, November): 9-13.

4. **L. Malaguzzi**, "The Importance of Interaction among Children and of Work in Small Groups: A Conversation with Loris Malaguzzi" (June 21, 1990). Unpublished interview by B. Rankin at Reggio Emilia, Italy.

5. **Municipality of Reggio Emilia**, *The Little Ones of Silent Movies: Make-believe with Children and Fish at the Infant-toddler Center* (Reggio Emilia, Italy: Reggio Children, 1996); Cf. **E. Turiel**, "Stage Transition in Moral Development," in *Second Handbook of Research on Teaching*, ed. R. M. W. Travers (Chicago: Rand McNally, 1973), pp. 732-757.

6. **L. Vygotsky**, *Mind in Society* (Cambridge, MA: Harvard University Press, 1978).

7. See also **J. Benenson**, "Understanding Social Competence in Peer Relations in Middle Childhood through Patterns of Sex Differences." Unpublished doctoral dissertation (Cambridge, MA: Harvard University, 1988); **J. Lever**, "Sex Differences in the Games Children Play," *Social Problems, 23* (1976): 479-487; **B. Sutton-Smith**, "The Play of Girls," in *Becoming Female: Perspectives on Development*, ed. C. B. Kopp and M. Kirkpatrick (New York: Plenum, 1979), pp. 229-257.

8. See, e.g., **G. A. Fine**, "The Natural History of Preadolescent Male Friendship Groups," in *Friendship and Social Relations in Childhood*, ed. H. C. Foot, A. J. Chapman, and J. R. Smith (New York: Wiley, 1980); **W. Hartup**, "Peer Relations," in *Handbook of Child Psychology: V. 4, Socialization, Personality, and Social Development*, vol. ed. E. M. Hetherington, series ed. P. H. Mussen (New York: Wiley, 1983), pp. 103-196.

9. Cf. **E. H. Erikson**, "Sex Differences in the Play Configurations of American Pre-Adolescents," *American Journal of Orthopsychiatry, 21* (1951): 667-692.

10. **W. Hartup** and **B. Laursen**, "Conflict and Context in Peer Relations," in

Children on Playgrounds: Research Perspectives and Applications, ed. C. Hart (Albany: State University of New York Press, 1995).

11. Cf. J. J. Gibson, *The Ecological Approach to Visual Perception* (Boston: Houghton Mifflin, 1979).

12. B. Rankin, "Curriculum Development in Reggio Emilia: A Long-Term Curriculum Project about Dinosaurs," in *The Hundred Languages of Children: The Reggio Emilia Approach—Advanced Reflections*, ed. C. Edwards, L. Gandini, and G. Forman (Greenwich, CT: Ablex, 1998), pp. 215-237.

13. See also H. Gardner, *Frames of Mind* (New York: Basic Books, 1983/93).

14. See also J. Harris, *The Nurture Assumption* (New York: Free Press, 1998); L. Kohlberg, "A Cognitive-developmental Analysis of Children's Sex-role Concepts and Attitudes," in *The Development of Sex Differences*, ed. E. Maccoby (Stanford, CA: Stanford University Press, 1966), pp. 82-183.

15. Municipality of Reggio Emilia, *The Hundred Languages of Children Catalogue* (Reggio Emilia, Italy: Reggio Children, 1996).

16. G. Bateson, *Mind and Nature* (New York: Bantam Books, 1979).

17. R. Nickerson, "On the Distribution of Cognition: Some Reflections," in *Distributed Cognitions: Psychological and Educational Considerations,* ed. G. Salomon (Cambridge, England: Cambridge University Press, 1993), pp. 229-261; quotation from pp. 223-224.

18. K. Popper, *Objective Knowledge: An Evolutionary Approach* (Oxford, England: Clarendon Press, 1972).

19. M. Scardamalia, C. Bereiter, and M. Lamon, "The CSILE Project: Trying to Bring the Classroom into World 3," in *Classroom Lessons: Integrating Cognitive Theory and Classroom Practice,* ed. K. McGilly (Cambridge, MA: MIT Press, 1994), pp. 201-228.

20. E. Duckworth, *The Having of Wonderful Ideas* (2nd ed.) (New York: Teachers College Press, 1996).

21. Municipality of Reggio Emilia, *The Fountains* (Reggio Emilia, Italy: Reggio Children, 1995).

22. Diana Preschool, *Paesaggi d'Ombra* [Shadow Landscapes: Explorations of Lights and Shadows] Unpublished manuscript (Reggio Emilia, Italy, 1995).

23. See, e.g., J. D. Bransford and D. L. Schwartz, "Rethinking Transfer: A Simple Proposal with Multiple Implications," *Review of Research in Education, 24* (1999): 61-100; D. Perkins and G. Salomon, "Teaching for Transfer," *Educational Leadership, 46*(1) (1988): 22-32.

24. A. L. Brown, "Analogical Learning and Transfer: What Develops?" in *Similarity and Analogical Reasoning,* ed. S. Vosniadou and A. Ortony (Cambridge, England: Cambridge University Press, 1989), pp. 369-412; A. L. Brown and M. J. Kane, "Preschool Children Can Learn to Transfer: Learning to Learn and Learning from Example," *Cognitive Psychology, 20* (1988): 493-523; A. L. Brown, M. J. Kane, and C. H. Echols, "Young Children's Mental Models Determine Analogical Transfer across Problems with a Common Goal Structure," *Cognitive Development, 1* (1986): 103-121; M. A. Crisafi and A. L. Brown, "Analogical Transfer in Very Young Children: Combining Two Separately Learned Solutions

to Reach a Goal," *Child Development, 57* (1986): 953-968.

25. **Municipality of Reggio Emilia**, *The Hundred Languages of Children Catalogue.*

26. **L. B. Cadwell**, *Bringing Reggio Emilia Home* (New York: Teachers College Press, 1997), p. 41.

27. **V. G. Paley**, "On Listening to What the Children Say," *Harvard Educational Review, 56*(2) (1986): 122-131; quotation from pp. 123-124.

Moving across the Atlantic (page 278 - page 283)

1. **R. Evans**, *The Human Side of School Change* (San Francisco: Jossey-Bass, 1996).

2. **J. Stevenson** and **J. Stigler**, *The Learning Gap: Why Our Schools Are Failing and What We Can Learn from Japanese and Chinese Education* (New York: Simon & Schuster, 1992).

3. **J. Nimmo**, "The Child in Community: Constraints from the Early Childhood Lore," in *The Hundred Languages of Children: The Reggio Emilia Approach—Advanced Reflections,* ed. C. Edwards, L. Gandini, and G. Forman (Greenwich, CT: Ablex, 1998), pp. 295-312.

4. **M. Spiro**, "On the Strange and Familiar in Recent Anthropological Thought," in *Cultural Psychology: Essays on Comparative Human Development,* ed. J. Stigler, R. Shweder, and G. Herdt (New York: Cambridge University Press, 1990), pp. 47-61.

5. **G. Dahlberg**, "Understanding the Theoretical Traditions of Education in Sweden," *Innovations in Early Childhood Education: The International Reggio Exchange, 6*(4) (1999): 4-5.

6. **H. Gothson**, "The Experiences of Swedish Educators Inspired by Reggio Emilia: An Interview with Harold Gothson and Gunilla Dahlberg, Interviewed by J. Kaminsky," *Innovations in Early Childhood Education: The International Reggio Exchange, 6*(4) (1999): 1-3.

7. **I. Calvino**, *Invisible Cities*, trans. W. Weaver (San Diego: Harcourt Brace Jovanovich, 1972), p. 82.

Four Features of Learning in Groups (page 284 - page 294)

1. **H. Gardner**, *Frames of Mind* (New York: Basic Books, 1983/93).

2. **G. Salomon** (ed.), *Distributed Cognitions: Psychological and Educational Considerations* (Cambridge, England: Cambridge University Press, 1993).

3. **J. V. Wertsch**, *Voices of the Mind: A Sociocultural Approach to Mediated Action* (Cambridge, MA: Harvard University Press, 1991); **B. Rogoff**, *Apprenticeship in Thinking: Cognitive Development in Social Context* (New York: Oxford University Press, 1990).

4. L. Vygotsky, *Mind in Society* (Cambridge, MA: Harvard University Press, 1978).

5. See, e.g., D. W. Johnson and R. T. Johnson, *Learning Together and Alone: Cooperative, Competitive, and Individualistic Learning* (4th ed.) (Boston: Allyn & Bacon, 1995); R. Slavin, *Cooperative Learning: Theory, Research, and Practice* (2nd ed.) (Boston: Allyn & Bacon, 1995).

6. R. Slavin, "Research for the Future: Research on Cooperative Learning and Achievement: What We Know, What We Need to Know," *Contemporary Educational Psychology, 21* (1996): 43-69.

7. W. Damon, "Peer Education: The Untapped Potential," *Journal of Applied Developmental Psychology, 5* (1984): 331-343; quotation from p. 341.

8. L. Gandini, "Celebrating Children Day by Day in Reggio Emilia: A Conversation with Amelia Gambetti by Lella Gandini," *Beginnings, Exchange 11/94* (1994): 52-55.

9. Municipality of Reggio Emilia, *Scarpa e Metro* [Shoe and Meter] (Reggio Emilia, Italy: Reggio Children, 1997).

10. C. Edwards, L. Gandini, and G. Forman (eds.), *The Hundred Languages of Children: The Reggio Emilia Approach—Advanced Reflections* (Greenwich, CT: Ablex, 1998).

11. E. Cohen, "Restructuring the Classroom: Conditions for Productive Small Groups," *Review of Educational Research, 64*(1) (1994): 1-35.

12. B. Rankin, "Curriculum Development in Reggio Emilia: A Long-Term Curriculum Project about Dinosaurs," in *The Hundred Languages of Children*, pp. 215-237.

13. N. M. Webb and A. S. Palincsar, "Group Processes in the Classroom," in *Handbook of Educational Psychology,* ed. D. C. Berliner and R. C. Calfee (New York: Simon & Schuster Macmillan, 1996), pp. 841-873.

14. Municipality of Reggio Emilia, *The Hundred Languages of Children Catalogue* (Reggio Emilia, Italy: Reggio Children, 1996).

15. L. Cadwell, *Bringing Reggio Emilia Home* (New York: Teachers College Press, 1997).

16. C. Edwards, L. Gandini, and J. Nimmo, "Promoting Collaborative Learning in the Early Childhood Classroom: Teachers' Contrasting Conceptualizations in Two Communities," in *Reflections on the Reggio Emilia Approach,* ed. L. Katz and B. Cesarone (Urbana, IL: ERIC, 1994), pp. 69-88.

17. D. W. Johnson, R. T. Johnson, and E. J. Holubec, *Cooperative Learning in the Classroom* (Alexandria, VA: Association for Supervision and Curriculum Development, 1994), p. 55.

18. E. Hutchins, "The Social Organization of Distributed Cognition," in *Perspectives on Socially Shared Cognition*, ed. L. B. Resnick, J. M. Levine, and S. D. Teasley (Washington, DC: American Psychological Association, 1991), pp. 283-307; J. M. Levine, L. B. Resnick, and E. T. Higgins, "Social Foundations of Cognition," *Annual Review of Psychology, 44* (1993): 585-612; J. L. Moore and T. R. Rocklin, "The Distribution of Distributed Cognition: Multiple Interpretations and Uses," *Educational Psychology Review, 10*(1) (1998): 97-

113; Salomon, *Distributed Cognitions*.

19. A. Brown and J. Campione, "Guided Discovery in a Community of Learners," in *Classroom Lessons: Integrating Cognitive Theory and Classroom Practice,* ed. K. McGilly (Cambridge, MA: MIT Press, 1994), pp. 229-270; A. Brown, D. Ash, M. Rutherford, K. Nakagawa, A. Gordon, and J. Campione, "Distributed Expertise in the Classroom," in Salomon, *Distributed Cognitions*, pp. 188-228.

20. J. Hewitt and M. Scardamalia, "Design Principles for Distributed Knowledge Building Processes," *Educational Psychology Review, 10*(1) (1998): 75-96; M. Scardamalia, C. Bereiter, and M. Lamon, "The CSILE Project: Trying to Bring the Classroom into World 3," in McGilly, *Classroom Lessons*, pp. 201-228.

21. R. Putnam, *Bowling Alone: The Collapse and Revival of American Community* (New York: Simon & Schuster, 2000); R. Putnam, "Bowling Alone: America's Declining Social Capital," *Journal of Democracy, 6*(1) (1995): 65-78.

22. R. Putnam, *Making Democracy Work: Civic Traditions in Modern Italy* (Princeton, NJ: Princeton University Press, 1993).

23. C. Rinaldi, Synthesis of February 17, 1998 Roundtable at Reggio Emilia, Italy; quotation from p. 6.

Understanding Documentation Starts at Home (page 304 - page 311)

1. H. Gardner, "Assessment in Context: The Alternative to Standardized Testing," in *Changing Assessments: Alternative Views of Aptitude, Achievement, and Instruction*, ed. B. R. Gifford and M. C. O'Conner (Weston, MA: Kluwer, 1991), pp. 77-119.

2. J. Q. Chen, M. Krechevsky, and J. Viens, *Building on Children's Strengths: The Experience of Project Spectrum* (New York: Teachers College Press, 1998).

3. W. S. Jackman, *Nature-Study* (Chicago: National Society for the Scientific Study of Education, Third Yearbook, 1904).

4. W. H. Kirkpatrick, *The Project Method* (1918), Teachers College Record, XIX.

5. E. C. Lagemann, *An Elusive Science: The Troubling History of Education Research* (Chicago: University of Chicago Press, 2000).

6. L. Cremin, *The Transformation of the School* (New York: Vintage Books, 1964).

7. H. Featherstone, *Changing Minds,* Bulletin 13 (Spring 1998), College of Education, Michigan State University.

8. M. Himley and P. Carini, *From Another Angle* (New York: Teachers College Press, 2000).

9. E. Duckworth, *The Having of Wonderful Ideas* (2nd ed.) (New York: Teachers College Press, 1996).

10. T. Blythe and the researchers and teachers of the Teaching for Understanding Project, *The Teaching for Understanding Guide* (San Francisco: Jossey-Bass, 1998); M. S. Wiske (ed.), *Teaching for Understanding: Linking Research with*

Practice (San Francisco: Jossey-Bass, 1998).

11. **S. Seidel** and **J. Walters**, "The Things Children Make in School: Disposable or Indispensable?" *Harvard Graduate School of Education Alumni Bulletin, 39*(1) (1994): 18-20.

12. **E. Winner**, *Arts Propel: An Introductory Handbook* (Educational Testing Service and Harvard Project Zero, 1991); **R. Zessoules** and **H. Gardner**, "Authentic Assessment: Beyond the Buzzword and into the Classroom," in Expanding Student Assessment, ed. V. Perrone (Yearbook of the Association for Supervision and Curriculum Development, 1991), pp. 47-71.

To Be Part of Something Bigger than Oneself (page 312 - page 321)

1. **S. Seidel**, *Stand and Unfold Yourself: A Report on the Shakespeare & Company Research Study.* Unpublished manuscript (Cambridge, MA: 1998), Project Zero, pp. 85-86.

2. Ibid, p. 87.

3. **A. Brown**, "The Advancement of Learning," *Educational Researcher, 23*(8), (November, 1994): 7.

4. **A. Brown** and **J. Campione**, "Guided Discovery in a Community of Learners," in *Classroom Lessons: Integrating Cognitive Theory and Classroom Practice*, ed. K. McGilly (Cambridge, MA: MIT Press, 1994), p. 261.

5. Ibid, p. 237.

6. Ibid, p. 229.

7. **I. Gaskell**, "An Economy of Seventeenth Century Clay Sculptors' Models," in "Sketches in Clay for Project by Gian Lorenzo Bernini," ed. I. Gaskell and H. Lie, *Harvard University Art Museums Bulletin, 6*(3) (Spring, 1999), p. 29.

"The Question Cannot Be Satisfied with Waiting": Perspectives on Research in Education (page 330 - page 334)

1. **W. Blake**, *The Complete Poetry and Prose of William Blake,* ed. D.V. Erdman (Berkeley: University of California Press, 1982).

2. **D. Wolf**, **J. Bixby**, **J. Glenn III**, and **H. Gardner**, "To Use Their Minds Well: Investigating New Forms of Student Assessment," in *Review of Research in Education*, ed. G. Grant (Washington, DC: American Educational Research Association, 1991), p. 57.

3. **E. Duckworth**, *The Having of Wonderful Ideas* (2nd ed.) (New York: Teachers College Press, 1996), p. 140.

4. **P. Carini**, *The Art of Seeing and the Visibility of the Person* (Grand Forks: North Dakota Study Group, 1979).

5. **T. A. Grotzer** and **B. Bell**, "Negotiating the Funnel: Guiding Students Toward Understanding Elusive Generative Concepts," in *The Project Zero Classroom:*

Views on Understanding, eds. L. Hetland and S. Veenema (Fellows and Trustees of Harvard, 1999).

6. Project Zero, The Evidence Process: A Collaborative Approach to Understanding and Improving Teaching and Learning, *24 Hours*, 2001, forthcoming.

7. P. Freire, *Letters to Cristina* (New York: Routledge, 1996).

Making Our Learning Visible (page 337 - page 340)

1. T. Kuhn, *The Structure of Scientific Revolutions* (2nd ed.) (Chicago: University of Chicago Press, 1973).

INTRO   ∩ JSB ∩ ?? ?

C.R.

MAePA-SPAsIALE

SALTO-NEL-iPERSP
AZiO

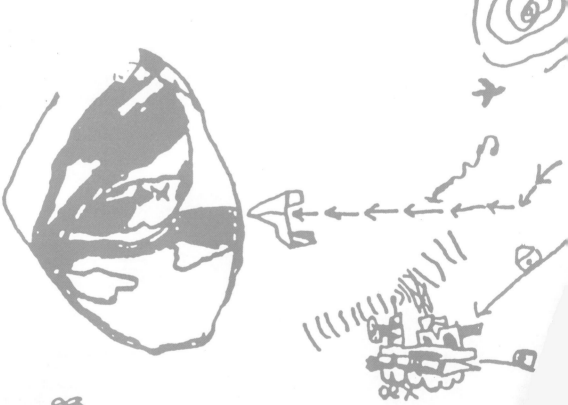

outer space map

INZIONE
ATE